Italian Soft-Skinned Vehicles of the Second World War

Motorcycles, Cars, Trucks, Artillery Tractors 1935–1945

Volume 2

Ralph Riccio

Mario Pieri

Daniele Guglielmi

Helion & Company

Helion & Company Limited
Unit 8 Amherst Business Centre
Budbrooke Road
Warwick
CV34 5WE
England
Tel. 01926 499 619
Email: info@helion.co.uk
Website: www.helion.co.uk
Twitter: @helionbooks
Visit our blog at blog.helion.co.uk

Published by Helion & Company 2023
Designed and typeset by Farr out Publications, Wokingham, Berkshire
Cover designed by Paul Hewitt, Battlefield Design (www.battlefield-design.co.uk)

Text © Ralph Riccio, Mario Pieri, Daniele Guglielmi 2023
Photographs © see Acknowledgements
Colour artwork by and © David Bocquelet 2023

Every reasonable effort has been made to trace copyright holders and to obtain their permission for the use of copyright material. The author and publisher apologise for any errors or omissions in this work, and would be grateful if notified of any corrections that should be incorporated in future reprints or editions of this book.

ISBN 978-1-804514-91-7

British Library Cataloguing-in-Publication Data.
A catalogue record for this book is available from the British Library.

All rights reserved. No part of this publication may be reproduced, stored in a retrieval system, or transmitted, in any form, or by any means, electronic, mechanical, photocopying, recording or otherwise, without the express written consent of Helion & Company Limited.

For details of other military history titles published by Helion & Company Limited contact the above address, or visit our website: http://www.helion.co.uk.

We always welcome receiving book proposals from prospective authors

Contents

List of colour plates	v
Acknowledgements	vii
Documentation sources	viii
Abbreviations	ix
Glossary	x
Prefixes and suffixes used in vehicle designations	xii
5 Medium and Heavy Trucks	13
6 Artillery Tractors	127
7 Special Purpose Vehicles	174
8 Trailers	189
Appendices	
I Camouflage and Markings	200
II Italian Vehicle Manufacturers	219
III Soft-Skinned Vehicles Produced in Italy while under German Control, September 1943-April 1945	222
Bibliography	224
About the Authors	226

List of colour plates

Fiat 634 NM standardised heavy truck, Balkans, 1940. (Artwork by and © David Bocquelet)	I
Lancia 3Ro NM standardised heavy truck, Eastern Front, 1941. (Artwork by and © David Bocquelet)	I
Fiat 626 NLM standardised medium truck, Libya, 1942. (Artwork by and © David Bocquelet)	II
SPA Dovunque 35 medium truck, Libya, 1942. (Artwork by and © David Bocquelet)	II
Breda 32 heavy artillery tractor, Eastern Front, 1941. (Artwork by and © David Bocquelet)	III
SPA TL37 light artillery tractor, Eastern Front, 1942. (Artwork by and © David Bocquelet)	III
A rare and interesting colour artwork from the user manual of the Lancia 3Ro. (see Appendix I)	IV
The German photographer Hugo Jaeger accompanied Hitler during his 1938 visit to Italy; this photo portrays a parade in Piazza del Plebiscito, in Naples. The two Pavesi P4-100 model 1926 tractors are painted in the regulation dark *grigioverde* (grey-green) colour. The circular bronze badge was fastened to the left of the white number plate. (See Appendix I)	V
A well-known photograph published by *Signal* magazine illustrates the landing of German material in the Tunisian port of Bizerte, at the end of 1942. The Italian Lancia 3Ro trucks are still in dark grey-green. The German Pz.Kpfw. III Ausf.N tanks are camouflaged in the *Tropen* colours in use since March 1942. (See Appendix I)	VI
In these photographs taken in Yugoslavia by an alpino soldier in April 1941, various Italian vehicles painted in the standard grey-green can be observed, including a damaged Alfa Romeo 800 RE, an OM Taurus and a Fiat 666. (See Appendix I)	VII
An OM Taurus crosses a German column in North Africa. The truck is grey-green and has the Italian flag painted on the cab roof. (See Appendix I)	VIII
In these photographs taken in Yugoslavia by an alpino soldier in April 1941, various Italian vehicles painted in the standard grey-green can be observed, including a damaged Alfa Romeo 800 RE, an OM Taurus and a Fiat 666. (See Appendix I)	VIII
This image is part of a series of poses taken on Agfa colour film by a German soldier during the transfer trip and stay in North Africa. It was taken perhaps in the port of Tripoli or Bengasi in 1942. Italian cars and trucks (on the right, a Fiat 634 seen from the front) are painted in *kaki sahariano* which, due to the effect of the sun and the quality of the photographic equipment, appears rather pale. (See Appendix I)	IX
Four M14/41 tanks ready for embarkation in Naples, bound for North Africa. Their colour is the factory applied *kaki sahariano* (sand-yellow). In the frame from a period newspaper there are other vehicles repainted in the same colour: on the right a Breda 41 tractor, left in the background a Lancia 3Ro and a Fiat 626 or 666. Some of them have visible residues of the pre-existing grey-green paint. (See Appendix I)	IX
During the campaign in North Africa, many Italian logistics vehicles remained painted in grey-green. In the absence of the regulation sand-yellow paint, the units often resorted to paints recovered on site and applied 'at best'. Here some *Bersaglieri* motorcyclists aboard Gilera 500 LTE two-seat motorcycles. (See Appendix I)	X

A column of Italian and German prisoners photographed in Tunisia in May 1943. Behind the grey-green trailer, Italian trucks of various models are painted in sand-yellow colour. (See Appendices I, II and III) (LIFE) XI

All army vehicles had to bear a special bronze badge that proved they belonged to the *Regio Esercito*. (See Appendix I) XI

Examples of number plates: A = front plate, metal, motorcycle (Gilera 500 LTE); B = rear plate, metal, motor tricycle (Guzzi Tralce); C = front plate, metal, car (Bianchi VM6 C); D = rear plate, metal, car (Lancia Aprilia Coloniale); E = front plate, painted, truck (OM 3 BOD); F = rear plate, metal, truck (Bianchi Miles); G = front plate, painted, tractor (Alfa Romeo, prototype); H = rear plate, metal, tractor (Breda 33); I = rear plate, metal, trailer; L = rear plate, Regio Corpo Truppe Coloniali in Libia, metal, truck (AS 37). (See Appendix I) (Colour artworks by M. Pieri) XII

About the Authors

RALPH RICCIO was born in 1939 and is a retired US Army officer who has had a life-long interest in military history, with a focus on Italian military history. He has authored or co-authored numerous books and magazine articles dealing with Italian as well as Irish military subjects. A native Italian speaker, he is actively involved in translating texts by various Italian authors from Italian to English. In 1981 he was awarded an honorary Italian knighthood for the fostering of relations between the US and Italy. Born in Connecticut, he has travelled extensively throughout Europe and South-East Asia while in the army and while later working for the Department of Defence and now resides in rural Pennsylvania.

MARIO PIERI is an Italian engineer, born in 1962 in Florence and currently residing in Rome. Always a military history researcher, focused on the military technology, Mario has used scale modelling primarily as an associative and educational medium. Actively publishing since the 1980s, his current pursuits are research, editing, and translations.

DANIELE GUGLIELMI is the author of many articles on both historical and modelling subjects and he has a large number of books, monographs and military maps to his credit. He was born in 1959 in Florence (Italy) and lives in the nearby town of Calenzano. He is a member of, or personally in charge of, several modelling and research associations, and works with many Italian and foreign authors, scholars, researchers and institutions.

Pignato, Nicola. *Le Autocarrette del Regio Esercito* (Trento: Gruppo Modellistico Trentino di studio e ricerca storica, 2021)

Pignato, Nicola and Cappellano, Filippo. *Gli Autoveicoli Tattici e Logistici del R. Esercito Italiano fino al 1943,* tomo primo (Roma: Ufficio Storico Stato Maggiore Esercito, 2005)

Pignato, Nicola and Cappellano, Filippo. *Gli Autoveicoli Tattici e Logistici del R. Esercito Italiano fino al 1943*, tomo secondo (Roma: Ufficio Storico Stato Maggiore Esercito, 2005)

Pignato, Nicola and Cappellano, Filippo. *Insegne, Uniformi, Distintivi e Tradizioni Delle Truppe Corazzate Italiane* (Repubblica di San Marino: T. & T. Edizioni, 2005)

Riccio, Ralph and Pignato, Nicola. *Italian Truck-mounted Artillery in Action* (Carrollton: Squadron/Signal Publications, 2010)

Riccio, Ralph. *Italian Tanks and Combat Vehicles of World War II* (Fidenza: Roadrunner, Mattioli 1885 Editore, 2010)

Salussoglia, Beppe and Vayl, Pascal. *Macchina e Rimorchio – Storie di Uomini e di Camion* (Cavallermaggiore: Gribaudo, 1999)

Santucci, Giovanni. *Le Grandi Moto Italiane 1930–1970* (San Giuliano Milanese: Edizioni Gaia, 2008)

Scolari, Attilio. *Dalla Russia noi Siamo Tornati* (Verona: Grafiche Duegi, 2000)

Spielberger, Walter J. *Beute-Kraftfahrzeuge und Panzer der Deutschen Wehrmacht* (Stuttgart: Motorbuch Verlag, 1989)

Squassoni, Costantino and Squassoni, Mauro Negri. *Storia Illustrata del Camion Italiano* (Brescia: Edizioni Negri, 1996)

Squassoni, Costantino and Squassoni, Mauro Negri. *Cent'anni di Camion Fiat* (Brescia: Edizioni Negri, 1999)

Squassoni, Costantino and Squassoni, Mauro Negri. *V. Orlandi – dal 1859 il Traino Dell'Autotrasporto* (Brescia: Edizioni Negri, 2000)

Squassoni, Costantino and Squassoni, Mauro Negri. *OM Officine Meccaniche – Una Storia nella Storia …* (Brescia: Edizioni Negri, 2000)

Squassoni, Costantino and Squassoni, Mauro Negri. *Camion Lancia* (Brescia: Edizioni Negri, 2001)

Tirone, Guido. *La Fiat 500 Topolino* (San Giuliano Milanese: Edizioni Gaia, 2008)

Tron, Ernesto. *Come Ottenere la Patente Diesel – 7a edizione* (Milan: Hoepli, 1944)

Valente, Luca. *Due Anni al Volante su Piste di Neve e Fango* (Schio: Edizioni Menin, 2008)

Vanderveen, Bart. *The Observer's Fighting Vehicles Directory, World War II.* (London: Frederick Warne & Co. Ltd., 1972)

Zampini, Carlo F. Salazar. *85 Anni di Camion Militari Fiat* (Turin: Stige Editore, 1987)

Magazines

4x4 Italia, several issues
Mezzi Corazzati, several issues
Notiziario GMT, several issues
Storia Militare, several issues

Original Manuals and Documents

The authors used a large number of technical manuals and original documents. A complete listing of these would be too long to publish here.

Bibliography

Books

Barlozzetti, Ugo and Pirella, Alberto. *Mezzi dell'Esercito Italiano 1935–1945* (Firenze: Editoriale Olimpia, 1986)

Benussi, Giulio. *Semicingolati, Motoveicoli e Veicoli Speciali del Regio Esercito Italiano 1919–1943* (Milan: Intergest, 1976)

Benussi, Giulio. *Veicoli Speciali del Regio Esercito Italiano Nella Seconda Guerra Mondiale* (Milan: Intergest, 1976)

Botti, Ferruccio, *La Logistica dell'Esercito Italiano (1831–1981) – vol. III* (Roma: Ufficio Storico Stato Maggiore Esercito, 1994)

Botti, Ferruccio, *La Logistica dell'Esercito Italiano (1831–1981) – vol. IV* (Roma: Ufficio Storico Stato Maggiore Esercito, 1995)

Carroll, John and Davies, Peter J. *The Complete Book of Tractors & Trucks* (London: Hermes House, 2002)

Cappellano, Filippo. *Batterie Volanti – Autocannoni e Artiglierie Portate Italiane (1915–1943), Storia Militare Dossier No.13* (Parma: Edizioni Storia Militare, 2014)

Cappellano, Filippo and Guglielmi, Daniele. *Il Cannone da 47/32 – Storia, Tecnica e Impiego, Storia Militare Briefing No.28* (Parma: Edizioni Storia Militare, 2021)

Ceva, Lucio and Curami, Andrea. *La Meccanizzazione dell'Esercito fino al 1943 – tomo primo* (Roma: Ufficio Storico Stato Maggiore Esercito, 1989)

Ceva, Lucio and Curami, Andrea. *La Meccanizzazione dell'Esercito fino al 1943 – tomo secondo* (Roma: Ufficio Storico Stato Maggiore Esercito, 1989)

Curami, Andrea, Ferrari, Paolo and Rastelli, Achille. *Alle Origini Della Breda Meccanica Bresciana.* (Brescia: Edizioni Negri, 2009)

Evangelista, Guglielmo. *Le Targhe e i Veicoli Dell'Esercito Italiano – Dal 1927 al 1947: Regio Esercito*

Evangelista, Guglielmo. *Le Targhe e i Veicoli Dell'Aeronautica Militare*

Evangelista, Guglielmo. *Le targhe e i Veicoli Della Marina Militare*

Finazzer, Enrico and Carretta, Luigi. *Light Trucks of the Italian Army in WWII* (Sandomierz: Stratus sp.j, 2017)

Finazzer, Enrico and Carretta, Luigi. *Le Camionette del Regio Esercito: Fiat-SPA AS 37, SPA-Viberti AS 42, Fiat-SPA AS 43, Desertica 43, I reparti che le impiegarono* (Trento: Gruppo Modellistico Trentino di studio e ricerca storica, 2020)

Frontalini, Giacomo and Frontalini, Costantino. *Moto Guzzi – Il volo dell'Aquila* (Roma: Polo Books, 2005)

Guglielmi, Daniele. *Italian Armour in German Service 1943–1945* (Fidenza: Mattioli 1885 Editore, 2005)

Guglielmi, Daniele. *Sd.Kfz.7 Mittlerer Zugkraftwagen 8 t* (Genova: Auriga Publishing International SRL, 2009)

Guglielmi, Daniele and Massacci, Luca. *Italian Armoured Vehicles 1940–1943, a Pictorial History* (Fidenza: Mattioli 1885 Editore, 2013)

Guglielmi, Daniele and Pieri, Mario. *Un "Milite" per il Regio Esercito* (Genova: Storia Militare, No.334, July 2021, pages 21–34)

Guglielmi, Daniele and Pieri, Mario. *Italienfeldzug Volume 4 – The German Ground Forces in the Italian Campaign 1943–1945* (Villatuerta: Ammo of Mig, 2020)

Leardi, Roberto. *Gilera – Storia e Modelli di un Marchio Leggendario* (San Giuliano Milanese: Edizioni Gaia, 2012)

Pignacca, Brizio. *Ruote in Divisa – Un Secolo di Veicoli Militari Italiani* (Vimodrone: Giorgio Nada Editore, 1989)

Pignato, Nicola. *Artiglierie e Automezzi Dell'Esercito Italiano Nella Seconda Guerra Mondiale* (Parma: Ermanno Albertelli Editore, 1972)

Pignato, Nicola. *Gli Autoveicoli del Regio Esercito Nella Seconda Guerra Mondiale* (Parma: Albertelli Edizioni Speciali, 1998)

Pignato, Nicola. *A Century of Italian Armored Cars* (Fidenza: Roadrunner, Mattioli 1885 Editore, 2008)

Pignato, Nicola. *I 'Dovunque' Fiat, SPA e Breda* (Fano: T. & T. Edizioni, 2006)

SOFT-SKINNED VEHICLES PRODUCED IN ITALY UNDER GERMAN CONTROL, SEPTEMBER 1943-APRIL 1945

Italian Denomination	German Denomination	Production
SPA AS 37, truck	Typ AS 37 (i)	44 in 1944
SPA TL 37, tractor	Radschlepper Typ TL 37 (i)	375 in 1944, 7 in 1945
SPA TM 40, tractor	Radschlepper Typ TM 40 (i)	153 in 1944
Breda 115, tractor	Radschlepper Typ 115 (i)	100 in 1944
Breda 61, half-tracked tractor	Zugkraftwagen 8t Typ 61 (i)	199 in 1944 and 1945
Fiat OCI 40, tracked tractor	Type OCI 40 PS (i)	64 in 1944

Note
Aside from these new production vehicles, German troops captured and employed thousands of other examples in Italy, France and the Balkans; the official data could be not completely verified, because of the destruction of the archives at the end of war, especially those referring to the last months. The table does not include models produced before 8 September 1943 and subsequently catalogued and registered in the German armed forces.

Appendix III

Soft-Skinned Vehicles Produced in Italy while under German Control, September 1943-April 1945

Italian Denomination	German Denomination	Production
Alfa Romeo 2500, car	Typ 2500 (i)	40 in 1944, 4 in 1945
Bianchi S4, car	Typ S4 (i)	100 in 1944
Fiat 500, car	Typ 500 (i)	102 in 1944
Fiat 1100, car	Typ 1100 (i)	1334 in 1944, 23 in 1945
Fiat 1500, car	Typ 1500 (i)	103 in 1944
Camionetta AS 43, weapon carrier	Typ 43 (I)	13 in 1944
Fiat 1100, truck	Typ 1100 LKW (i)	1640 in 1944, 37 in 1945
Fiat 1100, ambulance	Krankenkraftwagen 1100 (i)	11 in 1945
Alfa Romeo 500 RE, truck	Typ 500 RE (i)	}
and Alfa Romeo 430 RE, truck	Typ 430 RE (i)	} together, 176 in 1944 and 1945
Bianchi Miles, truck	Typ Miles (i)	90 in 1944
Breda 52, truck	Typ 52 (i)	29 in 1944
Fiat 626, truck	Typ 626 (i)	3346 in 1944 and 1945
Fiat 666, truck	Typ 666 (i)	77 in 1944 and 1945
Fiat 665, truck	Typ 665 (i)	2 in 1945
Isotta Fraschini 65D, truck	Typ D65 (i)	397 in 1944
Lancia 3Ro, truck	Typ 3Ro (i)	722 in 1944 and 1945
Lancia Esaro 267, truck	Typ 267 (i)	1228 in 1944 and 1945
OM Taurus, truck	Typ Taurus (i)	2305 in 1944 and 1945
SPA CL 39, truck	Typ CL 39 (i)	198 in 1944
SPA 38 R, truck	Typ 38R (i)	66 in 1944
SPA Dovunque 35, truck	Typ Dovunque 35 (i)	307 in 1944 and 1945
SPA Dovunque 41, truck	Typ Dovunque 41 (i)	191 in 1944 and 1945

Lancia was bought out by Fiat; since then, there have been a series of mergers and reorganisations, resulting in the Stellantis merger in 2021.

Moto Guzzi, Mandello del Lario

Moto Guzzi was established by Carlo Guzzi and Giorgio and Angelo Parodi in 1921 in Mandello del Lario (Province of Lecco). Guzzi motorcycles soon earned a reputation for being first-rate machines. During the Second World War, Moto Guzzi became well-known for its Alce and Trialce motorcycles. After the war, Moto Guzzi underwent a series of ownership changes until in December 2004 it became part of the Piaggio group.

Officine Meccaniche (OM), Milan

OM was founded in 1899 in Milan as the Società Anonima Officine Meccaniche; it was formed from the merger of two companies, Grondona Comi and Miani Silvestri. It began operations by manufacturing railway rolling stock and did not begin car production until 1918. In 1925 OM began to produce trucks and buses, licence building Swiss Saurer engines and other mechanical components. OM was taken over by Fiat in 1938 and ceased to produce passenger cars the following year, limiting its automotive manufacturing to a wide line of trucks. Despite its acquisition by Fiat, OM maintained strong ties to Saurer. In the post-war period, OM trucks were sold in Switzerland under the Saurer-OM or Berna-OM nameplate, and in Austria as the Steyr-OM, in France as Unic-OM and in Germany as Büssing-OM. In 1968 OM was merged into the commercial vehicles division of the Fiat group, and in 1975 was absorbed into Fiat's IVECO truck line and the OM brand name ceased to exist.

Società Piemontese Automobili (SPA), Turin

The Società Piemontese Automobili (SPA) was an automotive company founded in 1906 in Turin by Matteo Ceirano (brother of Giovanni Ceirano, founder of Ceirano Fabbrica Automobili) and Michele Ansaldi. In 1908 it merged with Fabbrica Ligure Automobili Genova; the new company, named Società Ligure Piemontese Automobili, was headquartered in Genoa but manufacturing remained in Turin. In 1923 the company was taken over by Fiat; passenger car production was terminated, but commercial and military vehicle production continued. By 1947 the company was fully absorbed into Fiat and the SPA mark ceased to exist.

Coachbuilders

Many Italian companies producing motor vehicles assigned to third parties the construction and assembly of the bodies, not only the special ones (for example tank trucker, ambulance, bus, van) but also the standard ones, including the truck beds.

Among the best known coachbuilders are Bartoletti, Bertone, Boneschi, Borsani, Brianza, Castagna, Cisitalia, Colli, Conta, Dalla Via, Fissore, Garavini, Ghia, Menarini, Pininfarina (Pinin Farina), Viberti, Vignale, Viotti, Zagato.

Over time, and especially with the increase in demand during the war, the automotive industries ended up incorporating all or part of the production of car bodies. For this reason, there are sometimes external differences between different specimens of the same vehicle model.

At the same time, some coachbuilders, such as the case of Viberti, independently produced a few brand-new models of vehicles based on Fiat, SPA et cetera chassis.

Regio Esercito, and produced some of the earliest examples of machine gun armed vehicles, the grandfather of the armoured car. During the years that followed, Bianchi continued to produce various types of vehicles for both the civilian and military markets. Its factory was heavily damaged by Allied bombing during the Second World War; however, it resumed production of bicycles as well as small numbers of motorcycles after the war, and in 1955 the company was merged with Fiat and Pirelli, giving rise to the Autobianchi company, which produced cars until 1995.

Società Italiana Ernesto Breda per Costruzioni Meccaniche, Milan

The Società Italiana Ernesto Breda is commonly referred to simply as Breda. It was founded in Milan in 1886 by Ernesto Breda and originally manufactured locomotives and other railway machinery. Breda later began manufacturing armaments and aircraft. During the Second World War, Breda manufactured machine guns, the excellent 20mm Breda model 35 anti-aircraft gun, trucks and aircraft. In 1962 Breda was nationalised but was liquidated in the 1990s. Breda's train and tram division merged with Ansaldo, and the armaments division became Breda Meccanica Bresciana, located in Brescia. Breda has a reputation for high-quality products.

Ceirano Fabbrica Automobili

Giovanni Battista Ceirano was the son of a watchmaker and a mechanics enthusiast. Towards the end of the nineteenth century, he moved from Cuneo to Turin to gain experience in the workshops. Later he opened his own business for the repair and sale of bicycles. In 1898 he founded the Accomandita Ceirano G. B. & C. company for the production of automobiles; together with him were some partners and employees including Vincenzo Lancia (later founder of the car manufacturer of the same name). The first car, called 'Welleyes', was built the following year and was a huge success, so much so that the small company was unable to cope with the demand due to a lack of capital and resources. Therefore, the entire assets were sold to Fiat, also founded in 1899. Giovanni Battista was also hired by Fiat, but after two years he left to found, together with his brothers Ernesto and Matteo, another car factory. Over time, the Ceirano family would create and incorporate other companies in the same sector, including Giovannni Ceirano Fabbrica Automobili, Scat (Società Ceirano Automobili Turin), Itala and Star (Società Torinese Automobili Rapid). The first Ceirano truck dates back to 1926, the 50 CM.

Fabbrica Italiana Automobili Turin (Fiat), Turin

Fiat traces its history to July 1889 when Giovanni Agnelli senior was part of the group of founding members of Fiat. The first Fiat plant opened in 1900, and by 1910 Fiat was the largest automotive company in Italy. During the First World War, Fiat produced large numbers of trucks and ambulances as well as aircraft engines and machine guns for the Italian armed forces. During the Second World War, Fiat made vehicles, including tanks, and aircraft for the Italian armed forces and later for the Germans. After the war, Fiat continued to produce cars and trucks, and in 1970 produced more than 1.4 million vehicles in Italy. In 2014, Fiat was merged with the Netherlands-based holding company Fiat Chrysler Automobiles NV.

Gilera, Arcore

In 1909 Giuseppe Gilera founded the Gilera motorcycle company, based in Arcore, near Monza. Its first motorcycle was the VT 317. During the Second World War, Gilera produced a range of motorcycles that were widely used by the Italian military. Production continued after the war, and in 1969 Gilera became part of the Piaggio group.

Isotta Fraschini, Milan

The company was born in Milan in 1900, with the name Società Milanese d'Automobili Isotta Fraschini & C. It was founded by Cesare Isotta together with the Fraschini brothers (Oreste, Antonio and Vincenzo) dedicating itself above all to car repairs. Over time the business expanded to the design and construction of cars, trucks, armoured cars, trolley buses, engines for airplanes and even weapons. The first military orders for trucks date back to 1911 and are related to the Libya Campaign (aka the Italo-Turkish War). The production of trucks obviously had a boost during the First World War, then it was suspended and finally resumed in the early thirties. During the Second World War they also manufactured trucks, in collaboration with MAN of Germany, as well as producing aircraft and marine engines. Isotta Fraschini suffered badly due to the war and economic disruption and stopped making cars in1949. In 1955 the company merged with Breda Motori, producing trolley buses and diesel engines. The company closed due to bankruptcy in 1999.

Lancia & C. Fabbrica Automobili, Turin

Lancia was founded in November 1906 in Turin by Vincenzo Lancia and Claudio Fogolin. Lancia had a reputation for building high-quality and innovative cars; Lancia was an industry leader in areas such as electrical systems, the monocoque chassis, the first five-speed gearbox in a production car, the first V4 engine and the first full-production V6 engine. During the Second World War it produced a number of staff cars as well as heavy trucks, the most notable of which was the Lancia 3Ro. In 1969

Appendix II

Italian Vehicle Manufacturers

Volugrafo Aermoto, Turin
The company was founded in Turin c.1936 by Claudio Belmondo, an engineer. Belmondo had designed a light motorcycle designed as a small vehicle for airborne troops. The company was born with the name Officine Meccaniche Volugrafo and subsequently took on that of Volugrafo Aermoto, keeping the same plant. After the war, Belmondo developed a small car; production of the car ended in 1948 and the company ceased to exist.

Officine Meccaniche Fausto Alberti, Milan
The Officine Meccaniche Fausto Alberti (in short, Alberti) was established in Milan in 1922, producing industrial and marine engines. In 1932 it began production of motorcycles under the Sertum brand name. Sertum motorcycles soon were competitive with other famous Italian brands (Benelli, Bianchi, Gilera and Moto Guzzi). During the Second World War, Sertum provided the MCM 500 machine to the Italian armed forces. Civilian production of the Sertum line resumed in 1946, but by 1952 financial reverses led to liquidation of the company.

Alfa Romeo, Milan
Alfa Romeo had its beginnings in 1910 when Cavalier Ugo Stella acquired the shares of the Società Italiana Automobili Darraq, the Italian plant of a French auto maker. Cars were initially produced in Naples, but the manufacturing facilities were subsequently moved to Portella, near Milan. By 1915 the company changed its name to ALFA, which was the acronym for Anonima Lombarda Fabbrica Automobili; the name Romeo was the surname of Nicola Romeo, who had taken control of the company. Alfa Romeo is traditionally associated with high-performance or luxury motor cars, but during both the First and Second World Wars was also engaged in military production of aircraft engines and other components. Alfa Romeo began manufacturing trucks in 1931 following commercial agreements entered into in 1929 with the German firms Deutz and Büssing-NAG. After the Büssing 50, the 80 and other models equipped with Deutz diesel engines built under licence, Alfa launched an entirely new model in 1935, the Tipo 350, followed two years later by the Tipo 500. In 1986 Alfa was taken over by Fiat, and in 2010 Alfa Romeo celebrated its 100th anniversary.

Fabbrica Motoveicoli Fratelli Benelli, Pesaro
The Benelli company was established in Pesaro in 1911 as a family business repairing bicycles and motorcycles, as well as producing spare parts. During the First World War, Benelli was engaged in repairing military vehicles, and in 1919 produced its first motorcycle. During the Second World War, Benelli manufactured motorcycles for military use. By the end of the war, however, much of the factory had been destroyed and production machinery damaged. The company resumed production and underwent a series of management changes; in 2005 it was acquired by the Chinese Quianjiang Motor Group, which produces small motorcycles, with production remaining in Pesaro.

Edoardo Bianchi, Milan
Edoardo Bianchi was born in Milan in 1865. At the age of eight he became an apprentice blacksmith. For approximately 10 years he gained experience, and in 1885 decided to set up a precision workshop and bicycle works. Bianchi still manufactures bicycles and is the oldest bicycle manufacturer in Italy. The company grew slowly but steadily, and at the end of the century began to produce motorcycles and cars; in 1905 the Società Anonima Fabbrica Automobili Edoardo Bianchi e C. was formed. During the Italo-Turkish War (the Libyan campaign) and during the First World War, Bianchi was a major supplier of vehicles to the

Moto Guzzi GT 17 machine gun carrier with *Carabinieri Reali* number plate. Little is known about the application of these plates, because it is common to see Carabinieri vehicles with markings of the *Regio Esercito*.

An OS 88 tractor with the German *Todt* Organisation number plate. The Società Nazionale delle Officine di Savigliano (SNOS, later simply OS), founded in the province of Cuneo in 1880 for the manufacture and repair of railway material, produced only one definitive example of this vehicle, which was equipped with the Tipo 102 engine of the Lancia 3Ro truck. (Viberti)

This Breda trailer bears an army number plate with the word *RIMORCHIO* (trailer) in full. (Breda)

A Viberti trailer, carrying a medium tank, has a regulation number plate, were 'R⁰ E^(TO)' (for *Regio Esercito*) and the final 'R' (*Rimorchio*) were red and numerals were black.

A standardised trailer belonging to the *Regia Aeronautica*. In this example the letters are red and numerals are black, but the final 'r' is lower case.

A plate, unfortunately not very recognisable, of the *Polizia Coloniale* (Colonial Police corps) on a motorcycle. (ACS)

In 1939, the *Polizia Coloniale* became *Polizia dell'Africa Italiana* (Italian African Police corps). Here two plates of AB40 armoured cars. (ACS)

Guzzi motorcycles belonging to the *Polizia dell'Africa Italiana*. (ACS)

A Fiat 634 truck with the *Regio Corpo Truppe Coloniali* (RCTC) number plate in Libya in 1942. (ACS)

Fiat 508 CM belonging to the *Polizia dell'Africa Italiana*.

A Gilera 500 LTE with the plate of the Milizia della Strada (Road Militia, equivalent to the modern traffic police). (ACS)

A member of the *Milizia Portuale* (Port Police) aboard of his Guzzi GT 17 in Naples in 1936.

A FIAT 618 of the Milizia Nazionale Forestale (National Forest Militia) in East Africa, 1937.

A Lancia 3Ro, from the *Regio Corpo Truppe Libiche* (RCTL).

A Benelli 175 Sport (1932) in service with the *Regia Marina*. (USMM/Guglielmo Evangelista)

A 708 CM tractor of the *Regia Aeronautica* engaged in towing a Cant Z. 1007 Alcione medium bomber. The plate is 'RA 126 T' with black numbers and red letters.

Accident between a German car and an Italian truck. The Fiat 634 in the foreground, with almost completely worn tires and no spare wheel, has the license plate of a requisitioned vehicle. (Bundesarchiv: Bild 101I-203-1679-06)

If a vehicle was transformed by changing its tactical role, the number plate still remained the same, as on this Autocannone da 75/27 on a TL 37 tractor. (ACS)

The civilian vehicles requisitioned by the *Regio Esercito* usually carried the number plate with numbers starting with zero, as on this Alfa Romeo Tipo 85, the previous model to the Tipo 350 and the more widespread Tipo 500.

Another truck requisitioned and incorporated in the Italian Army.

In this image of a CL 39 light truck the number plate on the rear is clearly visible; the letters were red and the numbers black. (ACS)

The letter 'M' on the plate of this Autocarretta 32 was a legacy of the First World War numbering system and indicated a special vehicle.

Later, these light trucks received a number plate identical to those of normal motor vehicles. Here a group of Alpini (mountain infantry) from a mortar company celebrate the victory in the Greek campaign aboard an Autocarretta OM 37.

The tractor number plates ended with the red letter 'T', as in this Breda 33 heavy tractor for engineers. (Breda)

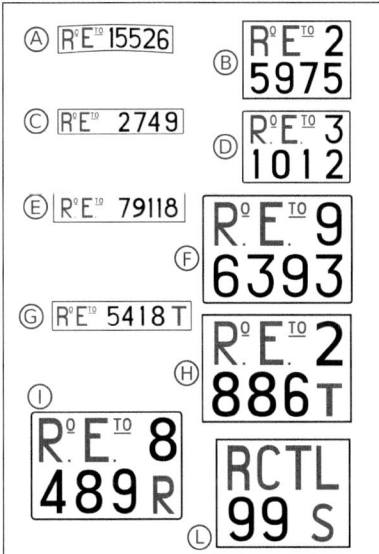

Examples of number plates: A = front plate, metal, motorcycle (Gilera 500 LTE); B = rear plate, metal, motor tricycle (Guzzi Trialce); C = front plate, metal, car (Bianchi VM6 C); D = rear plate, metal, car (Lancia Aprilia Coloniale); E = front plate, painted, truck (OM 3 BOD); F = rear plate, metal, truck (Bianchi Miles); G = front plate, painted, tractor (Alfa Romeo, prototype); H = rear plate, metal, tractor (Breda 33); I = rear plate, metal, trailer; L = rear plate, Regio Corpo Truppe Coloniali in Libia, metal, truck (AS 37). (Colour artworks by M. Pieri)

Bersaglieri aboard Guzzi Alce motorcycles. Note the number plate, curved to follow the profile of the mudguard. (ACS)

A Moto Guzzi GT 17 on the Eastern Front in 1941. The 'grandmother' of the Guzzi Alce had the front number plate made up of a regular rectangle. (ACS)

A Gilera 500 LTE with *Regio Esercito* number plate. Note the tyre inflation indication painted on the mudguard and the round badge under the headlight.

Number plates

Starting from 1927 all Italian vehicles, including AFVs, also had to carry a plate, different for the three arms of service (army, navy and air force). The plates of the army vehicles consisted of red letters and black numbers on a white background. The letters were 'R^O E^{TO}' (the abbreviation of *Regio Esercito*) and the numbers were progressive (theoretically, because photographic evidence testifies to various exceptions): from 1 to 9,999 for combat and special vehicles; from 10,000 to 49,999 for cars and light trucks; from 50,000 to 99,999 for trucks; motorcycles were assigned a rank from 1,000 to 29,999. The tractors had plates from 1 to 3,999 for the older ones and from 5,000 onwards for the more modern ones. Finally, no reliable information regarding the trailers was found.

The number plates of the requisitioned vehicles had a zero as the first digit, with exceptions relating, it would seem, to representative cars. However, the rules about numbering were not always respected and many non-standard plates are documented.

At the end of the numbering there could be a red letter, such as 'R' for trailer, 'B' for armoured car, 'T' for tractor, 'M' for special vehicles, and in some cases, some of the older autocannoni that originally had been issued registration plates during the First World War may have been encountered with plates that bore the letter 'C' (for *cannone autopropulso*, or self-propelled gun) in red, following the numbers.

Number plates of the *Regia Aeronautica* and *Regia Marina* were similar to the army plates, respectively with the initials RA (or R.A.) and RM (or R.M.). Other number plates were assigned to the vehicles of different corps, as the *Polizia Coloniale*, later *Polizia dell'Africa Italiana* (PAI), the *Milizia Nazionale della Strada* (MdS), the *Regio Corpo Truppe Coloniali* (RCTC) and other forces.

The size of the number plates varied over time, but when Italy entered the war the rear plates measured 230mm x 150mm for cars and motorcycles, and 320mm x 224mm for trucks and tractors, with letters and numbers arranged on two lines (but tractors could have everything on a single line), printed in relief on a thin metal plate.

The front number plates could also be made of metal (267mm x 52mm for cars) or painted directly onto the bumper or body, typically on trucks and tractors using the available space. Numbers and letters were arranged on a single line. The front number plate for motorcycles was fixed on the mudguard; it was always in metal and with a double face. It could be straight (250mm x 68mm) or curved (246mm x 58mm).

The badge on an Autocarretta 36 P.

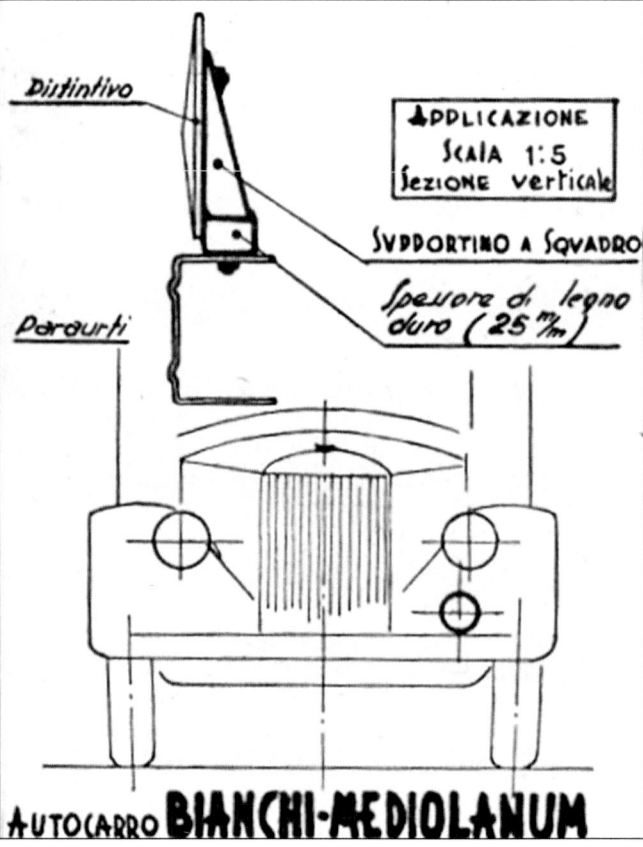

Application of the badge to the bumper sheet metal using a support and a small wooden board.

An uncommon example of black lettering on a Fiat 626.

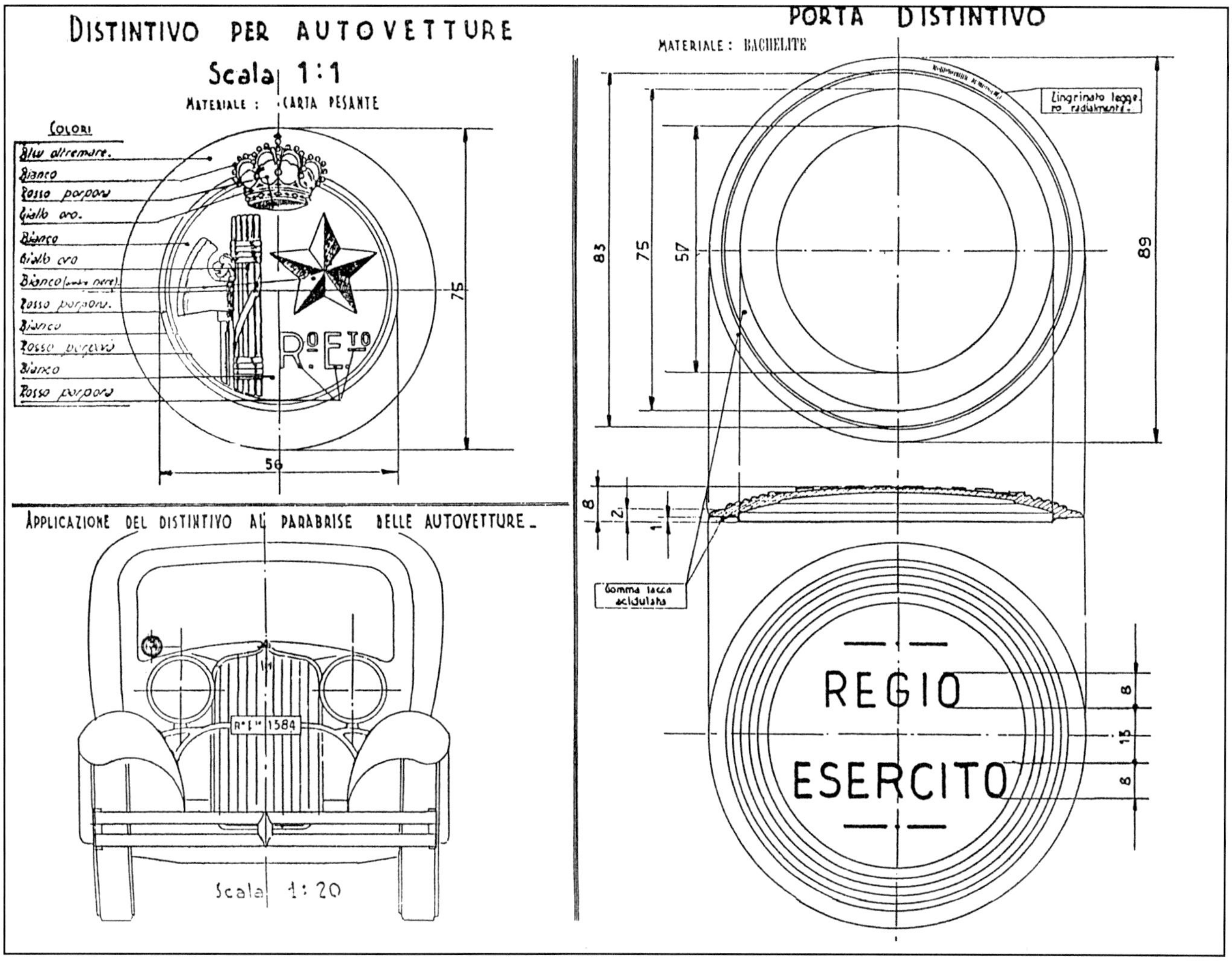

The characteristics of the cardboard badge to be applied to the windshield of cars and light trucks.

The Italian flag was sometimes painted on the roof of the truck cabs to facilitate aerial recognition.
At times, the sides of the vehicle's mudguards were painted in white to ease driving under blackout conditions.

The logistics writings were also white on the vehicles painted in *kaki sahariano*, like on this Fiat 665 Scudato.

All army vehicles had to bear a special bronze badge that proved they belonged to the *Regio Esercito*.

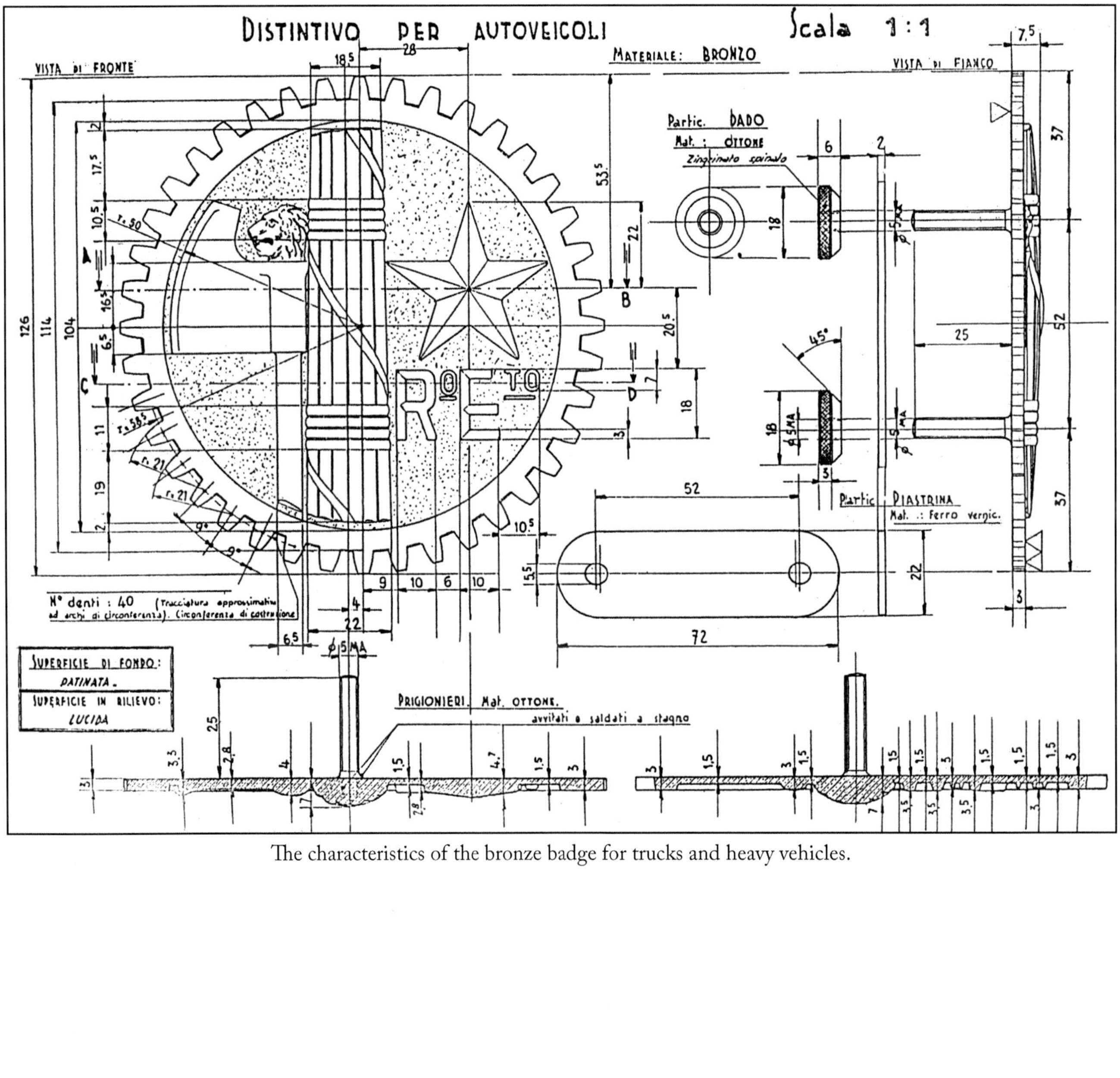

The characteristics of the bronze badge for trucks and heavy vehicles.

Markings

The wheeled vehicles of the Italian Army usually carried logistic marks useful above all for rail transport. In particular, the *tara* (unladen weight) and *portata* (carrying capacity) were specified, with values expressed in quintals (1 quintal = 100kg) or, more rarely, in kilograms. The colour of this writing and of the box that usually contained it was white both for the vehicles painted in *grigioverde* and for those in *kaki sahariano*, even if the photographic evidence reveals the occasional use of black lettering. Other writings, relating to tyre inflation pressure, could be painted on the outer edge of the fenders of all motor vehicles equipped with tyres, including motorcycles.

In addition, from 1935 all army vehicles had to bear a special badge that proved they belonged to the *Regio Esercito*. For the trucks it consisted of a cogwheel with 40 teeth, 126mm in diameter, cast in bronze. Inside and in relief, a bundle of fasces with an axe (a fascist emblem) surmounted by a lion's head were located on the left, a five-pointed star with the initials 'R.E.' below it was placed on the right. The emblem was worn on the front, usually fastened to the radiator grille.

Motorcycles had an almost identical marking, except for the diameter which was 90mm and a different attachment system.

Cars had a simplified emblem and displayed it on the windshield. In this case, however, it was made of cardboard, printed in colour, and had a diameter of 75mm; it was set in a Bakelite holder with an outside diameter of 89mm.

Trucks equipped with a closed cab could have a triangle (illuminated only on the civilian vehicles) installed on top, which had to be raised when a trailer was in tow.

Logistics information stencilled on the side of a Ceirano 50 CM. Below the windscreen, the round badge identifying an army vehicle is visible.

The cab of a Fiat 626 driven by men of the German 2. Fallschirmjäger-Division, in action in Italy.

The same writings could be enclosed in a box, as on this Lancia 3Ro. The winged letter 'V' visible below is the Officine Viberti trademark.

On this example of SPA Dovunque 35 both the on-road and off-road carrying capacity have been stencilled. (ACS)

During the campaign in North Africa, many Italian logistics vehicles remained painted in grey-green. In the absence of the regulation sand-yellow paint, the units often resorted to paints recovered on site and applied 'at best'. Here some *Bersaglieri* motorcyclists aboard Gilera 500 LTE two-seat motorcycles. (A. Tallillo)

A column of Italian and German prisoners photographed in Tunisia in May 1943. Behind the grey-green trailer, Italian trucks of various models are painted in sand-yellow colour. (LIFE)

original one (reference US FS 34159). At the same time, the authorities specified in a rule that: 'all vehicles currently coloured in yellow, grey-green or camouflaged must remain as they are'.

After the Armistice of 8 September 1943, the vehicles used by the Italian Social Republic (RSI) and German troops had various types of camouflage schemes, often non-standard. The *kaki sahariano* was mainly used, plain or with camouflage spots.

Until the end of the war, non-regulation camouflage schemes were sometimes adopted, using either captured or locally sourced paints in the area of operations. There are numerous testimonies and accounts in regard to this.

Generally, the vehicles built under German control maintained the Italian colours, but it is possible that some examples were repainted with German colours.

This image is part of a series of poses taken on Agfa colour film by a German soldier during the transfer trip and stay in North Africa. It was taken perhaps in the port of Tripoli or Bengasi in 1942. Italian cars and trucks (on the right, a Fiat 634 seen from the front) are painted in *kaki sahariano* which, due to the effect of the sun and the quality of the photographic equipment, appears rather pale.

North Africa, 1942. A grey-green Fiat 666 precedes a *kaki sahariano* Fiat 634 tank truck with trailer. The number plate and the circular bronze badge on the radiator grille are clearly visible.

The vehicles already present in Africa were repainted as soon as possible in *kaki sahariano* of a different intensity: in fact, from the images it is frequently observed that, the underlying grey-green showed through more or less evidently. Over time, but especially from the end of 1941 until the fall of Tunisia in May 1943, in many cases grey-green (and/or other colours) spots or stripes were applied to the *kaki sahariano* background to improve camouflage; these unofficial schemes were implemented only at the unit level and in a non-standard way.

From June 1943, because of the defeats suffered by the Axis on the African and Eastern Fronts and in view of the shift of operations to the Italian metropolitan territory, a new three-tone camouflage scheme was officially introduced for combat vehicles already in service and of future production. It was always made of *kaki sahariano* as a base, of shades – as far as we can see – tending to light (and in fact in some period documents it is simply called 'yellow'), with the addition of medium green and reddish-brown colours to complete the camouflage. The scheme was applied at the factory by means of a spray gun and in a standard way. Newly produced non-combat vehicles and artillery had to revert to the old grey-green, of which there was likely still ample supply; this colour, in the little documentation that has come down to us, seems to have a lighter shade than the

A Fiat 508 C Balilla sedan captured by Australian troops in the Bardia area, in December 1940, reveals the original colour showing through an improvised camouflage, perhaps made with mud or with a paint found on the spot. (AWM)

Four M14/41 tanks ready for embarkation in Naples, bound for North Africa. Their colour is the factory applied *kaki sahariano* (sand-yellow). In the frame from a period newspaper there are other vehicles repainted in the same colour: on the right a Breda 41 tractor, left in the background a Lancia 3Ro and a Fiat 626 or 666. Some of them have visible residues of the pre-existing grey-green paint.

Thus it was that the Italian troops took part in the Italo-Ethiopian War (1935–1936) and the Spanish Civil War (1937–1939) with cars, trucks and tractors painted in a solid grey-green colour, except for improvised camouflage schemes. It should be noted that vehicles operating in desert areas, such as eastern and northern Africa, were quickly covered with a layer of dust and sand – an effective natural camouflage effect.

We would add, especially for the benefit of modellers, that the seats made specifically for the *Regio Esercito* were normally in black faux leather (number 83) and the canvas roof covers and cargo covers were in light hazelnut or various shades of khaki (numbers 72, then 72A, and finally 72C), although some circulars called for painting them in camouflage schemes. It is almost superfluous to add that exceptions to the rules were numerous.

Starting from March 1941, following the guidelines of a circular that incorporated the observations coming from the battlefields, the production plants began to use a new *kaki sahariano* paint, named *kaki sahariano* (Sahara khaki, reference US FS 33434 or US FS 30260) aka *giallo sabbia* (sand-yellow) for the new vehicles destined for the North African Front. It was an intense sandy yellow colour, but its nuances – according to the examination of photos and finds – ranged from an ochre yellow typical of the new examples to a more or less faded and pale sand tone for those left under the desert sun or repainted in the field.

In these photographs taken in Yugoslavia by an Alpino soldier in April 1941, various Italian vehicles painted in the standard grey-green can be observed, including a damaged Alfa Romeo 800 RE, an OM Taurus and a Fiat 666.

A well-known photograph published by *Signal* magazine illustrates the landing of German material in the Tunisian port of Bizerte, at the end of 1942. The Italian Lancia 3Ro trucks are still in dark grey-green. The German Pz.Kpfw. III Ausf.N tanks are camouflaged in the *Tropen* colours in use since March 1942.

An OM Taurus crosses a German column in North Africa. The truck is grey-green and has the Italian flag painted on the cab roof.

Appendix I
Camouflage and Markings

Colours

In the period preceding the Second World War and until late 1943, various colour combinations were applied to Italian AFVs, motor vehicles, weapons and equipment, in accordance with the directions contained in the official memorandums. The painting was done in the factory, with good quality synthetic paints; it was also often applied in the theatre of operations at the level of an individual military unit, based on local conditions and the availability of paints. The main schemes are described below.

During the First World War the *grigio cenere* (ash grey, similar to US Federal Standard 595 code FS 36440) used since the beginning of the twentieth century gradually disappeared. In its place, and in particular from 1917, armoured cars, cars, motorcycles, trucks, tractors and guns received a dark grey-green colour named *grigioverde* (a good reference is US FS 34095). The first official document that has come to us relating to this colour is a circular dated 1925 which prescribes it 'for all artillery material', enclosing the 'recipe' of a mixture of various pigments to obtain it. This grey-green colour remained in force in the *Regio Esercito* during the Second World War with only the partial, but important exception, of the combat vehicles – which are not included in this work.

The German photographer Hugo Jaeger accompanied Hitler during his 1938 visit to Italy; this photo portrays a parade in Piazza del Plebiscito, in Naples. The two Pavesi P4-100 model 1926 tractors are painted in the regulation dark *grigioverde* (grey-green) colour. The circular bronze badge was fastened to the left of the white number plate.

152/37 guns being transported on Viberti heavy, two-axle cargo trailers in North Africa in November 1941. (ACS)

NB the trailer is equipped with pneumatic tyres, while the truck tractor still has semi-pneumatic tyres. Tobruk, Autumn 1941. (ACS)

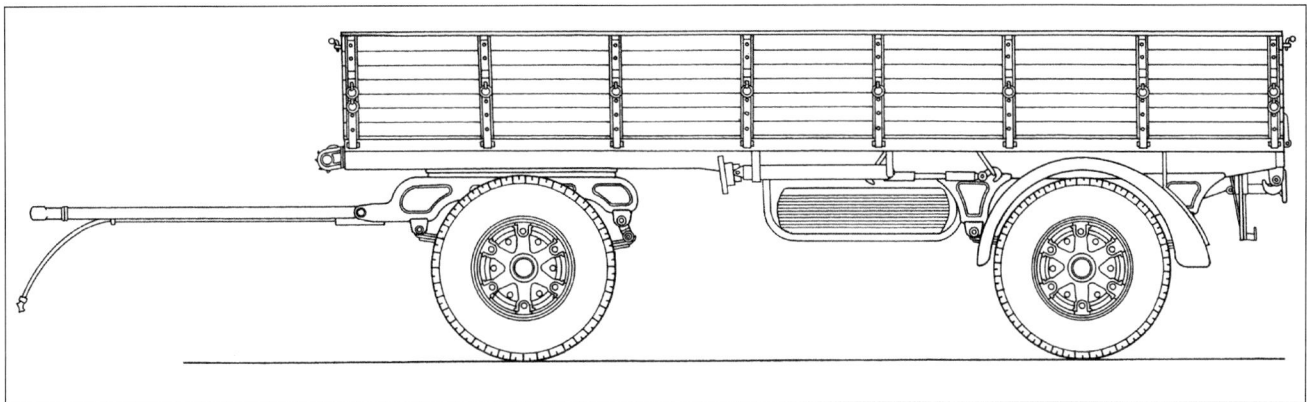

Regulation standard heavy trailer for medium tanks and derivatives. (Drawing by R. Ciuffoletti – GMT)

An M40 75/18 SPG being unloaded from the two-axle trailer. (ACS)

A column of two-axle trailers being towed by trucks in the Ukraine. In the foreground, a Benelli 500 VL and a Fiat 1100 Mimetica. (ACS)

Trucks and cargo trailers were also employed to transport troops and artillery pieces. (ACS)

An M40 75/18 SPG transported by a two-axle trailer in North Africa in 1942. (ACS)

An M40 75/18 SPG being unloaded from the two-axle trailer. (ACS)

One of the various trailers produced by Viberti, the Tipo 03 with steering wheels. (Viberti)

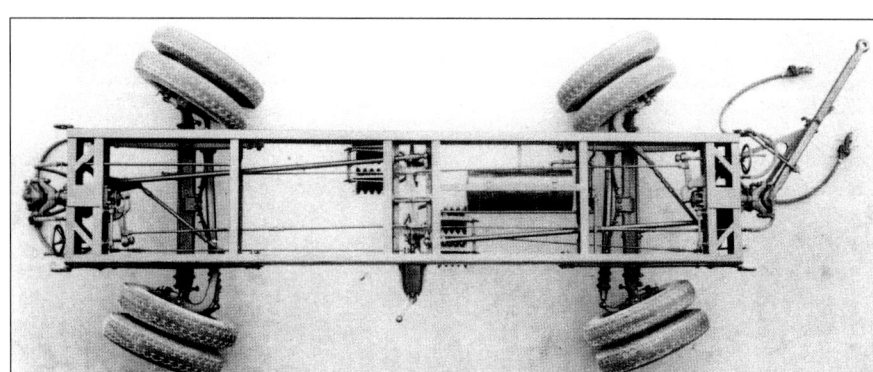

Top view of the frame of the standard 12 ton Viberti trailer. This model also has steering wheels (*a volta corretta*). (Viberti)

A trailer and related loading ramps for the ascent and descent of medium tanks and SPGs. (Viberti)

A Lancia 3Ro belonging to an *Autoreparto Pesante* while towing a M13/40 tank on a 12-ton two-axle trailer. (D. Zambon)

A Breda trailer *a volta corretta* (i.e. with steering wheels) with semi-pneumatic tyres. (Breda)

- Width: 2,000mm (6ft 7in)
- Turning radius: 7,800mm (25ft 7in)
- Tyres: 225 x 720.5

Two-axle cargo-type trailer (Viberti)
- Weight empty: 4,010kg (8,841lbs)
- Carrying capacity: 14,000kg (30,865lbs)
- Length: 6,770mm (22ft 2in)
- Width: 2,350mm (7ft 8in)
- Turning radius: 5,800mm (19ft)
- Tyres: 225 x 720.5

Two-axle cargo trailers, both military and civilian models, were commonly used for transporting tanks and SPGs because of the lack of specialist trailers. (IWM, ACS)

Of the two 12-ton cargo trailer manufacturers, initially the Viberti was favoured over the Bartoletti, as its compressed-air brakes were more reliable than those of the Bartoletti; however, based on user experience, the Viberti was judged to be too high off the ground and somewhat unstable.

In early 1942, an *autogruppo*, based on three *autoreparti*, was equipped with 246 heavy trucks and 225 trailers; this structure was later modified to an *autogruppo* with two *autoreparti* issued with 258 heavy trucks and 243 trailers. By March 1942 there were only 602 trailers of both categories (tank transporters and cargo trailers) spread throughout all operational theatres.

Specifications

Single-axle light tank transporter trailer (Viberti)
- Weight empty: 1,900kg (4,189lbs) with semi-pneumatic tyres; 1,742kg (3,840lbs) with pneumatic tyres
- Carrying capacity: 8,600kg (18,960lbs) with semi-pneumatic tyres; 7,600kg (16,755lbs) with pneumatic tyres
- Length: 4,400mm (14ft 5in)
- Width: 2,390mm (7ft 10in) with semi-pneumatic tyres; 2,500mm (8ft 3in) with pneumatic tyres
- Height: 690mm (2ft 3in)
- Tyres: 205 x 720.5 semi-pneumatic; 270 x 20 pneumatic

Two-axle medium tank transporter trailer (Strafurini)
- Weight empty: 4,940kg (10,891lbs)
- Carrying capacity: 14,000kg (30,865lbs)
- Length: 6,880mm (22ft 7in)

Two-axle cargo trailers, both military and civilian models, were commonly used for transporting tanks and SPGs because of the lack of specialist trailers. (IWM, ACS)

the Lancia 3Ro, the Fiat 634 or other heavy trucks. Although the general layout and the body type of these cargo trailers was similar, in addition to the differing cargo capacities there were many variations with respect to the type and arrangement of the wheels. Bodies consisted of wooden beds and wooden sides and tailgates, which could be lowered. The smaller capacity trailers had single pressed steel wheels front and rear, usually with four lightening holes and mounting semi-pneumatic tyres, whereas the higher capacity trailers had dual sets of pneumatic tyres front and rear, mounted on six-spoke, cast wheels, although some of the heaver trailers were reportedly fitted with dual semi-pneumatic tyres. All four wheels of the trailers could be steered, resulting in a tight turning circle, or, alternately, only the front two wheels could steer.

On the eve of the war, guidelines were issued for so-called *Rimorchi Unificati* (standardised trailers) with carrying capacities of 12,000kg for the heavy category and 6,500kg for the medium category; among the characteristics of these trailers were a frame consisting of parallel longerons, a towing yoke that could be used on either end, leaf spring suspension, with helical springs on the heavy capacity trailers, a standard pneumatic brake system on all four wheel sets, standardised spoke wheels, pneumatic tyres and an electrical system. There is a considerable amount of photographic evidence showing the cargo trailers in use in North Africa, often carrying tanks or heavy artillery pieces. When not carrying heavy equipment and when used as a cargo carrier, the use of trailers effectively more than doubled the carrying load capacity of a heavy truck.

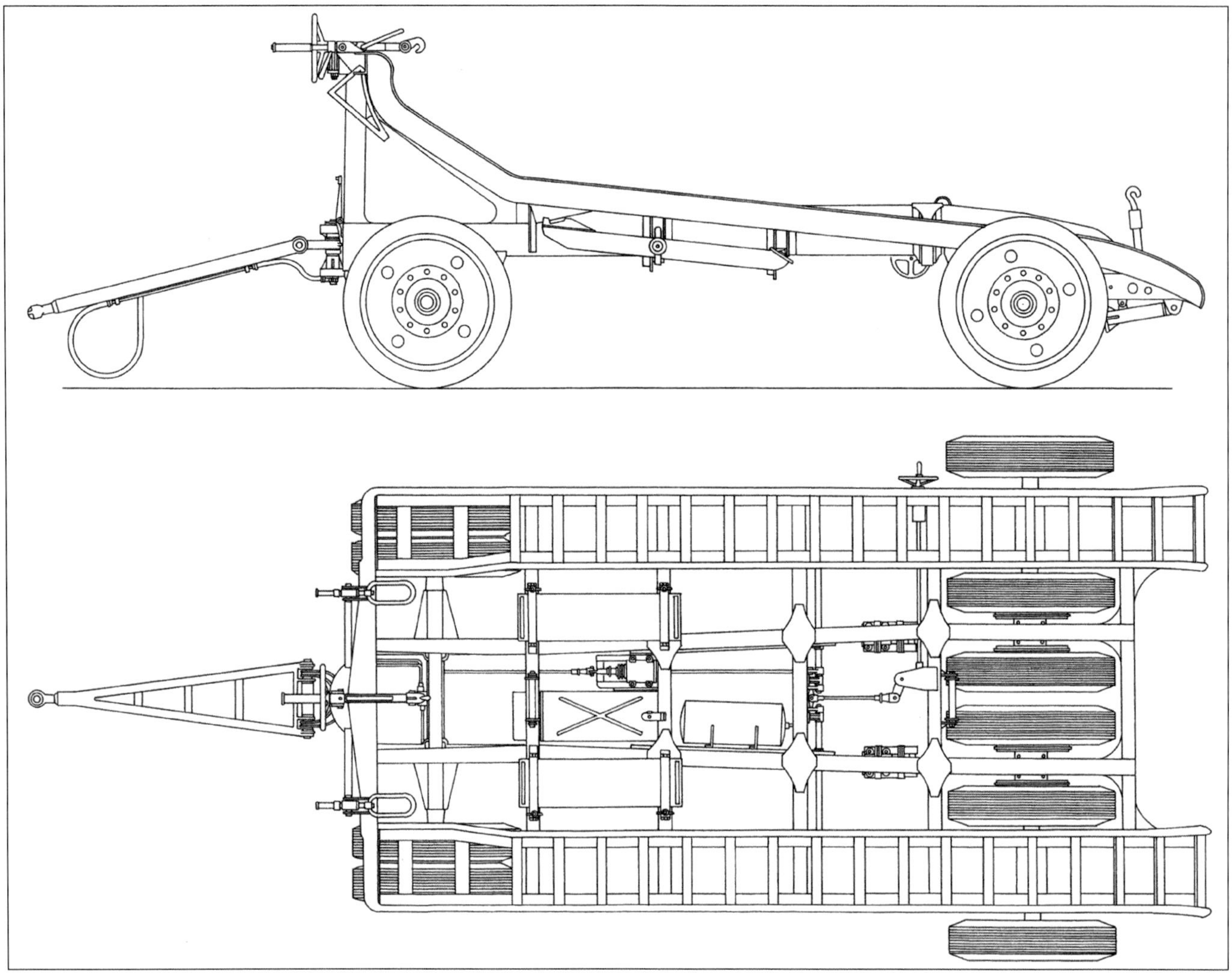

Special trailer for M15/42 medium tanks and derivatives. (Drawing by R. Ciuffoletti – GMT)

Two-axle cargo trailers, both military and civilian models, were commonly used for transporting tanks and SPGs because of the lack of specialist trailers. (IWM, ACS)

General Purpose Cargo Trailers

With respect to the general purpose cargo trailers, there was an extensive range of conventional two-axle platform trailers ranging in carrying capacity from 4 tons to 12 tons, produced mainly by Viberti and Bartoletti, and designed to be towed by

The prototype *biga* trailer for L6 light tanks built by Viberti. (Viberti)

An M11/39 medium tank on a Strafurini trailer; note the elaborate Strafurini name plate on each side of the track limiting bar. The trailer's tyres are Celerflex 720.5 x 225 semi-pneumatic tyres. (CSM)

profile joined by evenly spaced cross-members or sleepers for their entire length. The Viberti trailers could be fitted with either semi-pneumatic or pneumatic tyres.

These types of single-axle light tank trailers were called *biga*, the name of a chariot from the Roman era. They were towed by heavy trucks such as the Fiat 666, 634 or Lancia 3Ro. However, there is no information that the *biga* trailers were ever put into production or used in service. The photographic documentation reveals that light tanks and SPGs were carried on a truck bed, while the truck commonly towed a trailer with another tank on it.

A trailer for medium tanks (the M11/39, M13/40 and M14/41 and later the M15/42) and their derivatives (mainly SPGs), conceptually similar to the Viberti and Adige trailers but of significantly different configuration, was developed and produced by Strafurini and Viberti. The medium tank trailer had a two-axle design, with two sets of dual wheels on the front axle and six single wheels on the rear axle, two of which were outboard of the ramps and the other four of which were inboard. The wheels themselves were pressed steel discs with four lightening holes and which used semi-pneumatic tyres. The ramps were similar to those of the light tank trailers, with the end of each ramp ending in a marked upward curve which mated with the drive sprocket and forward portion of the tank's tracks.

A photograph from 31 July 1943 showing a M15/42 medium tank climbing onto a Viberti trailer towed by a TM 40 tractor. Note that the tank is painted *kaki sahariano*, but the other two vehicles appear in grey-green.

8

Trailers

During the inter-war years and throughout the Second World War, the Italians used a wide variety of types and sizes of trailers, many of them for logistic and specialised purposes such as animal transport, supply train use, ammunition transport for specific types of guns, and field kitchens, plus a number of types taken from the civilian market. A complete and detailed coverage of all trailers used by the Italian armed services is outside the scope of this work but it will cover, however, some trailers which were in widespread use and which significantly enhanced the ability of trucks to deliver equipment and goods quickly, and over long distances.

The trailers covered here fall into two broad categories: those that were designed to be used exclusively for transporting AFVs and which were basically ramps with varying numbers of wheels upon which the tanks were driven, and more conventional general purpose trailers with two axles which could accommodate tanks and artillery pieces as well as general cargo. The tank transporter trailers were used to save wear and tear on the tanks themselves as well to move them much more quickly over long distances. The cargo trailers were employed to move heavy artillery pieces more quickly and efficiently than towing by tractor on roads over long distances; also, they were used to carry other classes of cargo including ammunition, food, fuel, lubricants and other items of equipment.

Tank Transporter Trailers

Among the tank transporter type of trailer was a four-wheeled trailer built by the Adige company for transporting the L6/40 light tank and its derivatives; the four wheels had six cast spokes, used pneumatic tyres, and were all mounted along a single axis, two outboard of each of the two ramps and two inboard, between the ramps. A very similar trailer for the L6/40 was produced by Viberti; the chief difference between the Adige and Viberti trailers was that the ramps on the Adige trailers were linear, with an angled portion at the rear of the trailer which allowed the tank to climb. On the other side, the Viberti trailer had a downward curved section of each ramp to allow the tank to climb and a very pronounced upward curved section at the far end of each ramp that acted as a stop for the tank tracks. The ramps themselves consisted of side rails that had a roughly L-shaped

An L6 light tank on a single-axle prototype Adige *biga* trailer. (CSM)

to standardise what was done in Libya by the unit workshops (see the AS 37). In essence, the cab was reconfigured and simplified, while the bed was modified to house the 20mm Breda 35 cannon; there was also an 8mm Breda 37 machine gun. The few examples produced, perhaps 11, were delivered to the scout company of the *Battaglione d'Assalto Motorizzato* (Motorised Assault Battalion) which operated only in the Italian metropolitan area.

Specifications

- Designation: Camionetta SPA-Viberti AS 43
- Producer: Società Piemontese Automobili (SPA), Turin; Carrozzeria Viberti, Turin
- Years produced: 1943–1946
- Number produced: 63 or 66
- Length: 4,820mm (18ft 10in)
- Width: 2,060mm (4ft 9in)
- Height 2,175mm (7ft 2in)
- Combat loaded weight: 5,000kg (11,023lbs)
- Crew: 5 (commander/gunner, driver, assistant driver, 2 assistant gunners)
- Wheelbase: 2,500mm (8ft 2in)
- Front track: 1,600mm (5ft 3in)
- Rear track: 1,600mm (5ft 3in)
- Minimum turning radius: 7,600mm (24ft 11in)
- Minimum clearance: 345mm (1ft 1in)
- Fording depth: 700mm (2ft 4in)
- Tyres: Superflex Sigillo Verde 11.25 x 24 or Superflex Artiglio 9.00 x 24
- Engine: SPA 18 VT, four-cylinder, water-cooled, 4,053cc, 73 HP @2,600 rpm
- Transmission: five speeds forward, one reverse
- Fuel: Gasoline
- Fuel capacity: 120 litres (31.7 US gallons, 26.4 Imperial gallons), plus 200 litres (52.9 US gallons, 44 Imperial gallons) in fuel canisters
- Drive layout: 4x4
- Maximum speed: 68.5km/h (43mph)
- Range (on road): 750km (466 miles) without jerry cans; 1,120km (696 miles) with six 20-litre jerry cans

The Camionetta Desertica modello 1943, produced in only 11 units, was an independent project which should not be confused with the Camionetta AS 43.

Rear view of a Camionetta Desertica modello 1943.

Variants

The AS 43 served as the basis for an armoured car for the RSI (designated as Carrozzeria Speciale su SPA AS 43, or Special Body on SPA AS 43), completed in 1944 in only a few examples.

Although it was not a variant of the Camionetta AS 43, the Camionetta Desertica mod. 43, is worth mentioning because the two vehicles are sometimes confused with each other. The Camionetta Desertica mod. 43 was in fact built at the beginning of 1943 by the Centro Studi della Motorizzazione (CSM) by varying the bodywork of AS 37 trucks; the intention was probably

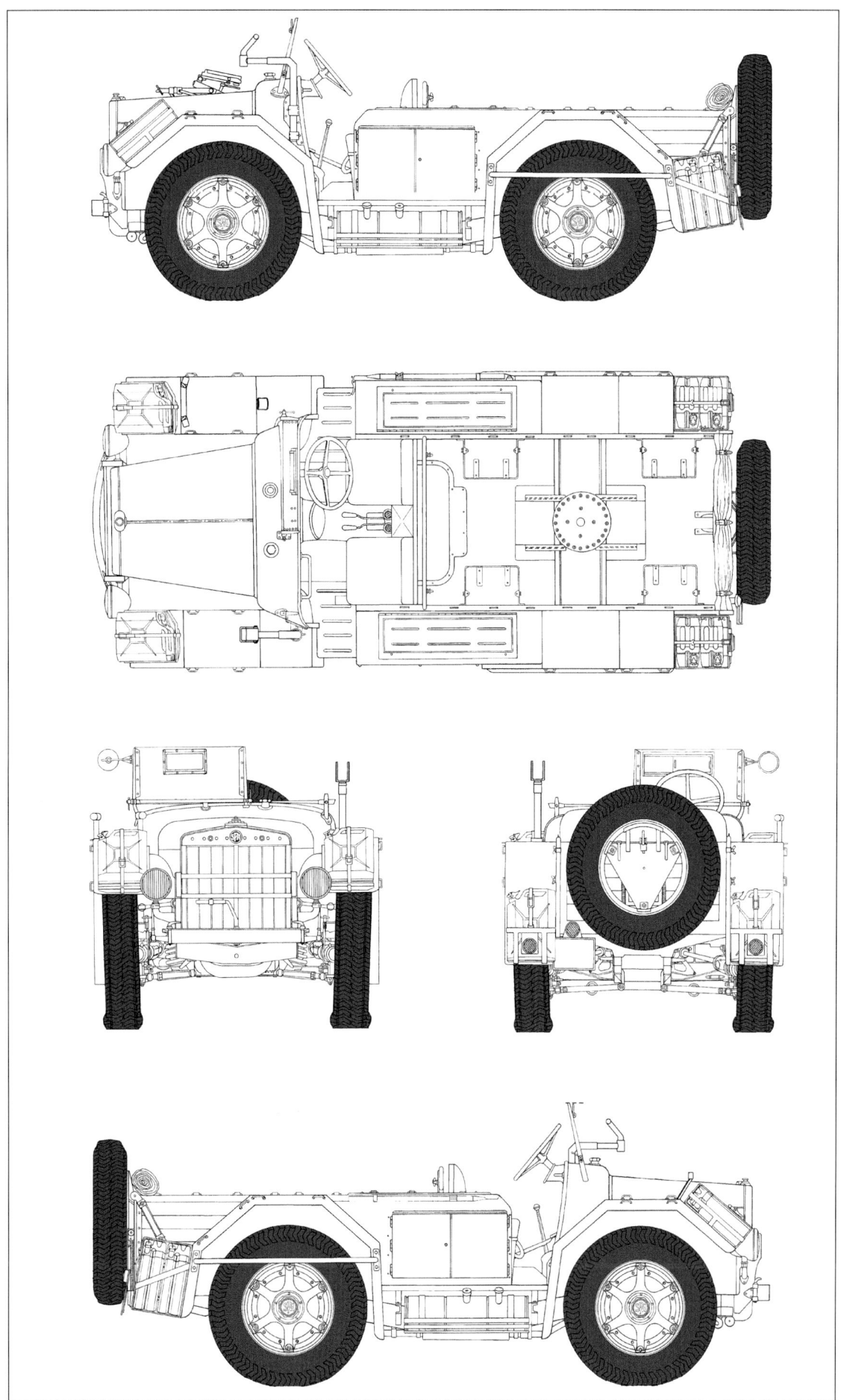

Camionetta AS 43. (Drawings by R. Calò – GMT)

This AS 43 with Superflex Artiglio tyres ready for delivery in the summer of 1943 shows the tyre pressure lettering painted white on the side of the mudguards.

Technical Description

Although based on the AS 37 chassis, the AS 43 was essentially a completely new vehicle that had few parts in common with the AS 37 itself. The body of the AS 43, built by Viberti, was of a completely different design to that of the AS 37. There were no doors to the vehicle, and access to the front seats was through a narrow gap between the front fender and the side storage lockers. An ammunition locker for the magazines for the on-board Breda model 37 machine gun was located between the seats. In common with most Italian military vehicles, the steering wheel was on the right-hand side.

It had a more powerful engine, independent spring suspension, hydraulic shock absorbers, on-board compressor for tyre inflation, hydraulic brakes, four-wheel drive with the rear wheels driving, and steerable front wheels only. Also, the minimum clearance was reduced in order to obtain lower-profile vehicle. Transmission was a five-speed manual.

Rear view of the same example. (Viberti)

This example of an AS 43 is almost identical to the previous one except for the standard Superflex Sigillo Verde tyres with diamond pattern tread. The camouflage is the three-tone scheme that became regulation in 1943. (Viberti)

The AS 43 in its almost final version, but without the rear spare wheel, the canisters on the mudguards and various accessories. An ammunition container is now present on the sides but the tyres are still the Superflex Raiflex Sigillo Verde. (Viberti)

More views of the same example, with the three-tone camouflage. (Viberti)

1946. Used and new vehicles were issued to the *Reparti Celeri* (Flying Squads) of the *Pubblica Sicurezza della Polizia di Stato* (national police public security agency).

Adding together all of the examples produced before and after the end of the Second World War, we arrive at a total of 63 or 66 vehicles, a figure that seems to be confirmed by military financial accounts.

The prototype of the Camionetta AS 43 equipped with Superflex Raiflex Sigillo Verde tyres. (Fiat)

Similar to the AS 42, the fuel canisters were located on the sides and the water canisters on the front and rear mudguards. (Fiat)

Rear view of the same prototype; on the side of the spare tyre is 'Pirelli Superflex, 11.25 x 24'. On the opposite side to the wording, an almost invisible letter 'R' indicates that it is a Raiflex rayon tyre. (Viberti)

During 1942, the *Regio Esercito* had ordered 180 of these vehicles. Viberti documents report between 167 and 169 examples to be made from June 1943 to January 1946, but it is unlikely that this figure was met, especially in view of the Armistice, so much so that researchers estimate a quantity actually delivered before 8 September 1943 equal to about 20 vehicles. The intention of the army was that the AS 43 was to have been armed, similarly to the AS 42, with the 47mm gun or the 20mm cannon to form special companies; however, this plan was not completed.

Following the Armistice, the German armed forces confiscated many of the AS 43s in service and had Viberti produce another 13 examples with a modified platform, so that they could rearm them with the 20mm Flak 30 or Flak 38 cannon.

Production of the AS 43 continued after the war, although in limited numbers, with deliveries being made as late as January

Two AS 42 Metropolitane patrolling in Rome on 23 March 1944. The PAI (Italian African Police) number plate, only visible under magnification, replaced the badge of the Regio Esercito in front left. Jerrycans had been removed. (Author's collection)

- Years produced: 1942–1943
- Number produced: between 120 and 140; some sources quote between 76 and 200
- Length: 5,626mm (18ft 5in)
- Width: 2,260mm (7ft 5in)
- Height: 1,800mm (5ft 11in)
- Weight: 4,500kg (9,921lbs) (empty weight); 6,000kg (13,228lbs) in combat trim
- Crew: four (the driver plus three others); six in the post-war Police variant
- Wheelbase: 3,200mm (10ft 6in)
- Track width: 1,750mm (5ft 9in)
- Minimum turning radius: 5,500mm (18ft)
- Minimum clearance: 350mm (1ft 2in)
- Fording depth: 700mm (2ft 4in)
- Tyres: Superflex 11.25 x 24 Artiglio or Libia Rinforzato 10T 9.75 x 24 or Superflex Sigillo Verde
- Engine: SPA ABM 3, six-cylinder, in-line, water-cooled, 4,995cc, 100 HP @2,700 rpm
- Transmission: five speeds forward, one reverse
- Fuel: Gasoline
- Fuel capacity: 145 litres (38.3 US gallons, 31.9 Imperial gallons), plus up to 400 litres (105.6 US gallons, 88 Imperial gallons) in fuel canisters
- Drive layout: 4x4
- Maximum speed (road): 84km/h (52mph)
- Maximum speed (cross-country): 50km/h (31mph)
- Range (on road): 300km (186 miles), plus 1,200km (745 miles) using fuel from on-board fuel canisters
- Range (cross-country): 5 hours (25 hours with fuel from additional canisters)

Camionetta SPA-Viberti AS 43

Developmental and Service History

In late summer 1942 the prototype of a new light desert truck, developed as a result of experience gained from operations in North Africa, was unveiled. The vehicle was built on the chassis of the AS 37 light desert truck (see separate entry) and was not armoured. The production model was not ready until January 1943, by which time the Axis forces in North Africa had suffered serious defeat, and the need for the vehicle there was no longer a priority. Some modifications were made to the vehicle as originally designed to make it more compatible for use in a European operational environment. In August 1943 the *Ispettorato per le Truppe Motorizzate e Corazzate* (Inspectorate for Motorised and Armoured Troops) issued a circular specifying the role of the AS 43 (Autocarro Sahariano 43, Saharan truck model 1943). Such vehicles were intended to equip coastal defence companies to repel landing attempts. The armament consisted of either a 20mm Breda model 35 cannon or a 47/32 gun on an interchangeable mount, in addition to an 8mm Breda model 37 machine gun, which was removable and could be used with a ground mount.

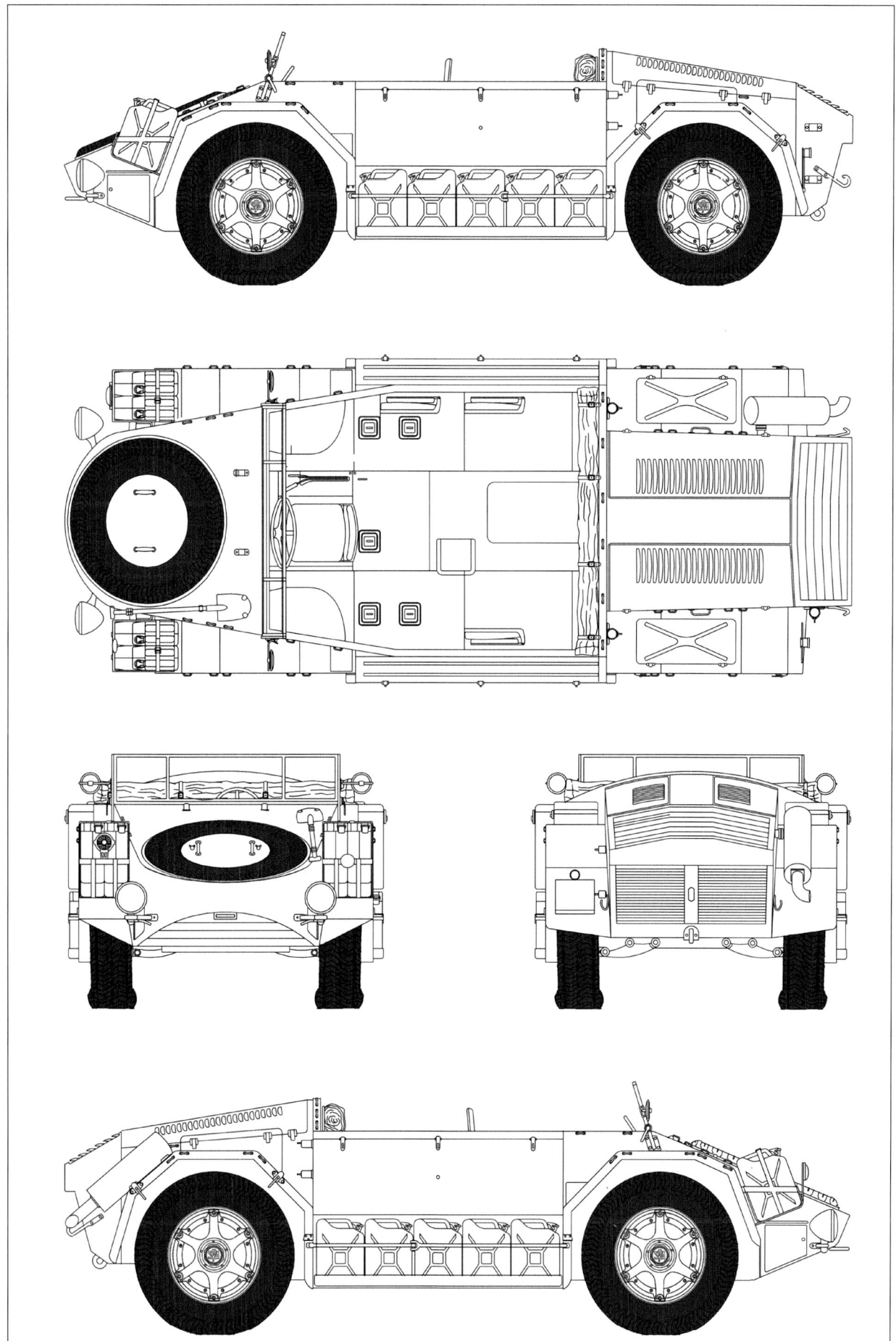

Camionetta AS 42 Tipo II Metropolitana. (Drawings by R. Calò – GMT)

A Camionetta AS 42 type 2 or 'Metropolitana'. The main differences with the type 1 Sahariana were the Superflex Artiglio tyres and the large multipurpose locker mounted in place of the upper row of side canisters.

Another view of the Camionetta AS 42 Tipo II

Variants

The original version or configuration of the AS 42, which had been developed for use in the desert, had racks on each side of the body which could carry ten 20-litre jerry cans of fuel per side; an additional four jerry cans for water were mounted on the front fenders, two per side. Sand channels could also be carried slung over the rear wheels.

Once the war in the desert ended in spring of 1943, the upper racks for the jerry cans on each side were replaced by large storage lockers. This version was designated the Tipo II (type 2), or more commonly referred to as the AS 42 Metropolitana (metropolitan), while the earlier version became designated as the Tipo I (type 1) or Sahariana (Saharan).

Specifications

Note. No factory technical manual was drawn up for this vehicle.

- Designation: Camionetta SPA-Viberti AS 42
- Producer: Società Piemontese Automobili (SPA), Turin; Carrozzeria Viberti, Turin

An AS 42 in North Africa mounting a 20mm Solothurn anti-tank rifle; the other weapon is an 8mm Breda 37 machine gun. Sand channels are fixed to the sides. In the background is an AS 37 armed with a 47/32 gun.

A pair of AS 42 Saharianas in North Africa; the vehicle on the right mounts a 20mm Breda anti-aircraft cannon, while that on the left mounts a 47/32 anti-tank gun. (AUSSME)

AB 41, the rear driving seat was eliminated and, while maintaining traction on all four wheels, the rear steering was also done away with. The body of the AS 42 was configured as a boat-hull, with a large open fighting compartment. The body was made up of pressed steel panels that resulted in a slab-sided vehicle with flat, angular fenders; but it was not an armoured vehicle. A wooden bulkhead at the rear of the fighting compartment provided access to the engine. The spare wheel and tyre were mounted in a recess on the front; the wheel disc was covered by a circular metal plate with lifting handles, while the tyre itself remained exposed. Depending on availability, Superflex tyres of different treads (Artiglio, Sigillo Verde, and Libia Rinforzato 10 Tele) could be mounted on the six-spoke 24 x 7 cast wheels. The AS 42 had a low-profile three-piece windshield. A canvas cover supported by two metal bows could be erected to protect the crew from inclement weather. The AS 42 frame consisted of two U-shaped channels on which the four independently sprung wheels with coil springs were mounted. The driver's position was offset just slightly to the left of the vehicle's centreline. The brakes were pedal operated hydraulically assisted mechanical brakes on all four wheels; the hand brake acted on the transmission. The electrical system ran off a 12 volt battery; starting was either by a rear-mounted hand crank or electrically by a Magneti Marelli starter.

The vehicle could be equipped with a variety of armament, including the 20mm Breda model 35 anti-aircraft gun, the 20mm Solothurn anti-tank rifle, and the 47/32 model 39 gun. In addition, there were up to three machine gun mountings for the 8mm Breda model 37 machine gun (one to the right of the driver, and two at the rear corners). The engine was a six-cylinder gasoline engine developing 100 HP, placed in the back; the transmission had five speeds forward and one reverse.

SPECIAL PURPOSE VEHICLES 177

The interior of an AS 42 with the windscreen down and the rear engine compartment bulkhead removed. The folding seats for the gunners are fixed to the internal sides.

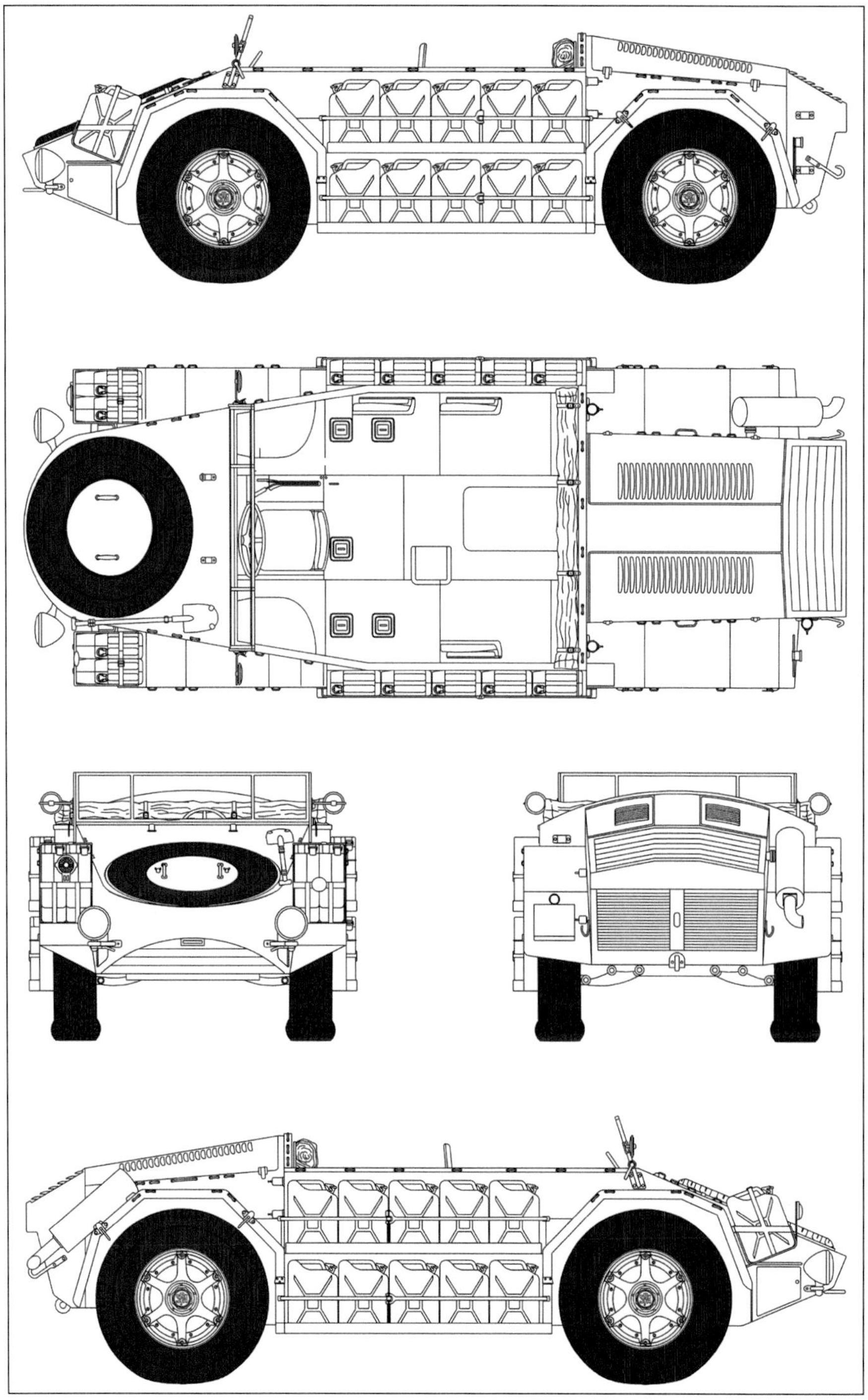

Camionetta AS 42 Sahariana.
(Drawings by R. Calò – GMT)

This other example, with its canvas top raised, has Superflex S.V. Libia tyres (except on the spare wheel).

View of the driver's seat.

they acted in a reconnaissance role between November 1943 and March 1944.

Ten examples were delivered to the *Polizia dell'Africa Italiana*, which employed them in Rome; one of these AS 42s was destroyed by US troops on 4 June 1944, during the operations to capture the city.

Following the war, the surviving eleven mod. 42s were turned over to the Italian *Pubblica Sicurezza* (State Police), and with minor modifications and sporting a burgundy paint scheme, constituted a company of the *Reparto Mobile Speciale di Pubblica Sicurezza* (State Police Special Mobile Unit).

Technical Description

The AS 42 was based on the chassis of the AB 41 armoured car and used many of its mechanical components. Compared to the

The Camionetta AS 42 Sahariana, rear three-quarter views.

The same vehicle with the windshield covered by a canvas case to reduce the reflection of the sun's rays and the consequent risk of detection by the enemy. On the front are a series of digging tools.

in August. An initial order was placed for 140 vehicles, later reduced to 80 vehicles, but then supplemented by a further order for 20.

Originally planned to be used for behind the lines raids against the Allies, it was used primarily as a reconnaissance vehicle (see also SPA AS 37). The AS 42 was initially employed operationally in late November 1942 in North Africa and continued to participate in operations until at least May 1943 in Tunisia. In April 1943 one company was sent to Sicily and fought there until the end of July, when it returned to mainland Italy. Following the 8 September Armistice with the Allies, some of the Camionette elements fought against the Germans, while others joined the Germans and continued fighting alongside them. A group of Italian volunteers accompanied the German *2. Fallschirmjäger-Division* (2nd Paratrooper Division) in Russia, where

7

Special Purpose Vehicles

Note

The two vehicles described in this chapter are somewhat anomalous in that they straddle two categories, i.e., they are soft-skinned vehicles while at the same time were expressly designed and built as combat vehicles. They have been included in this book because of their characteristics in the former category.

Apart from these series-produced fighting vehicles, Italian repair and workshop personnel produced some partially or completely armoured vehicles at unit workshops, based on wheeled cars and trucks.

CAMIONETTA DESERTICA SPA-VIBERTI AS 42

A Camionetta AS 42 Sahariana with Superflex Raiflex Sigillo Verde tyres ready for delivery. The 20 canisters placed on the sides were to contain fuel, those on the front (marked in white) were for drinking water. The on-board weapon mounts are visible.

Developmental and Service History

After the success obtained in the field with the first weapons carriers (based on trucks and light tractors), and impressed by the success of the British LRDG raiding parties, the Italian Army General Staff decided to form an equivalent organisation. Initially this was of battalion strength but it was later increased to regimental strength. The regiment had four battalions, each of which had an integral company of *Arditi Camionettisti* (vehicle-borne raiding parties). In order to properly equip these companies, the staff ordered the design and production of two special vehicles, the Camionetta mod. 42 (also referred to as the Camionetta Desertica, the Sahariana, or the AS 42) and the Camionetta mod. 43 (or AS 43 – see below).

The AS 42, jointly developed by SPA and Viberti, was built on a modified AB 41 armoured car chassis. In June 1942 the first prototype of the AS 42 was completed. Although it was not officially adopted until December 1942, deliveries had begun

A Breda document dated 29 January 1945 with the prices of some spare parts for the Breda 61 and the Breda 40 and 41 tractors. (Breda)

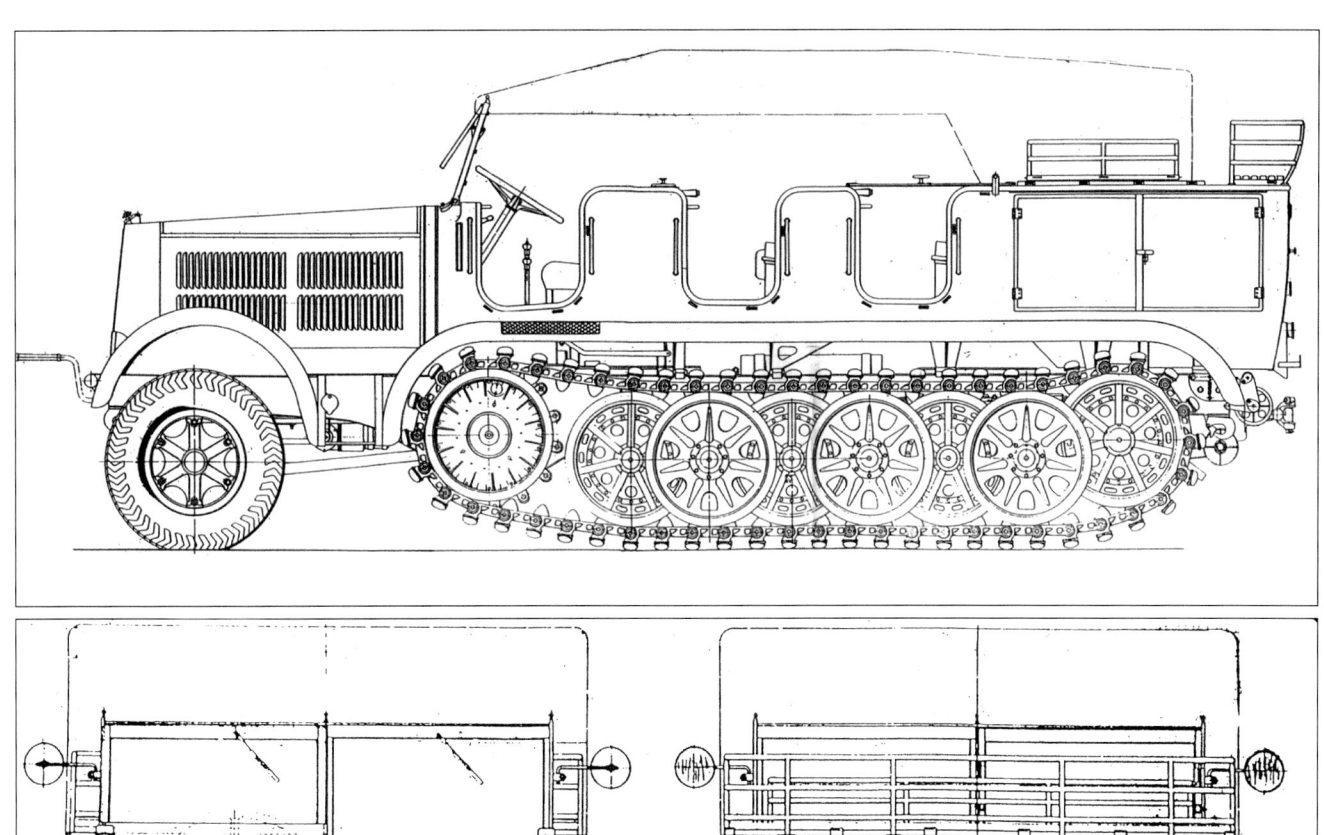

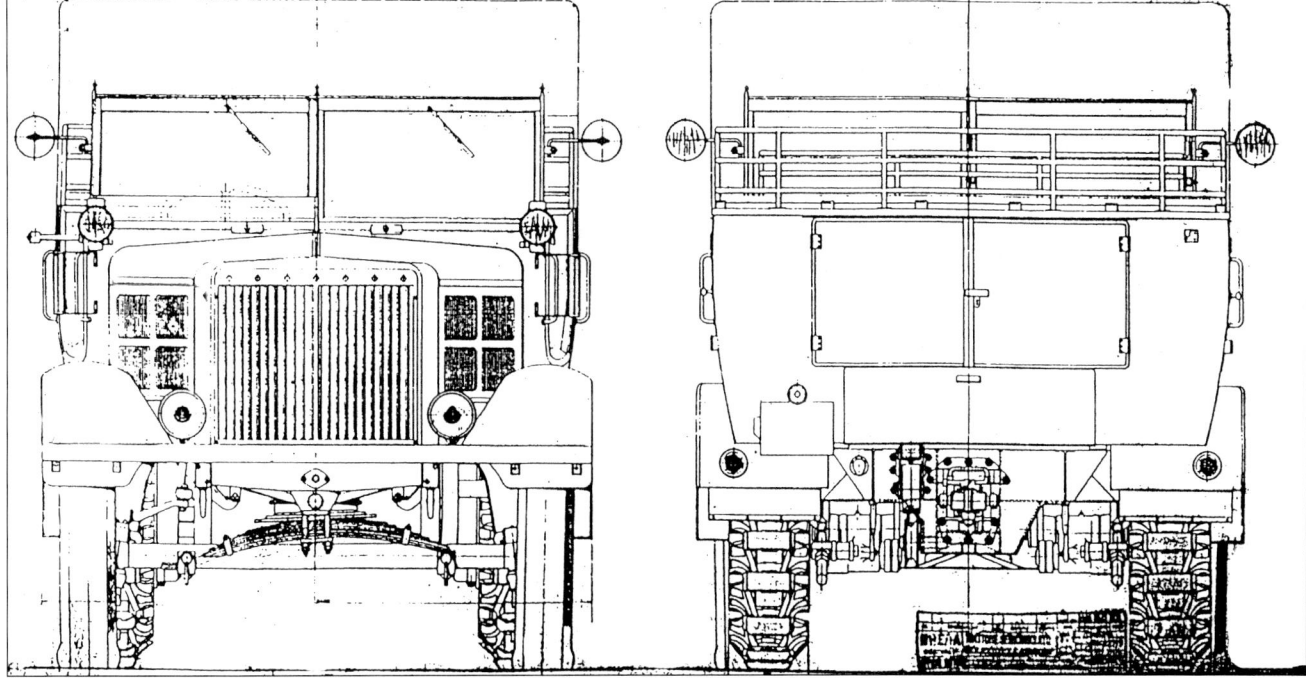

Original drawings of the Breda 61. (Breda)

A German-owned Breda 61 towing an Italian 149/19 howitzer, photographed in the outskirts of Bologna on 21 April 1945, when the Allied troops entered the city.

A Breda 61 abandoned by the Germans near the Po River. The 10 supports for the crew's individual weapons are visible in front of the centre and rear seats. The right-hand drive can be seen as well as the container located between the two rear seats. The number plate appears to be 'WH (or WL) 234117'.

- Width: 2,450mm (8ft)
- Height: 2,620mm (8ft 7in)
- Unladen weight: 11,200kg (24,692lbs)
- Carrying capacity: 1,800kg (3,968lbs)
- Towing capacity: 8,000kg (17,637lbs)
- Front track: 2,000mm (6ft 7in)
- Rear track: 1,800mm (5ft 11in)
- Minimum turning radius: 8,000mm (26ft 3in)
- Minimum clearance: 390mm (1ft 4in)
- Tyres (front): Superflex 9.75 x 20
- Engine: Breda T14, six-cylinder in-line, water-cooled, 7,412cc, 130 HP @2,400 rpm
- Fuel: Gasoline
- Transmission: five speeds forward, one reverse, with reduction gear
- Fuel capacity: 170 + 35 litres (45 US gallons, 37.4 Imperial gallons + 9.3 US gallons, 7.7 Imperial gallons)
- Drive layout: Half-track
- Maximum speed: 50km/h (31mph)
- Range (on road): 300km (186.5 miles)
- Range (cross-country): 170km (105.6 miles)

An example without canvas top. The windscreen glass could be partially or completely raised. The side openings were fitted with light chains to ensure that passengers did not fall out of the vehicle.

mounted inside the frame, under the rear seats. The driver and two other crew members could sit on the front seat and ten men on the two large rear seats. Personal equipment and ammunition could be stored in spacious rear lockers, and additional lockers were located under the seats. A waterproof canvas top could cover the top of the vehicle as far forward as the windshield. Starting was electrical or by a Bosch starter; the engine could also be cranked manually using a handle. In addition to the bumper-mounted headlights, there were also outdated acetylene headlights located on the sides of the windshield, at the bottom.

Specifications

- Designation: Trattore semicingolato da 8 tonnellate Breda 61
- Manufacturer: Società Italiana Ernesto Breda per Costruzioni Meccaniche, Milan
- Years produced: 1944–1945
- Number produced: 199
- Length: 6,900mm (22ft 7in)

The Breda 61 half-track in the Breda factory prior to being fitted with its centre and rear body work. The photo allows a clear view of the main fuel tank, the winch with its connection to the engine, the towing gear, the instrumentation, and the driver's controls. (Breda)

Trattore semicingolato Breda 61

The Breda 61 half-track, a close copy of the German Sd.Kfz. 7 half-track.

Developmental and Service History

As early as 1941 the Italian military authorities began to explore the idea of producing a half-tracked vehicle and consulted with German companies that had experience in half-track manufacture. In 1941 the Krauss-Maffei 8-ton Sd.Kfz. 7 was evaluated at the *Centro Studi della Motorizzazione* (Motorisation Studies Centre), and the following year Krauss-Maffei granted Breda a licence to manufacture the half-track, reproducing many components of German origin but also incorporating several components of its own design.

The artillery tractor prototype was sent to the technical evaluation centre in Rome in July 1943, while the plans included two other variants, such as a gun carriage for the 90/53 gun and an engineer vehicle. Nevertheless, as happened with other Italian equipment, the Breda 61 was not still ready at the time of the Armistice of 8 September 1943, so its production was carried out for the Germans, who ordered 300 examples of the Zugkraftwagen 8t Typ Breda 61 (i), as the tractor had been designated. At least 199 were completed at Breda plant, the majority being produced between March and December 1944.

The Breda 61s equipped artillery units of both the Wehrmacht and the Luftwaffe. After the war, in 1948, the Direzione Artiglieria dell'Esercito Italiano (Italian Army Artillery Directorate) asked Breda for the loan of two half-tracks for trials, but a 1952 proposal by Breda to resume production for the Italian Army was not accepted.

Technical Description

The Breda 61 was essentially a produced under licence version of the German Krauss-Maffei Sd.Kfz. 7 half-track, fitted with right-hand drive. The suspension and rear bogie were similar to the original German design, while the engine and several mechanical parts, including the front wheels, had been designed by Breda. The 130 HP gasoline engine was a Breda model T14, which was sophisticated for its time. The size and characteristics differed from those of the German engine, and the bonnet was larger and was fitted with a greater number of air vents. Other characteristics of the Italian version were a national model standard tow hook, the mudguards, the electrical and light system (comprising acetylene headlights), the tyres, the seats, the driver's position on the right-hand side instead of on the left, and the dashboard instrumentation.

Transmission was a German ZF with five forward gears and one reverse, with a reduction gear. The track system consisted of six interleaved road wheels (the typical design of German half-tracks called *Schachtellaufwerk*), a drive sprocket and an idler wheel on each side, plus the tracks themselves with 54 links per side, made of metal with synthetic rubber shoes. A winch was

Left side view of the Fiat 727 half-track; this vehicle never entered production. (Fiat)

The Fiat 727 half-track without body, allowing the radiator, engine and rear-mounted fuel tank to be clearly seen. (Fiat)

rows of three seats. The engine was the well-proven 4,170cc diesel, mated to a four-speed transmission with a reduction gear.

Specifications

- Designation: Trattore semicingolato da 3 tonnellate Fiat 727
- Manufacturer: Fabbrica Italiana Automobili Turin (Fiat), Turin
- Number produced: Prototype only
- Years produced: 1943
- Length: 5,550mm (18ft 2in)
- Width: 2,000mm (6ft 7in)
- Height to top of canvas cover: 2,150mm (7ft)
- Unladen weight: 3,000kg (6,614lbs)
- Carrying capacity: 1,500kg (3,307lbs)
- Towing capacity: 6,000kg (13,228lbs)
- Front track: 1,650mm (5ft 5in)
- Rear track: 1,660mm (5ft 5in)
- Minimum clearance: 320mm (1ft)
- Tyres (front): Superflex 8.25 x 20
- Engine: Fiat six-cylinder in-line water-cooled, 4,170cc, 100 HP @2,800 rpm
- Fuel: Gasoline
- Transmission: four speeds forward, one reverse, with reduction gear
- Drive layout: Half-track, the front axle was not a driving axle
- Maximum speed: 53km/h (33mph)
- Range (on road): 240km (149 miles)
- Range (cross-country): 140km (87 miles)

- Engine: Type 366, six-cylinder, 9,365cc, 105/110 HP @2,000 rpm
- Fuel: Diesel
- Transmission: five forward speeds and one reverse; four-wheel drive with lockable differential
- Fuel capacity: 140 litres (37 US gallons; 30.8 Imperial gallons)
- Drive layout: 4x4
- Speed (road): 43km/h (30mph)
- Range (on road): 300km (186.4 miles)

Trattore Semicingolato Fiat 727

A Fiat 727 half-track. Note the right-hand drive, the distinctive angled fenders and the German-style track system. (Fiat)

Developmental and Service History
Negotiations that had begun in 1941 between Krauss-Maffei and Fiat led to the German firm granting Fiat a licence in 1942 to produce the running gear and tracks for a half-track (*semicingolato* in Italian) based on the Krauss-Maffei 3-ton Sd.Kfz. 11 half-track. In June 1943 the prototype Fiat 727 made its appearance, with delivery having been scheduled to begin in early 1944, but due to the Armistice between Italy and the Allies in September 1943, production was cancelled. Photographs of the vehicle make it clear that the Fiat 727 closely copied contemporary German designs, while showing a more ample bodywork. It is not known to what extent, if any, Krauss-Maffei assisted Fiat with design and engineering of the Fiat 727. The more obvious differences between the Fiat 727 and the Sd.Kfz. 11 were the angled fenders, as well as the right-hand drive common to all medium and heavy wheeled Italian military vehicles.

Technical Description
The Fiat 727 was laid out on the German Sd.Kfz. 11, widespread and appreciated as well as produced in a number of variants. Its intended use as an artillery tractor dictated its open sides and provision for a canvas roof to cover the driving and crew compartments. Although the front section of the vehicle closely resembled the Sd.Kfz. 11, the bonnet and angular front fenders differed markedly, and the steering wheel was on the right. The engine, radiator, front axle (not a driving axle) and steering box were those of the Fiat 626 medium truck, while the tracks and running gear were closely patterned on the Krauss-Maffei original.

The track system consisted of, on each side, six interleaved road wheels, a front drive sprocket and a rear idler wheel. The bonnet and side panels covering the engine compartment were reminiscent of the configuration of those on the Fiat 634 N heavy truck. The two-piece split windshield could be opened forward for ventilation. In addition to the fender-mounted headlights, the 727 retained the anachronistic acetylene headlamps mounted on the firewall. A spare tyre was mounted on the rear of the crew compartment. In addition to the driver and the vehicle chief, there were spaces for six crew members in two

The TM 40 truck for the *Regia Aeronautica* was built in December 1942, but there is no information regarding the number of examples produced. It had a closed metal cab and a cargo body. (Drawing by A. M. Feller – GMT)

An Italian Spa TM40 medium tractor destroyed in Cervaro, near Frosinone, on 17 January 1944. This vehicle was also produced for the Germans in 1944.

Specifications

- Designation: Trattore Medio modello 40 or TM 40
- Producer: Società Piemontese Automobili (SPA), Turin
- Years produced: 1941–1945
- Number produced: NA
- Length: 4,680mm (15ft 4in)
- Width: 2,200mm (7ft 3in)
- Height: 2,800mm (9ft 2in)
- Unladen weight: 6,575kg (14,495lbs)
- Carrying capacity: 1,285kg (2,833lbs)
- Towing capacity: 5,000kg (11,023lbs)
- Wheelbase: 2,600mm (8ft 6in)
- Track: 1,630mm (5ft 4in) with pneumatic tyres; 1,665mm (5ft 7in) with semi-
- pneumatic tyres
- Minimum turning radius: 5,600mm (18ft 4in)
- Minimum clearance: 330mm (1ft 1in)
- Fording depth: 900mm (2ft 11½in)
- Tyres: pneumatic Cord 50 x 9 with Artiglio tread, or semi-pneumatic Celerflex

The truck on TM 40 chassis with *Einheits* cab and wooden bed produced for the German occupation forces. (Fiat)

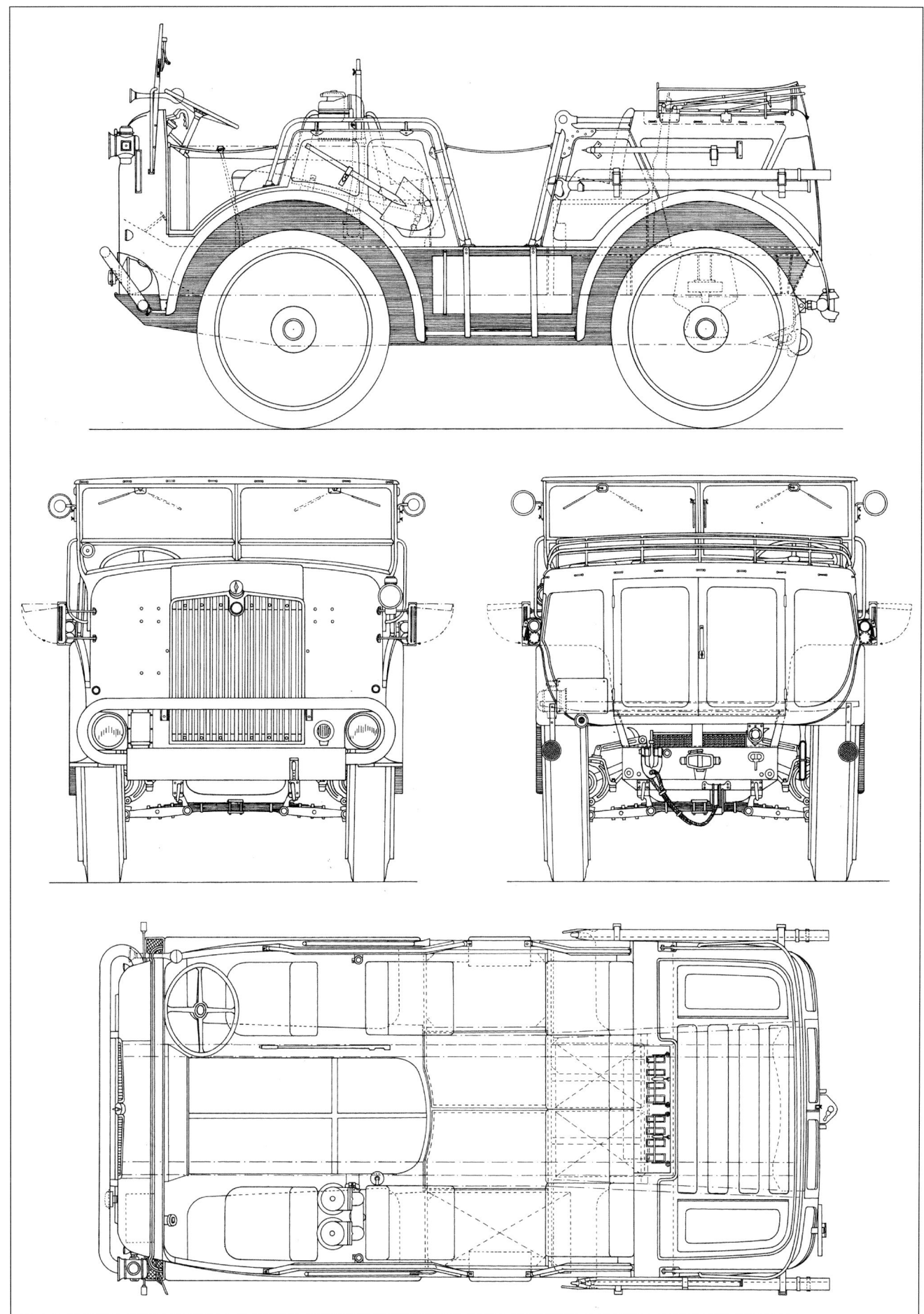

The SPA TM 40 with Celerflex semi-pneumatic tyres. (Drawings by A. M. Feller – GMT)

The tractor and trailer complex designed by Viberti for the transport of medium tanks.

A 90/53 mod. 1939 gun towed by a TM 40.

A TM 40 used in Italy by the German *Organisation Todt*. The *Organisation Todt* was in charge of civil and military building works at home and, using forced labour, in occupied countries; it was named after its founder, the engineer Fritz Todt.

Factory photo of the series TM 40 with canvas top and accessories. (Fiat)

Factory photo of the series TM 40 without canvas top and minus its accessory tools.

A TM 40 fitted with tyre chains in the Russian snow; the towed gun is almost invisible due to the exhaust fumes. Note the canvas door and the broken celluloid window.

A prototype of the TM 40 with spoked wheels and semi-pneumatic Celerflex tyres. (Fiat)

The prototype of the TM 40 but with pneumatic Superflex Artiglio tyres. (Fiat)

need for this type of tractor on all fronts, the chronic shortage of materials caused production to proceed very slowly. The TL 40s in service were just over 400 in April 1943. Following the 8 September 1943 Armistice, production continued on behalf of the German Army, with at least 153 examples delivered in 1944.

Technical Description

Like the earlier TL 37, the TM 40 was a four-wheel drive tractor with all four wheels steerable. Unlike the TL 37, the TM 40 was a cab-over-engine machine. The all-metal open bodywork of the TM 40 was divided into two sections, a forward section for the driver and a single passenger and the rear section for six crew seated face to face on two benches. There was also an ammunition locker in the rearmost portion of the body, with two doors that opened once the spare tyre was swung down out of the way; the locker could carry up to twelve 149mm rounds. A canvas top with side curtains for the crew compartment was stowed on board. The *Regia Marina* and *Regia Aeronautica* TM 40 tractors were fitted with a closed cab.

Drive was the typical right-hand drive. The large-diameter wheels could be fitted with either semi-pneumatic or pneumatic tyres; the diameter of the wheels provided excellent ground clearance. The TM 40 mounted a powerful winch in the rear with 50 metres of 20mm-thick cable. The independent suspension consisted of transversal leaf springs and hydraulic shock absorbers. A mechanical hand brake acted on the transmission while the brakes on all four wheels were hydraulic with a compressed-air booster. The electrical system used two 12 volt batteries. The front of the TM 40 was protected by a robust tubular bumper. The engine was a six-cylinder diesel developing 95 horsepower; the transmission had five forward and one reverse speeds, a locking differential and a backstop feature.

Variants

In early 1945 the SPA TM 40 chassis was used by Fiat to produce a low-cost truck for the occupying German forces, also known as T 40. The tractor body was replaced by a German-style *Einheits* wood cab over the engine and a cargo body, also of wood.

The TL 37 *Autoblindo* (armoured car) was made in 1941 as a prototype but lost in battle in North Africa.

An armoured personnel carrier version of the TL 37 was developed, designated as the TL 37 Protetto. It was open-roofed and was fitted with Superflex Sigillo Verde balloon tyres. A unique group of 150 examples was built in 1942.

The AS 37 Autocarro Sahariano (see separate entry) was a stand-alone model, being a light truck with an enclosed cab and cargo bed on the TL 37 chassis. It was developed in parallel with the tractor, starting in 1937, and it was conceived for operations in the African theatre. The bodywork consisted of a rigid cabin, with doors, for three people and a cargo bed made of wood and metal. The intended use was for the transport of troops, eight men, and of ammunition for self-propelled artillery. Some specialised variants also derived from the AS 37: bowser, recovery vehicle, radio truck.

Both the Camionetta AS 43 and the Camionetta Desertica mod. 43 light desert trucks, intended for use as a command and reconnaissance vehicle, were in turn a development based on the AS 37. They were produced in a few examples in 1943 and operated only on metropolitan Italian territory.

Specifications

- Designation: Trattore Leggero Modello 1937 or TL 37
- Producer: Società Piemontese Automobili (SPA), Turin
- Years produced: 1937–1945
- Number produced: 2,500 or more
- Length: 4,130mm (13ft 7in)
- Width: 1,830mm (6ft)
- Height: 2,180mm with canvas roof (7ft 2in)
- Unladen weight: 3,181kg (7,013lbs) with pneumatic tyres; 3,560kg (7,848lbs) with semi-pneumatic tyres
- Carrying capacity: 800kg (1,764lbs)
- Winch pulling capacity: 2,000kg (4,409lbs); 2,500kg. (5,511lbs) Coloniale
- Pulling capacity: 2,800kg (6,173lbs)
- Wheelbase: 2,500mm (8ft 2in)
- Track: 1,518mm (5ft) with pneumatic tyres; 1,440mm (4ft 8in) with semi-pneumatic tyres
- Minimum turning radius: 4,500mm (14ft 9in)
- Minimum clearance: 345mm (1ft 2in)
- Fording depth: 700mm (2ft 4in)
- Tyres: Celerflex 160 x 881; Superflex Artiglio 9.00 x 24; Superflex Sigillo Verde or Superflex S.V. Libia 9.75 x 24 or 11.25 x 24
- Engine: SPA Model 18 TL, four-cylinder, 4,053cc, 52 HP @2,000 rpm
- Fuel: Gasoline
- Transmission: manual transmission with five forward speeds and one reverse; four-wheel drive with lockable differential
- Fuel capacity: 100 litres (26.5 US gallons; 22 Imperial gallons)
- Drive layout: 4x4
- Speed (road): 38.2km/h (23.7mph) fully loaded
- Range (on road): 240km (149 miles)
- Range (cross-country): 215km (134 miles)

Trattore Medio SPA TM 40

Developmental and Service History

The TM 40 (*trattore medio*, or medium tractor) resulted from a request put forward by the *Regio Esercito* in 1938 for an artillery tractor to replace the old Pavesi tractors. The SPA company presented its prototype in competition with Alfa Romeo, Breda and Lancia, and after extensive tests the SPA was adopted in 1941 as TMa (*Trattore Medio per Artiglieria*, medium artillery tractor) then TM 40. Due to the high degree of satisfaction registered with the earlier TL 37, the TM 40 followed the same general construction principles as the lighter TL 37. The new medium tractor was intended to tow larger calibre guns assigned to army corps, while the TL 37 light tractor was suitable for field guns (called divisional artillery).

The tests carried out by the *Centro Studi della Motorizzazione* (Motorisation Studies Centre) with a 149/19 howitzer suggested the replacement of the stamped disc wheels (semi-pneumatic Celerflex 265 x 980) with dismountable spoked wheels (unified type) suitable for pneumatic tyres (Cord Artiglio 50 x 9). According to Fiat documents, special Superflex Libia tyres 12.75 x 32 and even Superflex 11.25 x 32 could be also be used.

Because of the shortage of raw materials, issue of the TM 40 to units of the *Regio Esercito* did not begin until early 1942; early examples of the TM 40 were assigned to the Russian Front. Despite the positive qualities of the TM 40 and the urgent

A TL 37 of the *Regia Aeronautica* tows a medium bomber Fiat Br. 20 M. (ACS)

A field modification of the TL 37 tractor in North Africa allowed the mounting of a 75/27 mod. 11 gun. (ACS)

Towing heavy trailers on the Eastern Front.

plate. The radiator consisted of eight separate elements. The TL 37 used the same Fiat model 18 engine as the SPA 38 R and Dovunque 35 trucks. The transmission was a five-speed transmission with a lockable differential. The clutch was a twin dry disc type. The TL 37 had a backstop device.

Variants

A number of variants for special uses resulted from the TL 37.

The so-called *Libia* version used Pirelli Superflex Libia tyres, had a 2,500kg winch, special filters, special radiator elements, a 150 litre supplemental fuel tank and two removable 35 litre tanks and a rear-mounted spare tyre. Similar to it was the *Coloniale*, without the supplemental fuel tanks. The *Pontiere* variant (for Bridging Engineers) was almost identical to the standard TL 37 but had double mufflers, a more powerful winch and Superflex Artiglio pneumatic tyres.

In the summer of 1941, the unit workshops of the *2° Autoparco* of the *12° Autoraggruppamento* mounted 75/27 mod.11 shielded pieces on as many adapted TL 37 chassis; with the 12 vehicles thus transformed, three batteries were set up. The vehicle is otherwise known as the Sahariana-Cannone.

A TL 37 of the *Regia Aeronautica* tows a medium bomber Fiat Br. 20 M. (ACS)

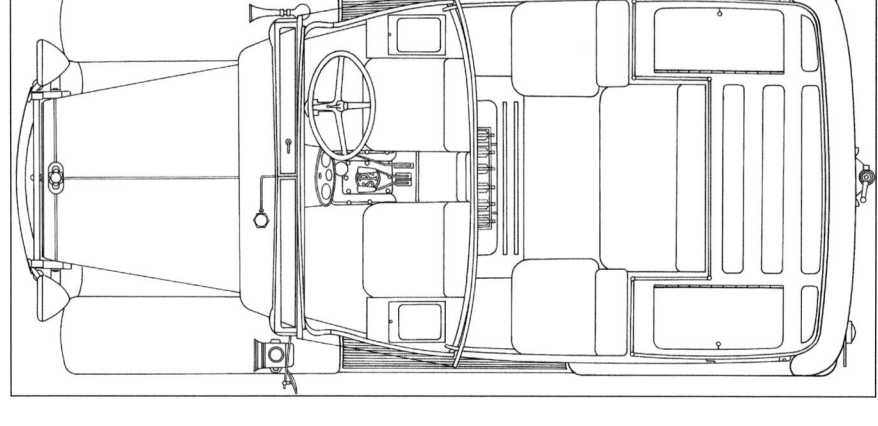

The SPA TL 37 with Celerflex semi-pneumatic tyres. (Drawings by A. M. Feller – GMT)

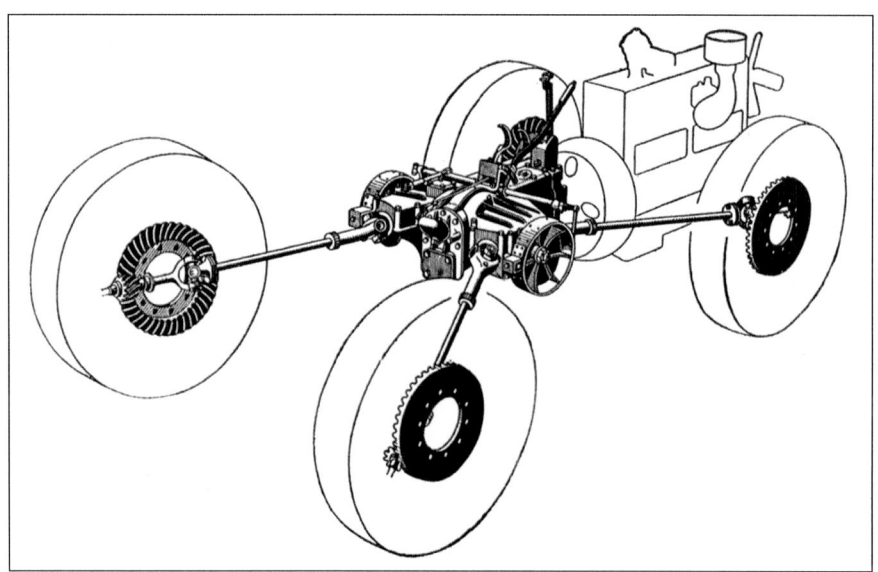

Transmission system.

Technical Description

The SPA TL 37 had a 'torpedo' structure, with an open body and had two openings per side, with no doors; a canvas roof, supported by two bows, that folded to the rear was provided. The TL 37 seated two in the front compartment and four in the rear compartment. Early production examples were fitted with semi-pneumatic Celerflex tyres on pressed steel rims. Later examples were fitted with pneumatic tyres on two types of pressed steel rims: the first type had eight holes in each wheel while the second type had no holes. All four wheels steered, which gave it a very tight turning circle. The independent front suspension consisted of coil springs with rubber block shock absorbers internal to the springs; inverted transversal leaf springs constituted the rear suspension. Braking occurred on all four wheels simultaneously; the handbrake acted on the transmission by means of two pulleys.

The 6 volt electrical system was a dynamo without battery; there were two headlights and a taillight over the number

The TL 37 with its characteristic Superflex Sigillo Verde balloon tyres for desert operations. (Fiat)

The 75/27 gun on the *carrello elastico* bogey arrangement towed by a TL 37. The tractor has no rear support for the spare wheel mounted, so a spare tyre is carried on its side.

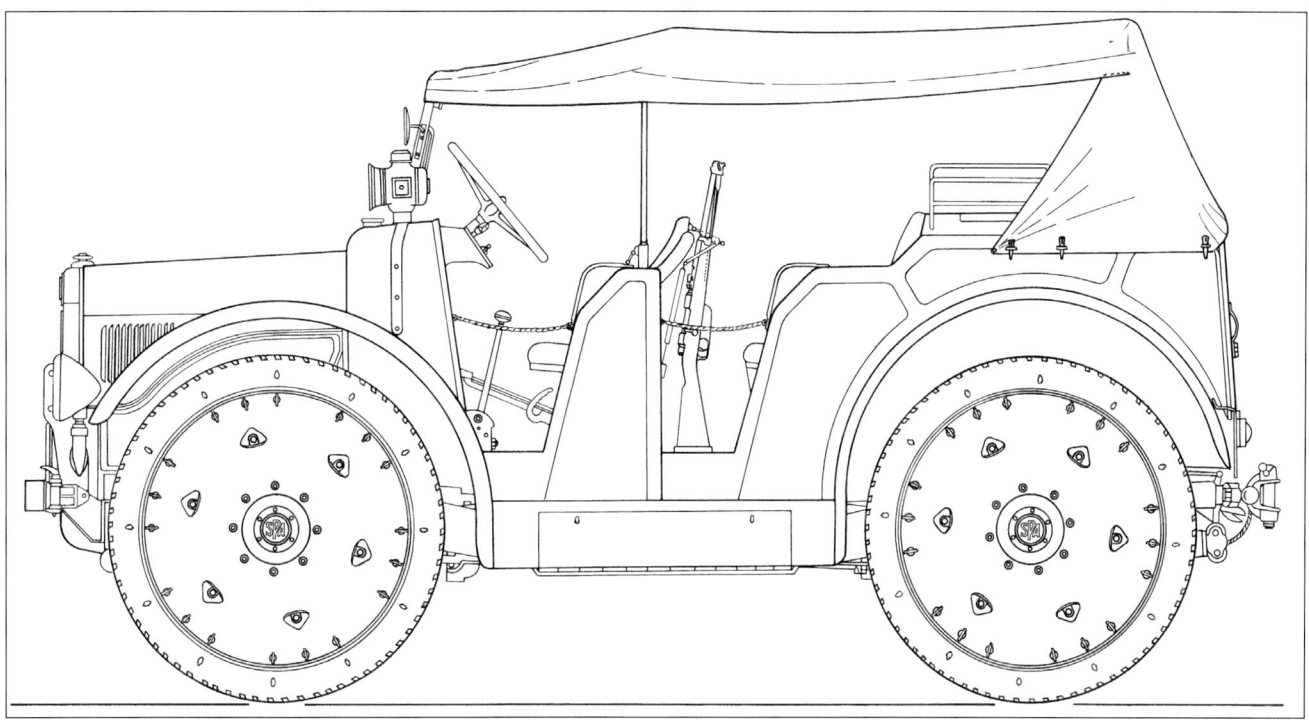

The SPA TL 37 with Celerflex semi-pneumatic tyres. (Drawings by A. M. Feller – GMT)

The *Libia* version was very similar to the *Coloniale* version. Externally it was characterised by having an additional 150 litre tank located on the rear luggage compartment. Here some examples captured in North Africa, probably in 1942.

The tractor could be equipped with chains to improve traction for use on snowy or muddy terrain.(Author's collection)

an artillery tractor, is attested to by a report by an Australian Commission in 1941 which, after having tested the TL 37, judged it to be the best artillery tractor available on either side in North Africa.

In addition to being issued to *Regio Esercito* units, the TL 37 was also used by the *Regia Marina* and the *Regia Aeronautica*. Following the 8 September 1943 Armistice, the Germans ordered 2,477 examples, only a few dozen of which were delivered in 1944 and 1945. There is some indication that a number of TL 37s were also furnished to the Hungarian and Bulgarian armies. Production of the TL 37 continued until 1948.

Another example with semi-pneumatic tyres from the *Divisione Pasubio* crossing the Dnieper River in the Ukraine. The bridge had been built by the Germans. Autumn 1941. (ACS)

An example with Superflex Artiglio tyres on display in May 1940.

The TL 37 Coloniale built from 1941, with standard Superflex Libia 9.75 x 24 tyres.

The TL 37 artillery tractor was issued to the motorised artillery batteries of infantry as well as cavalry motorised and armoured divisions and saw service in all Italian combat theatres, but saw its greatest use in North Africa. At the outbreak of war there were 1,142 of these tractors available, although not all had been delivered to the units. Prior to the Axis defeat in Tunisia, on 30 April 1943 the *Regio Esercito* had between 2,150 and 2,267 TL 37s of various versions in service (excluding the AS 37 light truck), according to different sources. That the TL 37 was a modern, high-quality vehicle well suited for its task as

The prototype of the TL 37 light tractor with semi-pneumatic tyres and pressed disc wheels.

The TL 37 Pontiere was externally very similar to the standard version. It is shown here with pressed steel wheels with lightening holes and fitted with pneumatic tyres.

A TL 37 with semi-pneumatic tyres pulling an ammunition trailer on the North African Front. (ACS)

Developmental and Service History

The Fiat OCI 40 tracked tractor was the evolution of the previous 708 C and went into production in 1939. It was more powerful than its predecessor, being able to use a new 40 HP engine designed by the engineer Fortunato Boghetto. For these reasons, the vehicle is otherwise known as Fiat 40 HP, Fiat 40 C and Fiat Boghetto.

In particular, Boghetto ensured that the engine, with minor modifications, could use not only gasoline and diesel, but also oil, methane gas, alcohol and wood gas. In this way, the tractor was suitable for both military and agricultural use, particularly in the colonies of East Africa where the supply of fuel was more difficult. The *Regio Esercito* acquired the tractor in 1941 and in addition to towing artillery pieces, such as the 105/28 gun, this tractor was assigned to units of Bridging Engineers (mainly on the Eastern Front). After the Armistice, its production was continued for the German occupiers.

Technical Description

From a mechanical point of view, the Fiat 40 took up many characteristics of the 708 C and modified others. The configuration was still one that provided for the engine placed in front and direction changes were made by means of a steering wheel, rather than levers, which acted on the steering clutches of the two-track suspension systems and, if necessary, also activated the relative drum brake.

The suspensions were different from the previous one, in fact they were not inspired by those of other Fiat tracked vehicles (such as the L3 light tank) but consisted of a rear drive sprocket, a front idler wheel, five road wheels and two small support rollers; also the track links were larger. The gearbox was four-speed (initially there were three) plus reverse. The engine, as mentioned, was multi-fuel, although the gasoline start was needed (gasoline was held in a small auxiliary tank) and external intervention was required for some fuels, such as the assembly of some components or additional tanks.

Specifications

- Designation: Trattore Fiat OCI 40
- Producer: Fiat/Officine Costruzioni Industriali, Modena
- Years produced: 1939–1950?
- Number produced: Not Known
- Length: 3,034mm (9ft 11in)
- Width: 1,504mm (4ft 11in)
- Height (to top of steering wheel): 1,710mm (5ft 7in)
- Unladen weight: 3,770kg (8,311lbs)
- Towing capacity: 3,500kg (7,716lbs)
- Towing power: 31 HP
- Minimum clearance: 310mm (1ft)
- Track width: 310mm (1ft)
- Engine: Fiat OCI tipo 40, four-cylinder water-cooled, 3,970cc, 40 HP @1,500 rpm
- Transmission: manual transmission with four forward speeds and one reverse
- Fuel: Gasoline, Diesel, petroleum, methane gas, alcohol, wood gas
- Fuel capacity: main tank 70 litres (18.5 US gallons, 15 Imperial gallons), auxiliary tank 5.5 litres (1.45 US gallons, 1.20 Imperial gallons); methane gas version carried two additional tanks of 40 litres (10.5 US gallons, 8.8 Imperial gallons) in total
- Drive layout: tracked
- Speed (road): 8.5km/h (5.3mph)

Trattore Leggero SPA TL 37

Developmental and Service History

In 1935 the *Regio Esercito* issued a requirement for a light 4x4 artillery tractor to tow the suitably modified 75mm and 100mm guns in its arsenal. In 1936 SPA engineers in competition with Breda, set to work developing a number of models. The Breda tractor was derived from the Breda 32, but the authorities preferred the SPA vehicle.

The prototype was called TLa, i.e. *Trattore Leggero per Artiglieria* (light artillery tractor) which was further developed into the standard pattern adopted by the *Regio Esercito* in 1937 and designated the SPA TL 37, the TL signifying *Trattore Leggero* or light tractor. In October 1937, 250 vehicles were ordered and a test group of 24 TL 37s was sent to Libya in 1938 where it was used to tow the 75/27 mod. 06 mounted on the *carrello elastico*, as well as towing ammunition trailers for the guns. The results proved to be entirely satisfactory, setting the stage for the mechanisation of Italian artillery in the desert. At the time it was thought that the TL 37 could also fill the need for a light reconnaissance vehicle.

Trattore Fiat OCI 40

The Fiat OCI 40, a development of the 708 CM.

A Fiat OCI 40 at work with a SPA 38 R truck in Ukraine in the summer of 1941. (ACS)

Close-up of the engine bonnet.

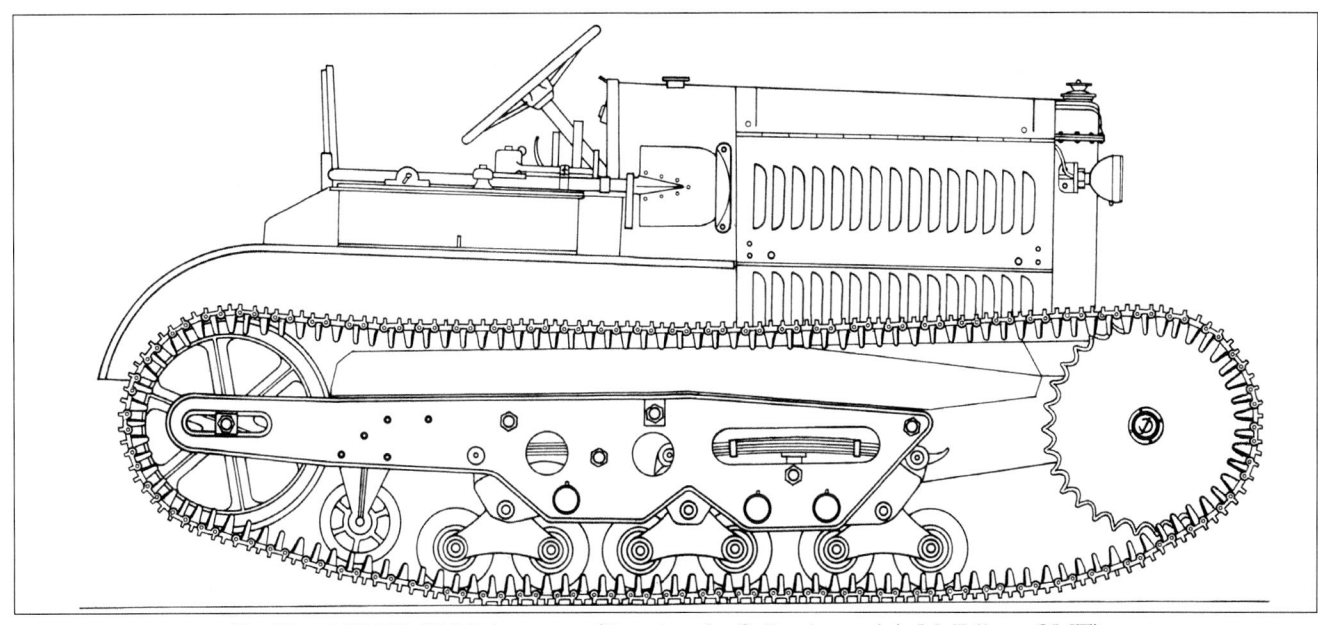

The Fiat OCI 708 CM light tractor. (Drawings by C. Pergher and A. M. Feller – GMT)

Technical Description

The OCI 708 CM was a very small crawler tractor; it was well suited to its intended role in mountainous terrain, although its civilian origins made it somewhat fragile in the military role. It was laid out as a typical crawler tractor with a front-mounted drive sprocket, bogies mounted on a rigid frame with six road wheels per side, a small tension roller and a large rear idler. The tracks of the agricultural version were replaced with others almost identical to those of the CV 33 light tank.

The cab was completely open, the engine was covered by a metal bonnet, and there was a conventional steering wheel, rather than levers, for steering; moving the steering wheel right or left acted on the clutches and applied the brakes to the appropriate track. The tractor had a modest towing capacity (2,200kg) and was quite slow. It was equipped with a winch.

The 708 CM performed very well off-road but did not stand up well over long distances on paved roads; it was often carried by trucks to minimise wear and problems. The engine was a Fiat gasoline engine developing 30 HP.

Specifications

- Designation: Trattore da montagna OCI 708 CM
- Producer: Fiat/Officine Costruzioni Industriali, Modena
- Years produced: 1934–1944
- Number produced: Not Known
- Length: 3,050mm (10ft)
- Width: 1,230mm (4ft)
- Height (to top of steering wheel): 1,470mm (4ft 10in)
- Unladen weight: 2,500kg (5,512lbs)
- Carrying capacity: 80kg (176lbs)
- Towing capacity: 2,200kg (4,850lbs)
- Track length: 2,278mm (7ft 6in)
- Front wheel track: 990mm (3ft 3in)
- Rear wheel track: 990mm (3ft 3")
- Wheelbase: 2,300mm (7'6in)
- Minimum turning radius: 1,500mm (4ft 11in)
- Minimum clearance: 290mm (11in)
- Track width: 190mm (7in)
- Engine: Fiat 708 C four-cylinder water-cooled, 2,520cc, 30 HP @2,300 rpm
- Fuel: Gasoline
- Transmission: manual transmission with four forward speeds and one reverse
- Fuel capacity: 84 litres (22 US gallons, 18.5 Imperial gallons)
- Drive layout: tracked
- Speed (road): 16km/h (10mph)
- Range (on road): 140km (87 miles)

A 708 CM tractor of the *Regia Aeronautica* towing a Cant Z.1007 Alcione medium bomber.

Italian troops advance on foot in the Libyan desert with light artillery in September 1940. (ACS)

A Fiat OCI 708 CM together with a Fiat 626 ambulance of the *Regio Esercito*.

Developmental and Service Background

The Fiat OCI 708 CM artillery tractor was Fiat's answer to a *Regio Esercito* request for a narrow wheel track tractor to tow the 75/18 howitzer for mountain troops. In mid–1934 the Fiat subsidiary, Officine Costruzioni Industriali (OCI) of Modena, presented a modified version of its tracked agricultural tractor, the OCI 708 C as a military prototype, designated the OCI 708 CM, with the letter C signifying *cingolato* (tracked) and M *militare* (military). In 1935 a total of 200 examples of the vehicle, officially designated as the Trattore da Montagna 708 CM (literally, mountain tractor), were ordered. The 708 CM was also used by the *Regia Aeronautica* as airfield tow vehicles, since the low weight and the tight track links limited the damage to the airstrips, especially the grass ones.

The 708 CM was first used operationally in Eritrea in 1935, where it was used to tow the 77/28 guns (Austro-Hungarian First World War booty) of two groups. In 1936 the tractor was assigned to units in Libya and Somalia, and later served in the Spanish Civil War. When Italy entered the Second World War in June 1940, there were 381 OCI 708 CM tractors assigned to the V Armata in Libya, but by October 1941 only 113 remained operational. The tractor was also pressed into service to tow 100/17 howitzers in the mountains and 75/27 guns in the desert, where it was heavily penalised by an average speed of only 10–12km/h and an air-cooling system that was prone to fail due to suction of sand.

Official photo of the Fiat OCI 708 second series. (Fiat)

Tests on rough terrain conducted in Italy in 1938. The car in the foreground is a Fiat 508 CM aka 1100 Mimetica.

OCI 708 CM tractors towing a 75/13 mountain gun and a single-axle trailer during an exercise in Italy, under the gaze of two Carabinieri.

had five forward speeds and one reverse.

Variants

The Breda mod. 41 was essentially a variant of the mod. 40 equipped with a 5-ton crane, to be mounted on the front of the tractor, and a 2-ton block and tackle, installable on the rear.

A civilian variant was also produced, characterised by a different bodywork. The front had a new bumper consisting of a single cross-member and equipped with a tow hook; the headlights were located on the bumper itself, on the sides of the engine hood; the compressed-air tank had been split into two tanks and placed under the cab, laterally. This vehicle is identified as a Breda 130 with Viberti bodywork, but others call it Tipo 40 Borsani (after the coachbuilder who allegedly built the bodywork).

Specifications

- Designation: Trattrice Pesante Breda 40
- Manufacturer: Società Italiana Ernesto Breda per Costruzioni Meccaniche, Milan
- Years produced: 1942–1945
- Number produced: Not known
- Length: 5,500mm (18ft)
- Width: 2,480mm (8ft 1in)
- Height: 2,610mm (8ft 7in) to top of cab; 2,920mm (9ft 7in) with canvas cover
- Weight (unloaded): 10,100kg (22,267lbs)
- Carrying capacity: 3,500kg (7,716lbs) on road; 2,500kg (5,512lbs) off-road
- Towing capacity: 10,000kg (22,046lbs)
- Wheelbase: 2,875mm (9ft 5in)
- Front track: 1,810mm (6ft)
- Rear track: 1,795mm (5ft 10in)
- Minimum turning radius: 8,550mm (29ft)
- Minimum clearance: 460mm (1ft 6in)
- Bed, internal length: 2,650mm (8ft 8in)
- Bed, internal width: 1,980mm (6ft 6in)
- Bed, internal height: 700mm (27½in)
- Tyres: high-pressure Cord pneumatic 50 x 9 with Artiglio tread
- Engine: Breda D11, six-cylinder, 8,850cc, 115 HP @1,800 rpm
- Fuel: Diesel
- Transmission: manual transmission with five forward speed and reverse; four-wheel drive with lockable differential
- Fuel capacity: 350 litres (92.4 US gallons, 77 Imperial gallons)
- Drive layout: 4x4
- Maximum speed (road): 36km/h (22.3mph)
- Range (on road): 500km (310 miles)
- Range (cross-country): 9 hours

Trattore da Montagna Fiat OCI 708 CM

A fresh from the factory OCI 708 CM light tractor of the first series. Note the automobile-type steering wheel used for steering instead of the lateral levers common on tracked vehicles. (Fiat)

The Breda 130 road tractor, a civilian variant with bodywork by Viberti also used in the post-war period. (Breda)

149mm calibre and above. However, this type of artillery was rarely used in the war; moreover, the entry into service of more modern pieces of ordnance allowed the Breda 32 tractors, already in active service, to tow them. For these reasons, the Breda 40 was little used.

A modified version of the mod. 40, with a slightly different body and mounting a retractable crane for use as a recovery vehicle, was designated the Breda mod. 41. Precise production figures are not known; at the end of April 1943, 1,354 Breda 32, 40 and 41 were still in service. Production of the Breda mod. 40 and 41 continued under German occupation following the September 1943 Armistice, and the tractor continued to be manufactured for a brief period in the post-war years.

The Breda 40 was also utilised by the Hungarian Army for the towing of its large calibre guns, some of which were of Italian production.

Technical Description

The Breda mod. 40 was a 4x4 tractor with an all-metal cab with full doors and a wooden cargo body (the prototype had a metal cargo body as well as a metal cab); the bed of the mod. 41 had higher sides than the mod. 40 bed. The roof-mounted storage bin of the mod. 32 was eliminated on both models. The Breda mod. 41 mounted a boom crane that was carried disassembled on the sides of the tractor but which could be mounted on the front of the frame.

Both versions of the tractor had lifting hooks mounted on the front and rear of the frames, and both had towing pintles on the rear. The large-diameter eight-spoke wheels were a carryover from the mod. 32, but mounted pneumatic tyres instead of the semi-pneumatic tyres of the mod. 32. Like the mod. 32, the mod. 40 had half-fenders over the front wheels. Suspension consisted of a transversally mounted semi-elliptical leaf spring in the front and leaf springs in the rear. The electrical system was fed by two batteries. The engine of the mod. 40 and mod. 41 was a four-cylinder diesel developing 115 HP. The transmission

A new Breda 41 parked on the Viberti factory premises.

A Breda 41 with its retractable boom in the extended position. (Breda)

Note

The Italian language uses two words for tractor: The masculine *trattore* and the feminine *trattrice*. In the past, the feminine form was generally used to indicate an agricultural machine, while the masculine had, and still has, a wider meaning and includes, for example, railway tractors and road tractors. The Italian armed forces used both forms of the word: initially, *trattrice* identified a power vehicle with great pulling power, capable of towing heavy artillery pieces and heavy loads on roads and – only under favourable conditions – off-road. The tractor was less powerful and was in more generalised use, and was more capable of operating on rough terrain. Often it was derived from a normal truck (*autocarro trattore*, truck tractor). In the end, the masculine form prevailed, probably because the use of such vehicles was not limited to towing artillery pieces.

Developmental and Service History

The Breda mod. 40 heavy tractor (TP 40) was a much-modernised development of the very successful Breda mod. 32 and was designed for use in Italy's African colonies. The general structure, in particular of the cabin and the body, and almost all the mechanical parts were the same as on the Breda 32. The most significant differences with respect to its predecessor were a diesel instead of gasoline engine and high-pressure Cord pneumatic tyres with Artiglio tread instead of the semi-pneumatic Celerflex tyres. A prototype was ready in 1940, but series production did not begin until 1942, with the first examples arriving in North Africa during the summer of 1942, not long before the El Alamein battles.

The intended use for the Breda 40 was the towing of heavy artillery (called *Artiglieria d'Armata*, army artillery), i.e. guns of

A Breda 40 with snow chains on its tyres during mobility tests.

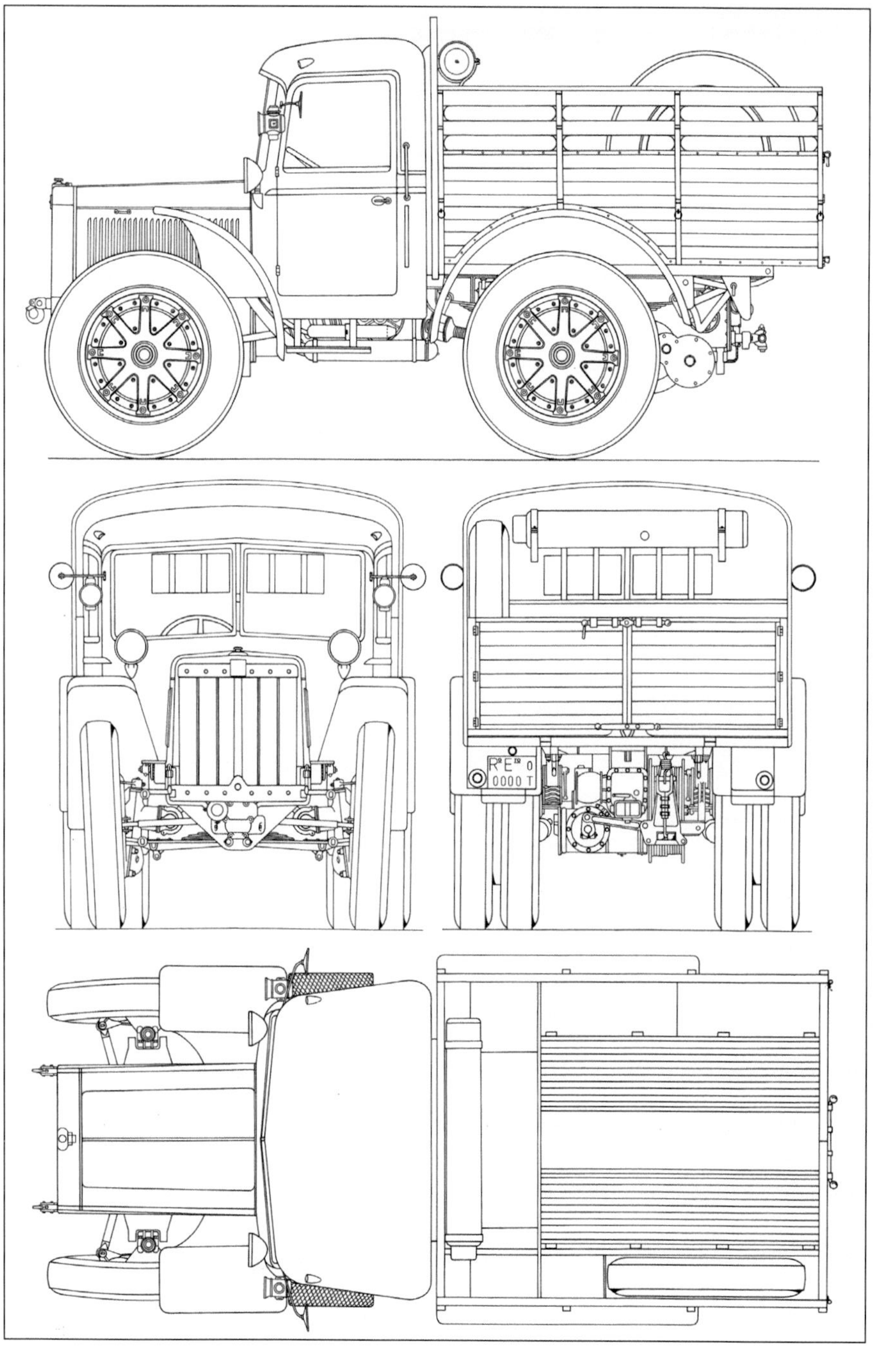

The Breda 40. (Drawings by A. M. Feller – GMT)

- Height: 3,000mm (9ft 10in) mod. 32; 2,910mm (9ft 6in) mod. 33
- Weight (unloaded): 8,400kg (18,519lbs) mod. 32; 8,500kg (18,739lbs) mod. 33
- Carrying capacity: 3,500kg (7,716lbs) mod. 32; 2,000kg (4,409lbs) mod. 33
- Towing capacity: 7,000kg (15,432lbs)
- Wheelbase: 2,650mm (8ft 8in) mod. 32; 2,800mm (9ft 2in) mod. 33
- Front track: 1,680mm (5ft 6in)
- Rear track: 1,615mm (5ft 3in)
- Minimum turning radius: 5,750mm (18ft 10in) mod. 32; 8,000mm (26ft 3in) mod. 33
- Minimum clearance: 390mm (1ft 3in)
- Bed, internal length: 2,500mm (8ft 2in)
- Bed, internal width: 1,770mm (5ft 10in)
- Bed, internal height: 700mm (2ft 3in)
- Tyres: semi-pneumatic Celerflex 205 x 980
- Engine: SPA Model T5, four-cylinder, 8,150cc, 84 HP @1,450 rpm
- Fuel: Gasoline
- Transmission: manual transmission with five forward speeds and one reverse; four-wheel drive with lockable differential
- Fuel capacity: 200 litres (52.8 US gallons, 44 Imperial gallons) mod. 32; 125 litres (33 US gallons, 27.5 Imperial gallons) mod. 33
- Drive layout: 4x4
- Maximum speed (road): 30km/h (18.6mph)
- Range (on road): 240km (149 miles) unladen; 150km (93 miles) with towed load
- Range (cross-country): 10 hours unladen; 6 hours with towed load

TRATTRICE PESANTE BREDA MOD. 40 AND 41

The final prototype of the Breda 40 heavy tractor, with and without canvas top. The vehicle had a closed cab and shows a noticeably short wheelbase.

The Breda 33 heavy tractor for engineers.

Variants
A version was developed as a tow truck/recovery vehicle with a boom and a winch; it was referred to colloquially as the *Giraffa* (giraffe).

Specifications
- Designation: Trattore Pesante Breda mod. 32 and mod. 33
- Manufacturer: Società Italiana Ernesto Breda per Costruzioni Meccaniche, Milan
- Years produced: 1932–1945
- Number produced: Not Known
- Length: 5,150mm (16ft 10in) mod. 32; 6,320mm (20ft 9in) mod. 33
- Width: 2,080mm (6ft 10in) mod. 32; 2,100mm (6ft 11in) mod. 33

One 149/40 gun of the Group, towed by a Breda 32.

The recovery truck version *Giraffa* (giraffe). Two halves of a crane were carried on either side of the vehicle. During operations, the crane was mounted on the front and used the winch.

Technical Description

The Breda mod. 32 tractor was a 4x4 vehicle and was laid out like a conventional truck. The all-metal cab had half-doors; the top of the cab was fitted with a form of storage bin for the tractor crew's personal items and consisted of raised metal sides which in turn had a canvas cover. The chassis of the vehicle had a particular shape being made of cast steel; it was a sort of 'cradle' made up of separate sections, joined by flanges and bolts, containing the engine and the transmission elements; there were three differentials, a central differential and two side differentials which transferred the movement to the wheels. The cargo body was made of stamped steel with wide reinforcing ribs; instead of a normal tailgate, there were two doors at the rear of the bed which opened outward.

The large-diameter eight-spoke wheels were fitted with Celerflex semi-pneumatic tyres; the rear tyres were twin. The mod. 32 and mod. 33 had distinctive slanting half-fenders over the front wheels. The rear suspension consisted of traditional semi-elliptical longitudinal leaf springs; at the front, however, there was a large traverse leaf spring connected to the two wheels. In this way, the sprung mass, i.e. the frame with everything that weighs on the suspension (engine, transmission, et cetera) was flexibly connected to the unsprung mass (wheels) at only three points; this allowed the vehicle to adapt well to the irregularities of the terrain. This type of arrangement was also adopted on other vehicles produced in Italy.

Starting was by hand crank; later production models also had an electric starter. The engine was a four-cylinder in-line gasoline engine developing 84 HP. The transmission had five forward speeds and one reverse.

ARTILLERY TRACTORS 139

An example in an unusual camouflage design taking part in a parade.

A Breda 32 towing a 149/35 gun; despite the apparently cold environment of the spring of 1941, the engine side panels are raised to assist in cooling. (ACS)

A Fiat 508 C Balilla Berlina precedes a column in Libya in 1942. The four Breda 32 tractors tow 149/40 guns as a battery of Artillery Group of XXI Army Corps, of the Italian XXXIII Army.

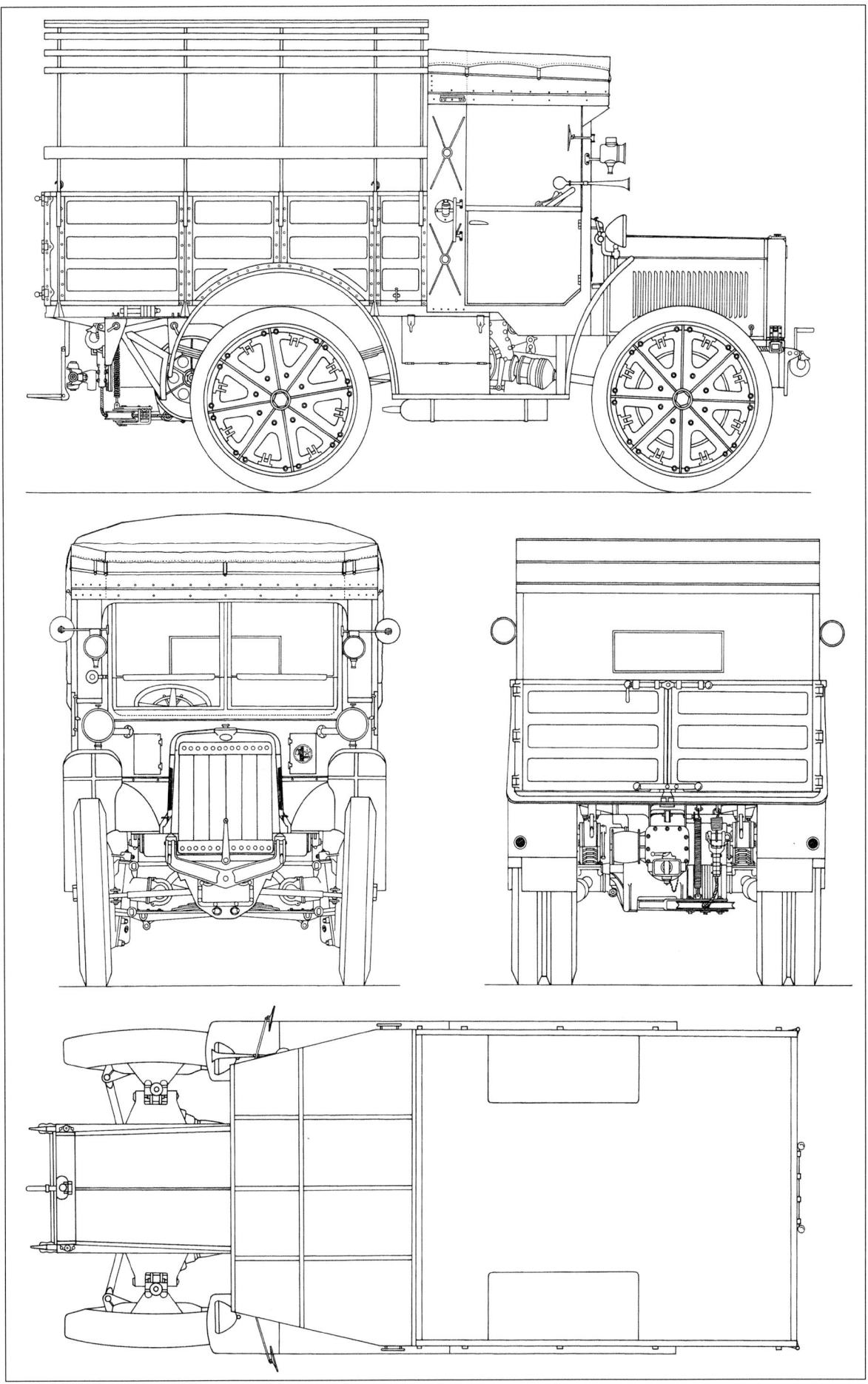

The Breda 32. (Drawings by A. M. Feller – GMT)

A Breda 32 belonging to the *4° Reggimento Artiglieria Pesante*. (N. Pignato)

Front view of Breda 32. The number plate is incomplete. (C. Pergher)

of the Second World War all of the Italian Army's heavy artillery regiments had been equipped with this tractor. The Hungarian Army also used the Breda mod. 32, mainly to tow the 210/22 howitzers, which were also of Italian origin. During the post-war period some of the Breda mod. 32 tractors were modernised and continued to be used by the Esercito Italiano. The Italian state railway system, which had adopted the mod. 32 around 1935 for towing freight cars, used the tractor well into the 1980s.

- Fuel capacity: 75 litres main tank, 25+5 litres auxiliary tank, total 105 litres (27.7 US gallons; 23 Imperial gallons) mod. 26; 75 litres main tank, 25 litres auxiliary tank, total 100 litres (26.4 US gallons, 22 Imperial gallons) mod. 30
- Drive layout: 4x4
- Speed (road): 22km/h (13.7mph) fully loaded
- Range (on road): 280km (174 miles) Mod. 26; 265km (165 miles) Mod. 30

Trattore Pesante Breda mod. 32 and 33

The almost definitive prototype of the Breda 32 during towing tests.

The Breda 32 heavy artillery tractor in a factory photo. The 8-spoke wheels and abbreviated front fenders were distinctive features.

The chassis of the Breda 32 had a particular 'cradle' shape made in cast steel. (Breda)

Developmental and Service History

Breda manufactured a wide range of machinery including locomotives, railway cars, trucks and artillery. The Breda mod. 32 heavy tractor (or TP 32) was the first of a series of Breda heavy artillery tractors used by the *Regio Esercito*. It was based on the earlier Autocarro Trattore Breda 4x4 of 1927, one of the first examples in Italy of a heavy four-wheel drive vehicle. It was adopted in 1932 with the name Trattrice Pesante 32 and began to be supplied to units in 1933. It was a powerful machine that performed well off-road as well as on paved or metalled roads. A modified model of the Breda 32, designated the Breda mod. 33, was developed for the engineers and differed from the mod. 32 in its greater length, a modified body and differences in the transmission and winch.

In 1938 an example of the Breda 32 equipped with a front crane, to be used as a recovery vehicle, was sent to Italian East Africa for testing.

The mod. 32 was first used in Spain during the Civil War to tow the Spanish Nationalists' heavy artillery, and by the outbreak

Two Modello 30A tractors with Superflex Sigillo Verde 11.25 x 30 pneumatic tyres in North Africa in 1942. (ACS)

Specifications
- Designation: Trattore Pavesi Tipo P4-100 Modello 26, Modello 30 and Modello 30A
- Producer: Motomeccanica Pavesi; Società Piemontese Automobili (SPA), Turin
- Years produced: 1926–1939
- Number produced: NA
- Length: 4,115mm (13ft 6in)
- Width: 2,050mm (6ft 9in)
- Height: 2,400mm (7ft 10in)
- Unladen weight: 4,680kg (10,318lbs) Mod. 26; 4,780kg (10,538lbs) Mod. 30
- Carrying capacity: 1,000kg (2,205lbs)
- Towing capacity: 12,000kg (26,455lbs) on road; 3,800kg (8,378lbs) off-road
- Wheelbase: 2,420mm (7ft 11in)
- Front track: 1,565mm (5ft 2in)
- Rear track: 1,565mm (5ft 2in)
- Tyres: semi-pneumatic Celerflex 150 x 1160 on Mod. 26 and Mod. 30; Superflex Sigillo Verde 11.25 x 30 on Mod. 30
- Minimum turning radius: 4,750mm (15ft 7in)
- Minimum clearance: 490mm (1ft 7in)
- Fording depth: 800mm (2ft 8in)
- Engine: P4-100 four-cylinder water-cooled, 4,720cc, 52 HP @1,500 rpm Mod. 26; 57 @1,800 rpm Mod. 30
- Fuel: Gasoline and Diesel Mod. 26; gasoline Mod. 30
- Transmission: manual transmission with 4 forward speed and 1 reverse; four-wheel drive with lockable differential

Pavesi Modello 26 tractors with complete gun crews towing a group of 105/28 guns. Turin, 9 August 1939 (AUSSME)

Italian troops parade in Tripoli in March 1941 aboard Pavesi P4 Mod. 30A tractors and Fiat 626 trucks. (ACS)

tilt independently by turning on the longitudinal axis, a feature that guaranteed a considerable vertical excursion of wheels and, therefore, optimal grip on all terrains.

The open body of the Pavesi mods 29, 30 and 30A was of stamped steel; the right-hand drive forward body had seats for the driver and a mechanic, and the rear body had six seats for the crew. The crew seats could be rotated downwards to obtain a flat bed allowing a 1,000kg cargo load to be carried instead. Both the front and the rear bodies had canvas covers. The very large diameter wire wheels provided very high ground clearance; the wheels measured 1.30 metres (4ft 3in) in diameter including the semi-pneumatic tyres that replaced the solid rubber tyres. In the late 1930s the Pavesis began to be fitted with pneumatic tyres, and following experience gained in Libya, in 1938 Pirelli pneumatic tyres fitted on eight-spoke cast wheels were adopted for the Pavesis. Starting was by hand crank thanks to a high-tension magneto, but it was possible to install an electrical system with battery and starter.

The Pavesis had oil and acetylene headlamps and from the mod. 30 A the headlamps were electric. The pedal brake system was connected to two belt (strap) brakes – flexible metal ribbons covered with braking material – operating on the left and right axle shafts connected to the front differential. The hand brake acted on a drum mounted on the transmission shaft. An interesting feature was that two or more tractors could be joined to add power for very heavy loads.

The engine was a four-cylinder water-cooled engine; the transmission had four forward and one reverse speeds. The model 26 retained the complex, but economical, gasoline and petroleum fuel system of its predecessors. Starting with the model 30, only gasoline and a new carburettor were used.

Variants

As described above, the Pavesi was produced in three series or models, the Modello 26, 30 and 30A. In addition, there was a derivative version, the Modello 31 which was similar to the earlier versions but was more manageable cross-country and was faster on paved roads. Their frame and suspension differed slightly, it had a somewhat less powerful engine and a battery.

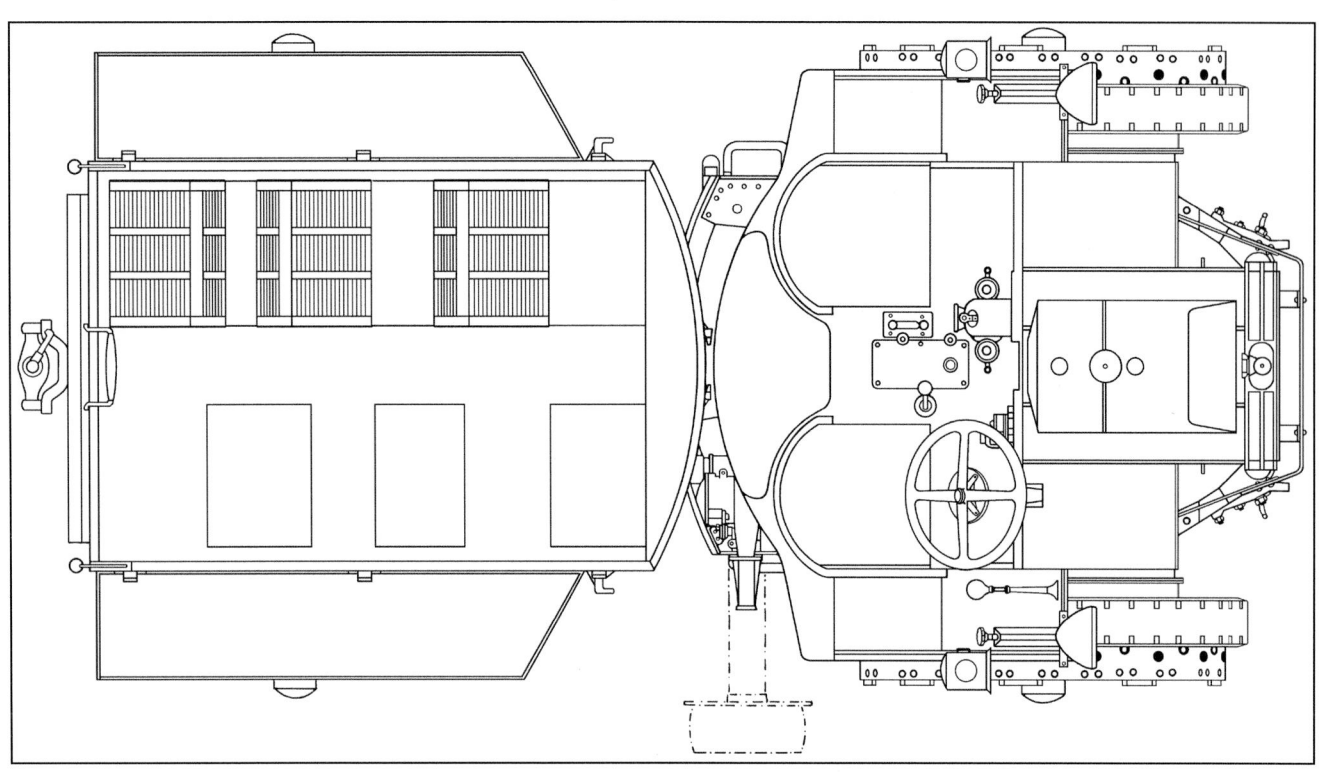
Pavesi P4-100 Modello 30A. (Drawings by GMT)

Pavesi tractors towing 149/35 guns during the Greek campaign in November 1940 and in North Africa in the same year. It was an antiquated artillery piece which entered service way back in 1901. (C. Pergher)

The Pavesi Modello 30A, very similar to the 30. (MMM)

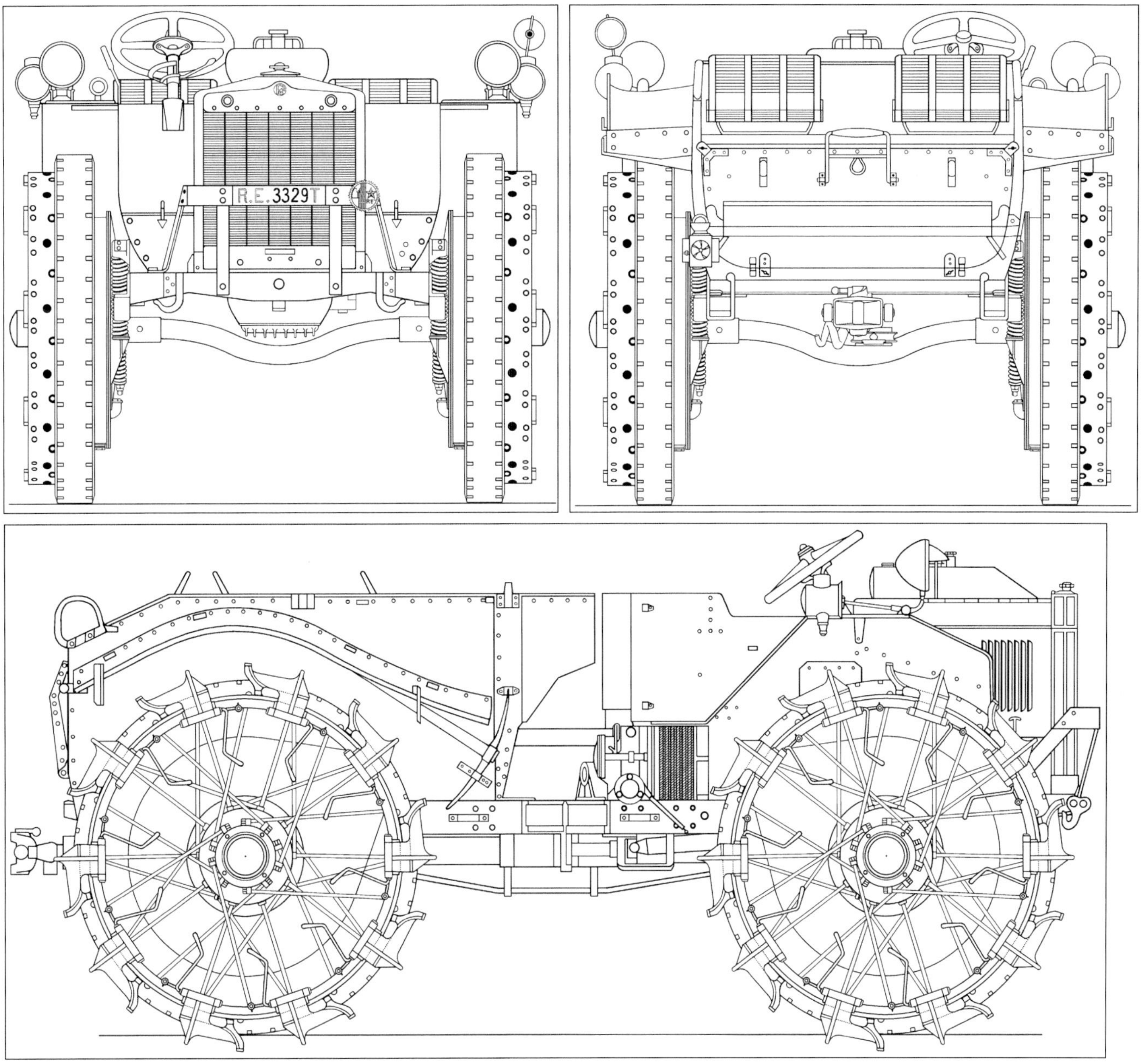

Pavesi P4-100 Modello 30A. (Drawings by GMT)

The side and top views allow you to observe the winch, the casings containing the wheel gears, the two flat cylinders of the band brakes on the front axle shafts, and the cylinder of the handbrake located immediately behind the rear differential. (MMM, Fiat)

The Pavesi Modello 30. (MMM)

Typ P 40-100 (i), to tow their own artillery and, in some cases, as recovery vehicles.

Pavesi tractors were tested and adopted by several other countries. Between 1930 and 1938 a total of about 100 tractors of various models (26, 30 and 30A) were delivered to Bulgaria. Greece, Finland, Poland and Spain also used the Pavesi acquired from Italy, and the United Kingdom, Sweden and Hungary produced Pavesis under licence.

Technical Description

As explained in the Pavesi P4 description, this family of Pavesi tractors had traction on all four wheels and a unique layout made of two separate frames connected by an articulated assembly consisting of gears, racks and a tubular bar; a transmission shaft with universal (Cardan) joint allowed the connection between the engine unit located in the front frame, together with the driving compartment and fuel tanks, and the parts located in the rear frame, essentially a platform for the gun crew to sit on, just as a trailer follows. The system, effective though mechanically complex, first of all allowed a very tight turning circle thanks to the synchronised steering system; this was achieved by rotating the two halves on the horizontal plane, although the wheels did not change position with respect to the frame, remaining integral with the axles. Secondly, the two frames could also

Trattore Pavesi P4-100 Modello 26 and Modello 30

The Pavesi P4-100 Modello 26 heavy field tractor. (MMM)

Developmental and Service History

As we wrote in the previous entry, in 1924 Motomeccanica Pavesi with its P4 (later called model 25) was the winner of a tender called by the *Regio Esercito* for an artillery tractor. Soon after, the military authorities placed an order for 45 machines with various improvements suggested by the approval trials. After a cycle of pre-series and severe field tests, numerous modifications to the model 25 were made, which led to the P4-100 or model 26; this garnered a production order for 1,000 vehicles over the course of four years. Since the Pavesi Company was unable to satisfy the production needs, Fiat – through its subsidiary SPA – took over the military production of the P4-100 tractors, while Pavesi maintained that of the same models for the civilian market.

In 1930 a further improved model was introduced, designated the Modello 30 or PC 30. At first sight it can be distinguished by the auxiliary tank located on the engine hood, slightly smaller and flattened instead of cylindrical. In 1934 the model 30A appeared, incorporating further improvements but being nearly identical in appearance to the previous one, except for the electric headlights.

By 1937 a total of 2,300 were on hand, with a further 270 on order. Pavesi tractors were issued on a scale of five machines per artillery battery. Operationally, these tractors first saw service in Ethiopia and later were used by Italian troops in the Spanish Civil War. At the outbreak of the Second World War they were still issued to corps level artillery regiments to tow guns up to 149mm as well as anti-aircraft guns and saw service on all fronts. Subsequently, they were used to tow the lighter 100/17 howitzer and the 75/46 anti-aircraft gun. Beginning in 1942, the Pavesi was replaced by the much more modern SPA TM 40 tractor. Following the September 1943 Armistice, German forces in Italy used captured Pavesis, named Radschlepper Pavesi

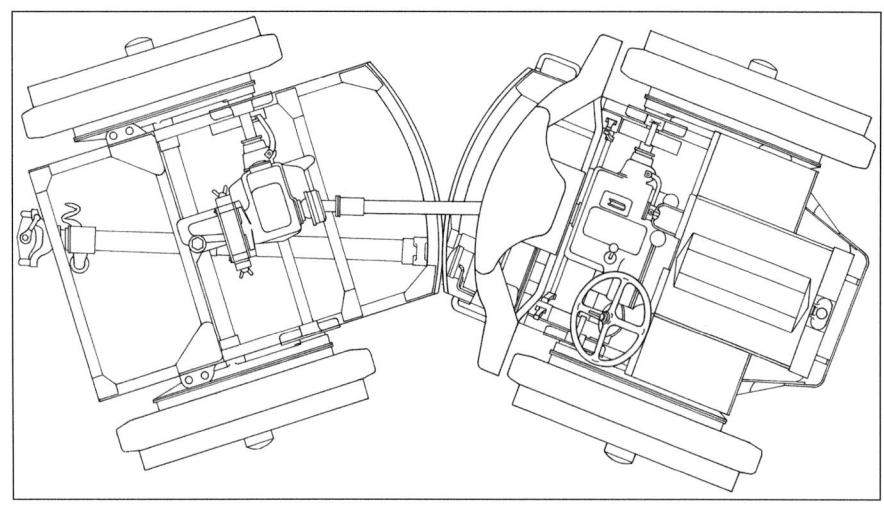

The tractor chassis at its maximum steering angle, when the two frames were completely horizontal. The bigger longeron, ending with the towing hook (left end) is the coupling bar. (Drawings by A. M. Feller – GMT)

Specifications

(Unless otherwise specified, data refer to P4-100 Mod. 25)

- Designation: Trattore Pavesi P4 and Trattore Pavesi P4-100 or Modello 25 pr PC 25
- Producer: Motomeccanica Pavesi, Milan
- Years produced: 1922–1926
- Number produced: NA
- Length: 3,900mm (12ft 9in)
- Width: 2,050mm (6ft 9in)
- Height: 2,400mm (7ft 10in) with canvas cover; 1,450mm (4ft 9in) without cover
- Unladen weight: 4,500kg (9,921lbs)
- Carrying capacity: 1,000kg (2,205lbs)
- Towing capacity: 3,000kg (6,614lbs)
- Wheelbase: 2,320mm (7ft 7in)
- Front track: 1,530mm (5ft)
- Rear track: 1,530mm (5ft)
- Minimum turning radius: 4,750mm (15ft 7in)
- Minimum clearance: 490mm (1ft 7in)
- Tyres: 1,600x50 solid rubber tyres
- Engine: two-cylinder opposed, 4,520cc, 15–20 HP @900 rpm the P4; four-cylinder, in-line, water-cooled, 4,700cc, 48 HP @1,250 rpm the P4-100 Mod. 25
- Fuel: Gasoline/petroleum
- Transmission: manual transmission with two forward speeds and two reverse – P4; manual transmission with three forward speeds and one reverse, four-wheel drive with lockable differential – P4-100 Mod. 25
- Fuel capacity: 75 litres main tank, 25+5 litres auxiliary tank, total 105 litres (27.7 US gallons, 23 Imperial gallons)
- Drive layout: 4x4
- Speed (road): 10km/h (6.3mph) the P4; 20km/h (12.6mph) the P4-100 Mod. 25
- Range (on road): 100km (62 miles) estimated

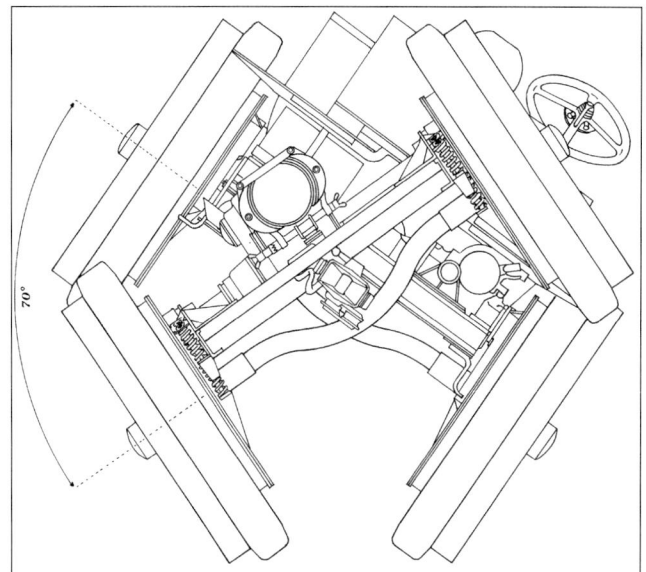

Theoretical rotation of the two frames with respect to their own axes. (Drawings by A. M. Feller – GMT)

Bottom view of the same chassis. The tubular longitudinal longeron (coupling bar) was pivoted to the front of the engine block. Also note the axles, the rack on the parts in contact with the two articulated frames, and the coil spring suspensions.

The front frame accommodated the engine, driving commands, transmission, front differential and fuel tanks, while the rear frame held the rear differential. The 4,520cc two-cylinder engine could run on petroleum with gasoline starter, and developed 15–20 HP. The 75 litre main tank, containing gasoline, was located forward between the seats; the 30 litre auxiliary tank for starting on gasoline was fixed on top of the engine hood. Basically, the engine was started cold thanks to the gasoline; subsequently, by means of a device that exploited the heat of the exhaust gases, the oil was vaporised, creating the air-gas mixture for feeding in normal mode. Instead of gasoline, benzene or diesel fuel could be used, at the time they were all cheaper and more available than gasoline.

The driver sat on a simple tractor-style metal seat. The large-diameter iron wheels were fitted with solid rubber tyres that had 10 metal grousers; these latter could be folded inward while the tractor travelled on roads but could be opened outward to provide ground contact while working on soft or muddy ground. The P4 suspension consisted of double coil springs, with other springs used as shock absorbers. The pedal controls activated two belt (strap) brakes which operated on the two axle shafts protruding from the front differential; the handbrake acted by means of a metal cable on a pulley keyed to the final end of the propeller shaft, behind the rear differential. In both cases, all four wheels were braked by the action of the transmission.

The P4-100 Modello 25 (or PC 25) artillery tractor was a modified and improved P4, while retaining the mechanical structure of the previous model. The rear frame was configured to hold six men, in addition to the driver and mechanic seated on the front frame. The engine was a 4,700cc four-cylinder gasoline engine developing 40 HP. The transmission had three forward speeds and one reverse, compared to the two forward and two reverse of the P4 agricultural machine.

Variants

The P4 Modello 25 served as the basis from which all successive Pavesi models 26, 30, 30A and 31 were developed (see next entry).

Among experimental models or variants were a model powered by a gas generator engine, one with twin disc wheels on both front and rear axles, one with the wheels replaced by eight small pneumatic tyres, and one which replaced the wheels with tracked bogies.

6

Artillery Tractors

Trattore Pavesi P4

Propaganda image from 1924 of a Pavesi P4 tractor. It portrays the test driver during the tests of the tender organised by the *Regio Esercito*.

The complete pre-series Pavesi P4 chassis showing the arrangement of the mechanical parts. The propeller shaft connects the front differential block (on the right, connected to the engine) with the rear differential. Below the two frames the connection bar can be seen.

Developmental and Service History

In 1918 Ugo Pavesi designed the P4 agricultural tractor; the P4 was the first Italian 4-wheel drive tractor and incorporated a number of innovations such as the articulated frame and four large-diameter road wheels of equal size. It proved to be an exceptional machine in terms of performance, but because of its complexity was very expensive (almost double the most popular models) compared to its contemporary agricultural tractors and thus was unaffordable by small and medium-size farms. Its speed on roads, even without a towed load, was very low. Starting in 1922 a lightened version was manufactured – the P4 Modello Leggero.

However, Pavesi made a number of further modifications to the P4 aimed at making it attractive to the military market. In 1923 the *Regio Esercito* invited proposals for an artillery tractor to tow army and corps level artillery pieces, and Pavesi submitted its proposal for the P4 Modello Pesante heavy tractor. The vehicle was selected over the other competitors (Fiat and Ansaldo, who, however, ultimately failed to propose any vehicle) and was adopted in 1925 with the name Modello 25 (or PC 25 – PC is for Pesante Campale, Heavy Field in English) to tow the new 149/19 howitzer as well as the 105/28 gun from 1939 to 1942. The PC 25 was further modified, leading to the 26, 30 and 30 A models (see appropriate sections).

Technical Description

Compared to other tractors, the P4 was characterised by two major features: its articulated frames and its large-diameter, steel, wire-spoke wheels. The P4 had two separate frames, one front and one rear, connected by a tubular longeron that allowed the frames to flex independently to conform to uneven terrain, at the same time the two frames could be steered in the same direction contemporaneously. This mechanical arrangement ensured that all four wheels maintained contact with the ground regardless of undulations in the terrain. The height of the wheels from the ground could be regulated by hand cranks for ploughing on consistently sloped ground so that the tractor maintained a level horizontal trim.

- Minimum clearance: 400mm (1ft 4in)
- Fording depth: 1,000mm (3ft 3in)
- Tyres: pneumatic Cord 40 x 8 or Superflex 9.75 x 24 with Sigillo Verde or Artiglio tread
- Engine: Breda D11 six-cylinder in-line water-cooled injection, 8,850cc, 110 HP @ 1,700 rpm Breda 51; 115 HP @ 1,800 rpm Breda 52
- Fuel: Diesel
- Transmission: four speeds forward and one reverse, with reduction gear, Breda 51; five speeds forward and one reverse, with reduction gear, Breda 52
- Fuel capacity: 480 litres (127 US gallons, 105.5 Imperial gallons)
- Drive layout: 6x4
- Speed: 50km/h (31mph) Breda 51; 53km/h (33mph) Breda 52
- Range (on road): 500–800km (311–497 miles) depending on version

MEDIUM AND HEAVY TRUCKS 125

This Breda 52 mounting a 90/53 gun is shown abandoned in Sicily and being inspected by British soldiers.

- Wheelbase: 2,769mm (9ft) front axle to leading rear axle; 3,400mm (11ft 2in) from front axle to centreline of rear bogey; 4,040mm (13ft 3in) front axle to trailing rear axle
- Front track: 1,810mm (5ft 11in)
- Rear track: 1,880mm (6ft 2in)
- Minimum turning radius: 9,750mm (32ft)

The Breda 52, or Autocarro 52 according to the manuals, was also intended to be used as an artillery tractor for mobile batteries. A cargo bed box could be mounted on the chassis to obtain a truck. A total of 262 examples were produced before the interruption following the Armistice of 8 September 1943.

The Autocarro 52 was actually used as a platform for the 90/53 gun. More variants were envisaged on the same chassis, such as ammunition carrier, battery command vehicle, group command vehicle and finally tool carrier.

Specifications

- (unless otherwise specified, data refer to Breda 51 model)
- Designation: Autocarro Pesante 51 (Breda 51) and Autocarro 52 (Breda 52)
- Producer: Società Italiana Ernesto Breda per Costruzioni Meccaniche, Milan
- Years produced: 1938–1951
- Number produced: 48 (estimated) Breda 51; 262 Breda 52
- Length: 6,750mm (22ft 2in)
- Width: 2,500mm (8ft 2in)
- Height: 3,000mm (9ft 10in) Breda 51; 2,650mm (8ft 8in) Breda 52
- Unladen weight: 8,500kg (17,739lbs) Breda 51; 8,900kg (19,621lbs) Breda 52
- Carrying capacity: 7,000kg (15,432lbs); 5,000kg (11,023lbs) off-road
- Towing capacity: 12,000kg (26,455lbs)
- Towing capacity of winch: 7,500kg (16,535lbs).

The Breda 51/52 prototype used as a platform for an anti-aircraft gun. The cab is an open type with a canvas top.

The final version of the Autocannone da 90/53 on Breda 52 chassis. The spare wheels had to be removed to put the gun into battery.

drum brakes on all wheels, boosted by an air compressor; the mechanical handbrake acted on the transmission. The winch, if present, guaranteed a towing capacity of 7,500kg.

Variants

In 1941 the Royal Army was looking for truck frames suitable for mounting guns on, in particular the 90/53 anti-aircraft gun, as had been done on the Lancia 3 Ro. Thus Breda, in collaboration with Viberti, created a modified version of the 51, with a strengthened frame, which later took the name of Breda 52. The most evident external modifications, compared to the Breda 51, concerned the cab, which resumed the shapes seen on the previous Breda 5T, i.e. only partially closed and with half-doors equipped with side canvas. However, the windshield appeared to be divided into three parts, with the smaller central one fixed and the lateral ones opening outwards. The electrical system was 12 V, without a battery; the latter could be mounted on request together with the starter motor. Apart from the bodywork, the main changes include the gearbox, which was upgraded to five forward gears and one reverse, with reduction gear.

The Breda 52 differed from the Breda 51 in bodywork and other elements, mainly the simplified cab with half-doors and the windshield divided into three pieces.

Technical Description

The Breda 51 was a three-axle 6x4 all-terrain truck and artillery tractor. The traction was on the two rear axles equipped with twin wheels. The design was modern for the time, with a closed metal cab over engine designed for civilian and military use in the Italian colonies. It housed two berths behind the driver and passenger seats. There was a double windshield, with the right and left portions further divided into two parts: the lower part was fixed and the upper one could be opened outwards for ventilation. The windshield wiper was electric.

The frame consisted of two longerons in pressed steel plate, connected to each other by three crossbars of the same type. The lifting hooks were welded to the ends of the longerons, while the regulation tow hook was fixed to the rear crossbars. The cargo bed was made of wood.

Free-wheeling spare wheels were mounted just behind the cab on each side, helping to avoid bellying. Tyres were pneumatic, mounted on six-spoke wheels; on the rear wheels special chains to improve traction could be mounted. It is interesting to note that the manual suggested mounting, if the terrain conditions made it necessary, the spare wheels alongside the front ones so as to have twin wheels on the front as well.

Wheels had leaf spring independent suspension, one spring arranged transversely on the front axle and four longitudinally at the rear. Oil-filled shock absorbers were only present on the front suspension. An auxiliary gasoline engine (two-cylinder, 584 cc, 14 HP) was used for starting; an electric starter could be included under request, as there was a battery.

The 125 HP six-cylinder diesel engine of the 5T model was replaced with a 110 HP engine. The transmission had four forward and one reverse speed, doubled when the reduction gear was activated. The truck had a backstop device. The brakes were

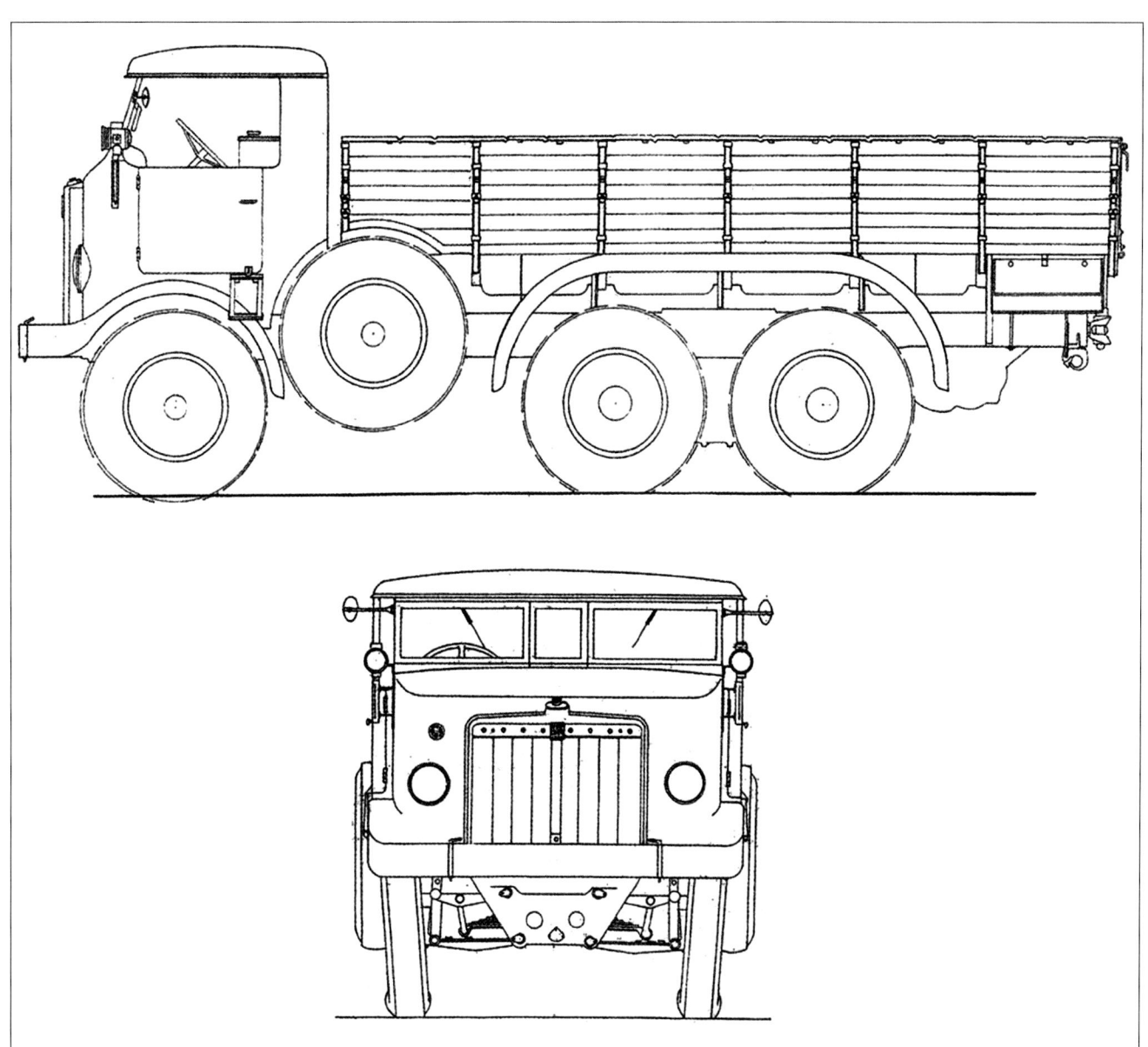

The Breda 52, or Autocarro 52, styled by Viberti. (Breda)

MEDIUM AND HEAVY TRUCKS   121

Trials with a trailer of the Breda 5T, aka Autocarro Coloniale. Addis Ababa, 1938. (Breda)

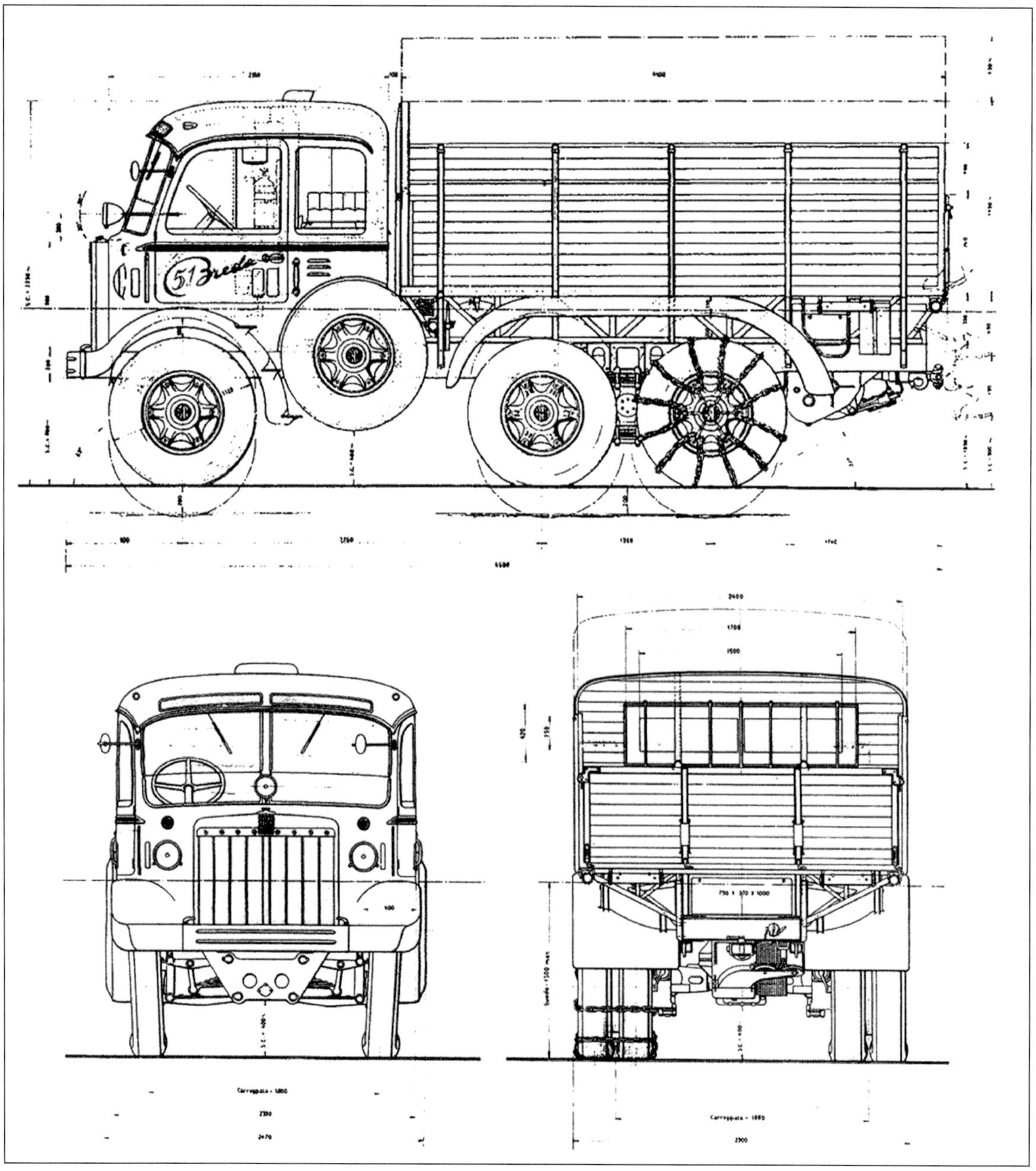

The Breda 51 Autocarro Coloniale Militare, drawing dated 5 April 1940. (Breda)

Although it served on all fronts, operational employment of the Breda 51 was rather limited; precise figures concerning total production are not available, but the numbers are believed to have been relatively modest. The first batch included 48 examples; later reports cite an order in progress for 200 frames to which another 52 were to be added, to be used above all for the construction of *autocannoni*, or gun trucks (see below).

Breda tried to market a commercial version of the truck following the war, but it was not successful.

The Breda 51 was initially baptised Dovunque, but then the nickname was removed to avoid confusion with the Dovunque manufactured by Fiat.

Traction tests with chains on snowy ground. The vehicle appears camouflaged.

The Breda 5T was the forerunner of the Breda 51; this photo highlights the vertical excursion of the axes. The wheels are of the stamped disc type with holes. (Breda)

The Trattore Medio Dovunque 41, artillery tractor version of the truck.

Specifications
- Designation: Autocarro SPA Dovunque 41
- Producer: Società Piemontese Automobili (SPA), Turin
- Years produced: 1943–1948
- Number produced: Not known
- Length: 7,040mm (23ft 1in)
- Width: 2,350mm (7ft 8in)
- Height: 3,124mm (10ft 3in) full loaded with canvas top, 3,285mm (10ft 9in) unloaded
- Unladen weight: 8,800kg (19,401lbs) without refuelling, 9,210kg (20,305lbs) laden
- Carrying capacity: 4,200kg (5,512lbs); 2,000kg (4,409lbs) off-road
- Towing capacity: 3,000kg (6,614lbs)
- Wheelbase: 3,900mm (12ft 9in) front axle to leading rear axle; 5,500mm (18ft) front axle to trailing rear axle
- Front track: 1,985mm (6ft 6in)
- Rear track: 2,000mm (6ft 7in)
- Minimum turning radius: 9,050mm (29ft 8in)
- Minimum clearance: 360mm (1ft 2in)
- Tyres: Superflex 11.25 x 24 or 12.75 x 24 with Artiglio tread
- Engine: Fiat 366 six-cylinder water-cooled, 9,365cc, 110 HP @2,000 rpm
- Fuel: Diesel
- Transmission: five speeds forward, one reverse; reduction gear; central lockable differential
- Fuel capacity: 130 litres (34.4 US gallons, 28.6 Imperial gallons)
- Drive layout: 6x6
- Speed: 50km/h (31mph)
- Range (on road): 270km (168 miles)

AUTOCARRO BREDA 51 AND 52

Developmental and Service History
The Dovunque Breda 51 was an evolution of the Breda Tipo A Dovunque of January 1936, equipped with a 95 HP gasoline engine, and of the subsequent Dovunque Pesante Breda, or Breda 5T, of December 1936, which had a 125 HP diesel engine. Both had been developed to meet the needs of the Italian Army, but were never mass produced.

The second prototype, modified and upgraded, of the Breda 5T (with the provisional name of Autocarro Coloniale) was sent to Italian East Africa where it underwent a long test period, mainly focused on cross-country performance as well as on both unimproved tracks and on paved roads; it performed well under all circumstances.

The definitive version of the vehicle was presented in April 1940, designated as the Breda 51. Since 1936 Breda had advertised the vehicle as a Dovunque, but in 1941 – perhaps to avoid disagreements with Fiat, which already had a Dovunque in its catalogue (see separate entry) – had changed the description to Autocarro Campale Pesante (heavy field truck). The new truck, in its definitive configuration, had a fuel-injected six-cylinder engine rated at 110 HP, could carry up to 36 men and had a range of 800 kilometres. With further modifications it was offered in both the truck as well as artillery tractor versions.

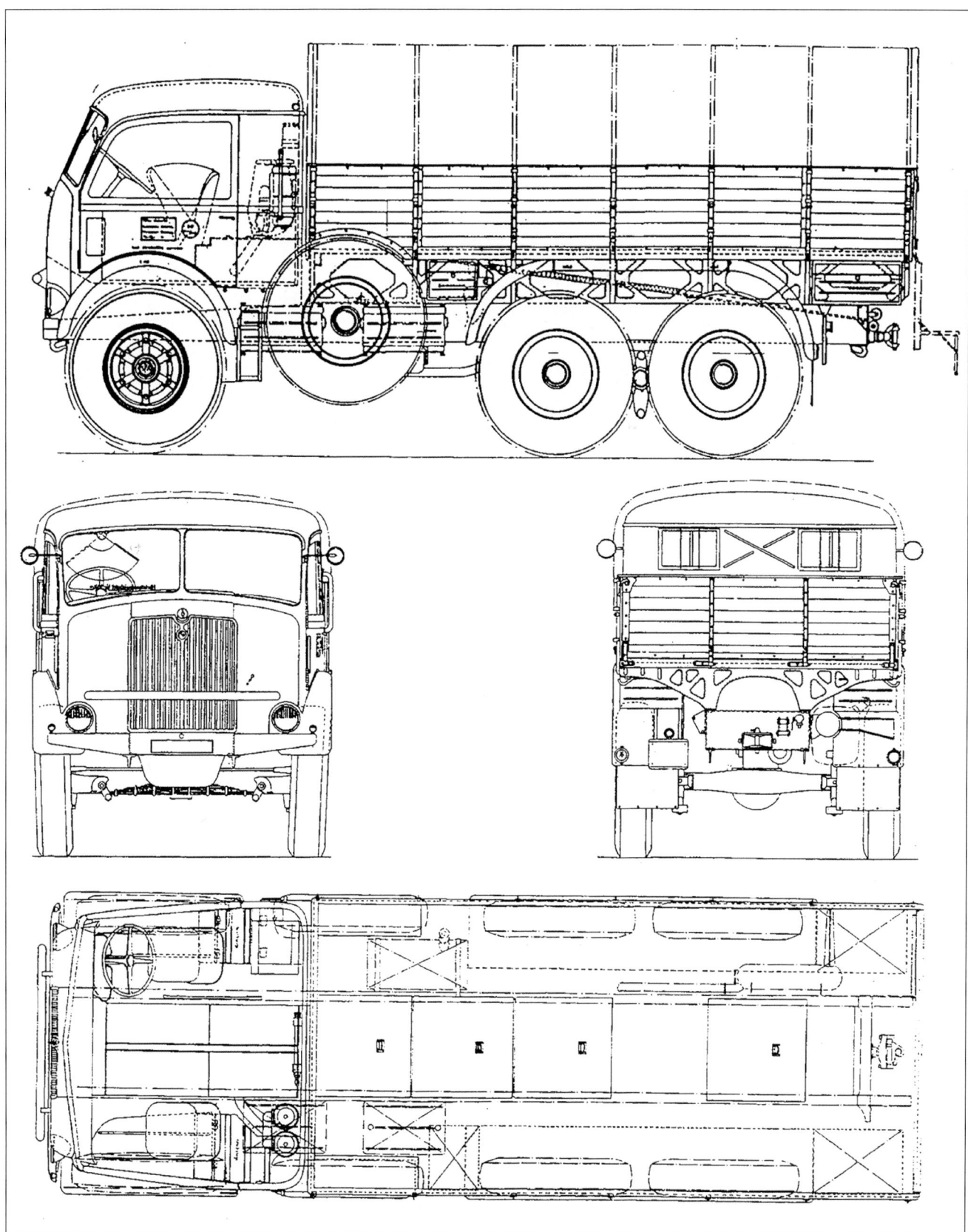

The Dovunque 41 produced for the Wehrmacht. Line drawing dated 31 May 1944. (Fiat)

plans to produce a lighter, gasoline-powered version, designated the SPA Dovunque 42, which was to have entered production in February 1944, but, because of the Armistice in late 1943, production never began.

Following the end of the war, the Dovunque 41 served as the basis for development of the TP 41/50 and 41/51 heavy tractors which remained in service with the Italian Army until the 1970s.

A *Luftwaffe* column made up of vehicles of various types and origin, comprising some Dovunque 41 towing 8,8 cm Flak guns in Italy, just after the armistice of 8 September 1943. (Bundesarchiv: Bild 101I-570-1604-21A)

The German unit is heading towards Popoli (near Pescara), and the Italian vehicles still carry the Regio Esercito number plates. Some trucks equipped with single 20mm cannons give antiaircraft protection to the column. (Bundesarchiv: Bild 101I-570-1604-22A)

The engine on the Dovunque 41 was a Fiat diesel engine developing 110 HP. Details of the transmission are uncertain, but presumably the vehicle had five forward speeds and one reverse, and it is likely to have had a reduction gear given its reported excellent cross-country capabilities. It is also likely that the vehicle had a backstop system. The suspension included a single transverse leaf spring on the front axle and two sets of longitudinal leaf springs for the rear wheels. Brakes were hydraulic on all wheels with an air booster; the handbrake was mechanical acting on the reduction gear shaft.

Variants

A recovery vehicle variant was produced, and although there were plans to utilise the chassis of the Dovunque 41 as a platform for the 90/53 gun (the *autocannone* version), the plans apparently never progressed beyond the design stage. Likewise, there were

- Bed, internal height: 635mm (2ft)
- Tyres: Cord 32 x 6 with Artiglio tread Dovunque 33 and 35; Ultraflex 200 x 20 or 210 x 20 with Sigillo Verde tread Dovunque 35
- Engine: Fiat 122B six-cylinder water-cooled, 2,953cc, 46 HP @2,400 rpm Dovunque 33; Fiat 18T, four-cylinder in-line water-cooled, 4,053cc, 55 HP @2,000 rpm Dovunque 35
- Fuel: Gasoline
- Transmission: four speeds forward, one reverse; reduction gear; lockable differential
- Fuel capacity: 100 litres (75 + 25) (26.4 US gallons, 22 Imperial gallons) Dovunque 33; 115 litres (90 + 25) (30.4 US gallons, 25.3 Imperial gallons) Dovunque 35
- Drive layout: 6x4
- Speed: 47km/h (29mph) Dovunque 33; 50km/h (31 mph) Dovunque 35
- Range (loaded vehicle, on road): 250km (155 miles) Dovunque 33; 280km (174 miles) Dovunque 35

Autocarro SPA Dovunque 41

Developmental and Service History

In early 1935, Fiat announced that, in response to requirements established by the *Regio Esercito*'s Automobile Inspectorate, it was developing a heavy version of its Dovunque 33/35 truck. However, the gestation period for the new vehicle was quite prolonged, partly due to the slowdown in military investment following the Italo-Ethiopian War. For these reasons the 6x6 Dovunque 41 truck version, equipped with closed cab, did not make its appearance until mid–1942. The open cab artillery tractor version, designated the Trattore Medio TM 41 and especially conceived for towing the anti-aircraft gun Cannone da 90/53 mod. 1939, was delivered in early 1943. According to Fiat's claims, the vehicle's cross-country performance exceeded that of contemporary German half-tracks.

Because of the late date at which it appeared, the Dovunque 41 saw only limited service, and only 87 examples were delivered before 31 May 1943. It therefore did not have time to arrive on the Eastern Front, the theatre for which it was designed. Following the September 1943 Armistice, production of the Dovunque 41 continued under German auspices with 153 examples being delivered. Following the end of the war, modest numbers of the Dovunque 41 continued to be produced until 1948.

Technical Description

The SPA Dovunque 41 was a three-axle 6x6 all-terrain truck and artillery tractor; it was the only 6x6 truck fielded by the *Regio Esercito* during the war. As a departure from almost all other Italian medium and heavy military trucks, the rear axles had single rather than double wheels, so as to ensure good performance both on and off road. Free-wheeling spare wheels were mounted just behind the cab on each side, helping to avoid bellying. The truck version of the Dovunque 41 was a typical Fiat cab-over-engine design with an all-metal cab with full doors and windows, whereas the artillery tractor version had an open cab that could be covered by a folding canvas top. The cargo body on both types was made of wood. The tractor had a body with two rows of three seats each for the gun crew, and a powerful winch mounted on the rear of the frame. Superflex Artiglio pneumatic tyres were mounted on six-spoke wheels. The electrical system was fed by two 12 volt Marelli batteries.

The SPA Dovunque 41 6x6 heavy truck was mainly employed as an artillery tractor.

The Dovunque 33 (Fiat 612) searchlight platform.

Specifications
- Designation: Autocarro Fiat Dovunque 33 and SPA Dovunque 35
- Producer: Fabbrica Italiana Automobili Turin (Fiat), Turin; Società Piemontese Automobili (SPA), Turin
- Years produced: 1933–1948
- Number produced: At least 1,050, to which perhaps must be added the 307 produced for the Germans and the 701 exported to Hungary
- Length: 4,996mm (16ft 5in) Dovunque 33; 5,030mm (16ft 6in) Dovunque 35
- Width: 2,000mm (6ft 7in)
- Height: 2,910mm (9ft 6in)
- Unladen weight: 3,790 (8,356lbs) Dovunque 33; 4,440kg (9,789lbs), 4,530kg (9,987lbs) with winch, Dovunque 35
- Carrying capacity: 2,000kg (4,409lbs) on road, 1,500kg (3,307lbs) off-road Dovunque 33; 2,500kg (5,512lbs) on road, 2,000kg (4,409lbs) off-road Dovunque 35
- Towing capacity: 3,300kg (7,275lbs) Dovunque 33; 3,600kg (7,937lbs) Dovunque 35
- Wheelbase: 2,700mm (8ft 10in) front axle to leading rear axle; 3,700mm (12ft 1in) front axle to trailing rear axle
- Front track: 1,470mm (4ft 10in)
- Rear track: 1,500mm (4ft 11in)
- Minimum turning radius: 6,500mm (21ft 4in)
- Minimum clearance: 250mm (10in)
- Fording depth: 700mm (2ft 3in)
- Bed, internal length: 3,200mm (10ft 6in)
- Bed, internal width: 1,880mm (6ft 2in)

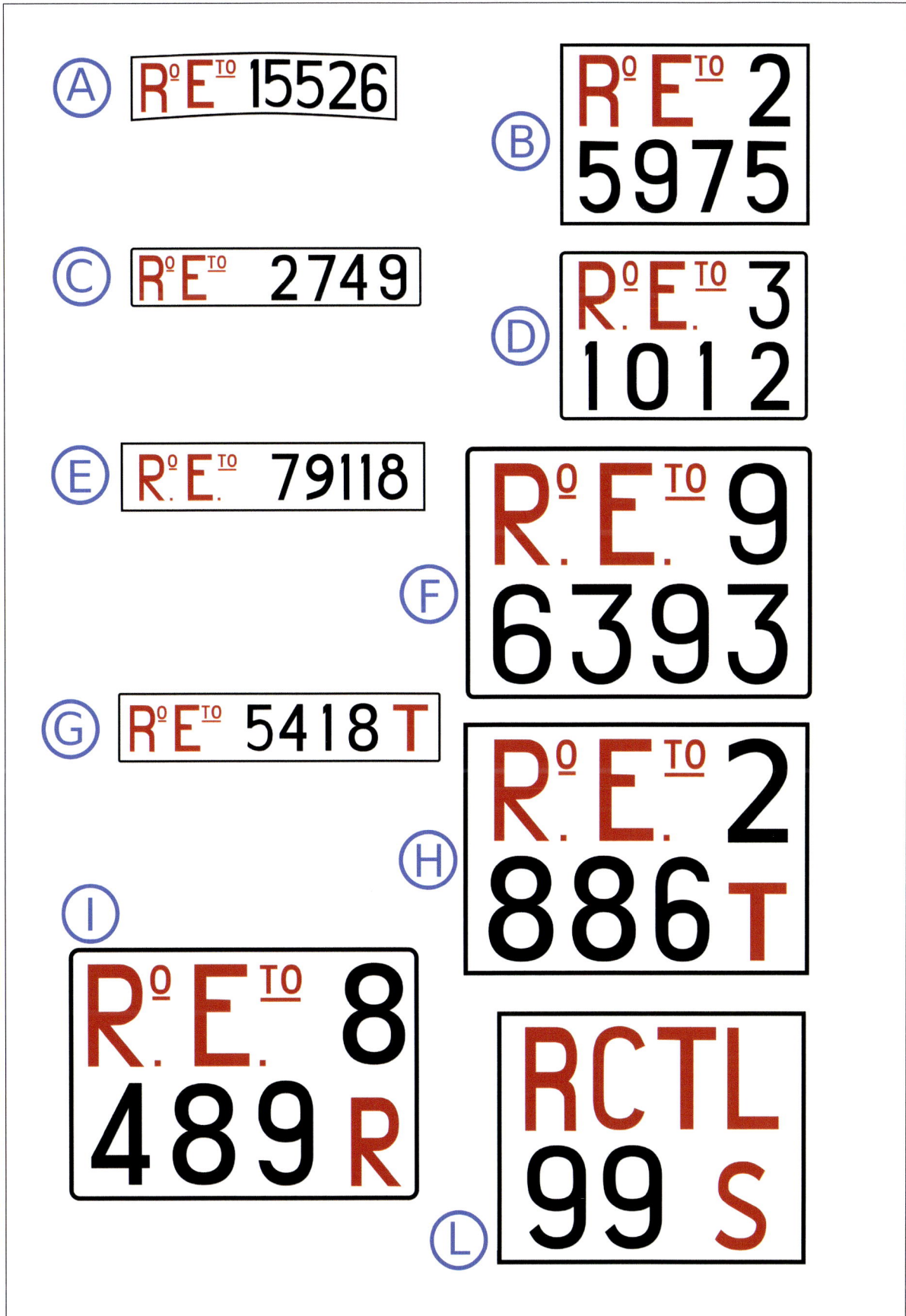

Examples of number plates: A = front plate, metal, motorcycle (Gilera 500 LTE); B = rear plate, metal, motor tricycle (Guzzi Trialce); C = front plate, metal, car (Bianchi VM6 C); D = rear plate, metal, car (Lancia Aprilia Coloniale); E = front plate, painted, truck (OM 3 BOD); F = rear plate, metal, truck (Bianchi Miles); G = front plate, painted, tractor (Alfa Romeo, prototype); H = rear plate, metal, tractor (Breda 33); I = rear plate, metal, trailer; L = rear plate, Regio Corpo Truppe Coloniali in Libia, metal, truck (AS 37). (See Appendix I) (Colour artworks by M. Pieri)

A column of Italian and German prisoners photographed in Tunisia in May 1943. Behind the grey-green trailer, Italian trucks of various models are painted in sand-yellow colour. (See Appendices I, II and III) (LIFE)

All army vehicles had to bear a special bronze badge that proved they belonged to the *Regio Esercito*. (See Appendix I)

During the campaign in North Africa, many Italian logistics vehicles remained painted in grey-green. In the absence of the regulation sand-yellow paint, the units often resorted to paints recovered on site and applied 'at best'. Here some *Bersaglieri* motorcyclists aboard Gilera 500 LTE two-seat motorcycles. (See Appendix I)

This image is part of a series of poses taken on Agfa colour film by a German soldier during the transfer trip and stay in North Africa. It was taken perhaps in the port of Tripoli or Bengasi in 1942. Italian cars and trucks (on the right, a Fiat 634 seen from the front) are painted in *kaki sahariano* which, due to the effect of the sun and the quality of the photographic equipment, appears rather pale. (See Appendix I)

Four M14/41 tanks ready for embarkation in Naples, bound for North Africa. Their colour is the factory applied *kaki sahariano* (sand-yellow). In the frame from a period newspaper there are other vehicles repainted in the same colour: on the right a Breda 41 tractor, left in the background a Lancia 3Ro and a Fiat 626 or 666. Some of them have visible residues of the pre-existing grey-green paint. (See Appendix I)

An OM Taurus crosses a German column in North Africa. The truck is grey-green and has the Italian flag painted on the cab roof. (See Appendix I)

In these photographs taken in Yugoslavia by an alpino soldier in April 1941, various Italian vehicles painted in the standard grey-green can be observed, including a damaged Alfa Romeo 800 RE, an OM Taurus and a Fiat 666. (See Appendix I)

In these photographs taken in Yugoslavia by an alpino soldier in April 1941, various Italian vehicles painted in the standard grey-green can be observed, including a damaged Alfa Romeo 800 RE, an OM Taurus and a Fiat 666. (See Appendix I)

A well-known photograph published by *Signal* magazine illustrates the landing of German material in the Tunisian port of Bizerte, at the end of 1942. The Italian Lancia 3Ro trucks are still in dark grey-green. The German Pz.Kpfw. III Ausf.N tanks are camouflaged in the *Tropen* colours in use since March 1942. (See Appendix I)

The German photographer Hugo Jaeger accompanied Hitler during his 1938 visit to Italy; this photo portrays a parade in Piazza del Plebiscito, in Naples. The two Pavesi P4-100 model 1926 tractors are painted in the regulation dark *grigioverde* (grey-green) colour. The circular bronze badge was fastened to the left of the white number plate. (See Appendix I)

A rare and interesting colour artwork from the user manual of the Lancia 3Ro. (see Appendix I)

Breda 32 heavy artillery tractor, Eastern Front, 1941. (Artwork by and © David Bocquelet)

SPA TL37 light artillery tractor, Eastern Front, 1942. (Artwork by and © David Bocquelet)

Fiat 626 NLM standardised medium truck, Libya, 1942. (Artwork by and © David Bocquelet)

SPA Dovunque 35 medium truck, Libya, 1942. (Artwork by and © David Bocquelet)

COLOUR SECTION

Fiat 634 NM standardised heavy truck, Balkans, 1940. (Artwork by and © David Bocquelet)

Lancia 3Ro NM standardised heavy truck, Eastern Front, 1941. (Artwork by and © David Bocquelet)

Italian vehicles captured by Australian troops. In the foreground are some CV 33 light tanks. Behind them, a Dovunque 35 converted into a tow truck; note the machine gun on board. (AWM)

each side. Thanks to these suspensions equipped with articulated and independent connections, the vehicle could perform wide transverse oscillations. Both differentials were lockable.

The engine on the Dovunque 33 was a Fiat gasoline engine developing 46 HP, which proved to be underpowered. Therefore, during production of the Dovunque 35 it was replaced by the proven and reliable 55 HP Fiat 18T engine, that was used on the SPA 38 R truck. The fuel supply was by gravity, through a 25 litre tank placed on the dashboard; this was supplied by the main tank, fixed to the right side longeron of the chassis, by means of a mechanical pump controlled by the camshaft.

The transmission had four forward speeds and one reverse, which with a reduction gear doubled the speeds. A winch attached to a gearbox power take-off could be installed, but only on the Dovunque 35; it had a pulling capacity of 3,000kg. The electrical system was 6 V without battery, so the crank start was necessary.

Variants

A *coloniale* version for tropical environment was prepared; it was equipped with an oil-filled air filter, and an additional 225-litre tank connected to the main one. The wheels were different, having 20 x 6 stamped wheels with two holes and 210 x 20 Ultraflex balloon tyres; they could be inflated with a compressor connected to the gearbox power take-off.

The Dovunque 33 could be fitted out as a *Stazione Autofotoelettrica da 120cm* (120cm searchlight platform)

Many examples of Dovunque 33 and 35 were configured as special vehicles for chemical service, equipped with a sprayer equipment (*Attrezzatura Irroratrice* model 33 A or B, later model 40), decontamination equipment (*Attrezzatura Bonificatrice* model 33) or fogging equipment (*Attrezzatura Nebbiogena* model 33). The first was supposed to be used to spread mustard gas, while the other two were designed for defence; a few dozen of each type were built.

Tow truck (likely a field modification), mobile observation tower and mobile photo lab variants were also made.

A radio van with a Viberti (or other firms) body was built in some variants for the *Regio Esercito* and the *Regia Aeronautica*; long folding antennas were placed on the roof.

The armoured version of the Dovunque, called Autotrasporto Armato SPA Dov. 35 or more simply Dovunque 35 Protetto, remained in its design state until after the Armistice of 8 September 1943. At least one prototype was built by Viberti, perhaps more, in 1945.

Another example of a Radio Campale Mobile, camouflaged, with number plate 'RA30270' and whip antenna shown in two positions. (Viberti, Moncalvo)

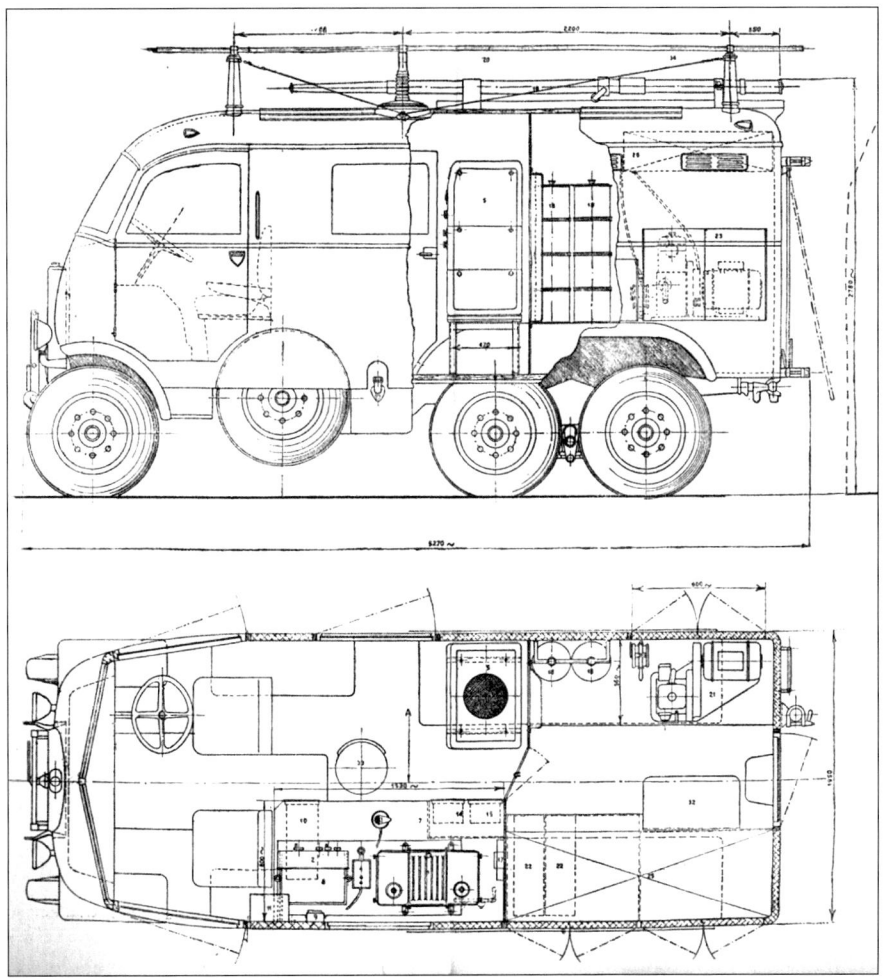

Factory scheme of the radio van. (Viberti)

A Radio Campale Mobile R.T. field radio van built by Viberti for the *Regia Aeronautica*. The number plate is 'RA30252'. (Viberti, Moncalvo)

the spare wheel; the Dovunque 33 had them on the left-hand side, the 35 on the right; there were stowage lockers on the opposite side. Brakes were hydraulic on the front wheels and the leading set of rear wheels (on the Dovunque 33 and on the first 250 examples of the Dovunque 35, manufactured until 1937, they were compressed-air brakes). A mechanical brake acted on the transmission. The backstop device acted on the brake drum on the transmission. A transverse semi-elliptical leaf spring suspension was designed for the front axle, while the two rear axles used a double longitudinal semi-elliptical leaf spring on

MEDIUM AND HEAVY TRUCKS 111

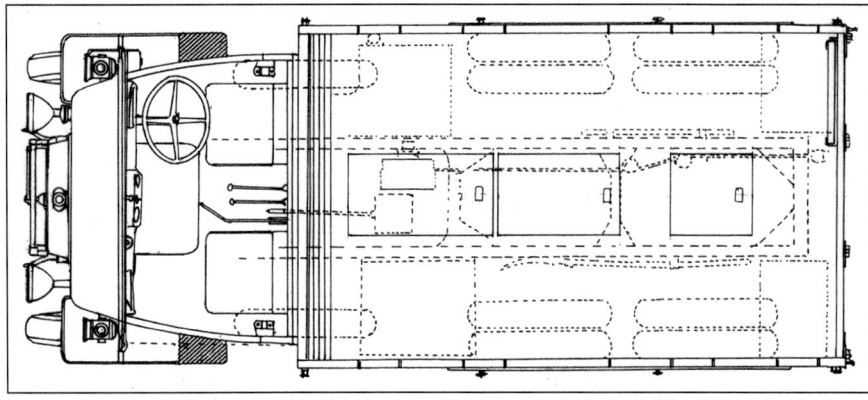

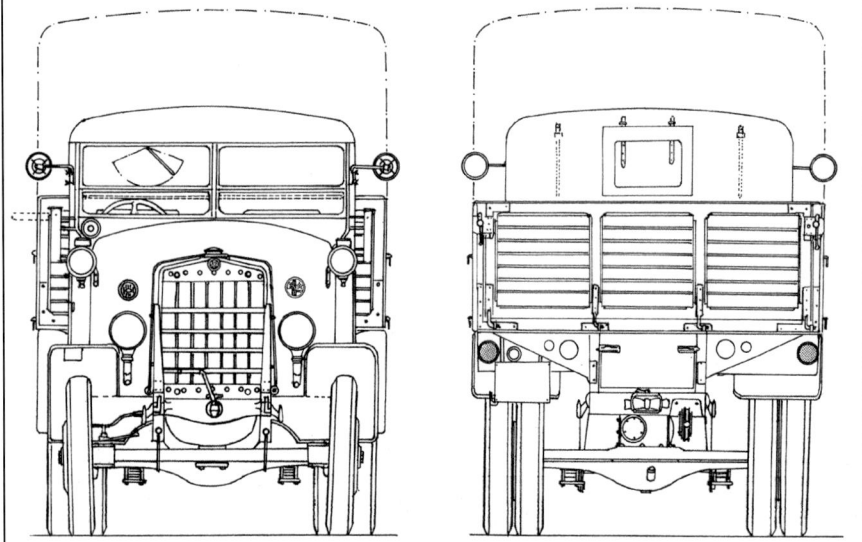

The Dovunque 35. (Drawings by N. Pignato via GMT)

The Stazione A 310 R.E. radio with the umbrella antenna mounted. (Viberti)

Note the number plate that ends with the letter 'G' (*Corpo del Genio*, Corps of Engineers). (Viberti)

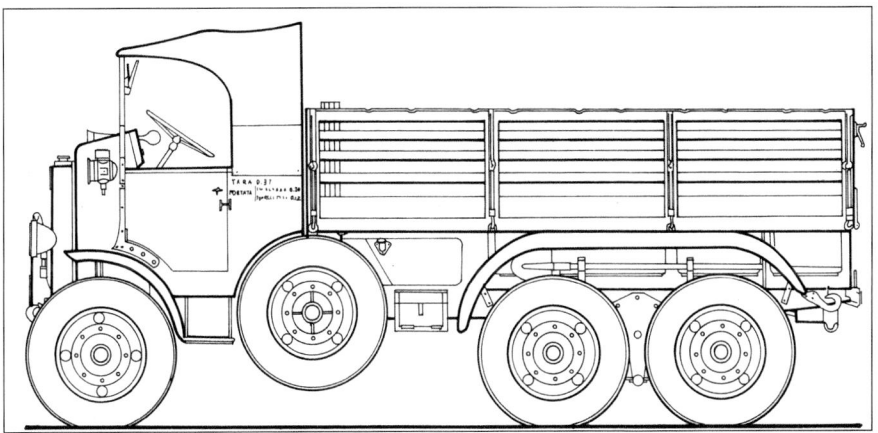

The Fiat 612 (Dovunque 33). (Drawings by A. Barozzi – GMT)

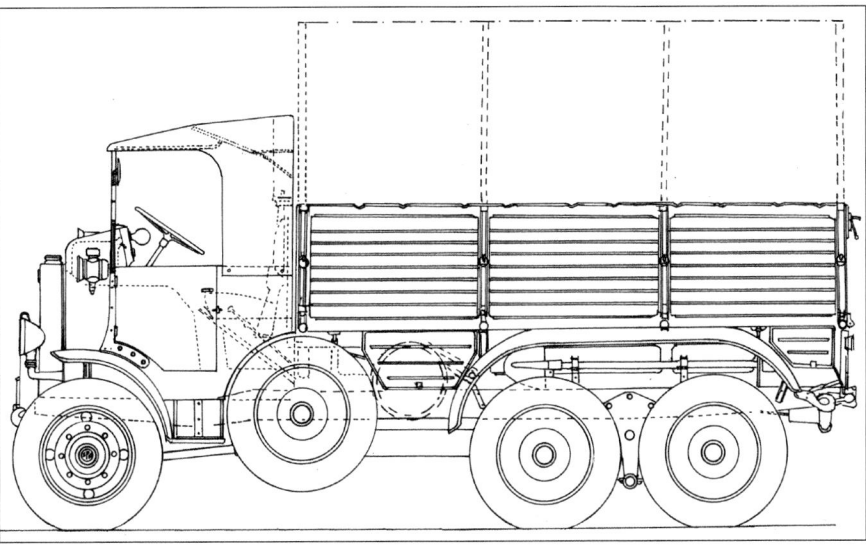

The Dovunque 35. (Drawings by N. Pignato via GMT)

metal, while the rear was wood. The truck bed, sides and tailgate were made of wood. Five removable troop transport benches were placed in the cargo bed. The windshield, with safety glass, could be opened; the wiper was operated by a vacuum motor.

Tyres were Cord Artiglio 32 x 6 pneumatic tyres mounted on 20 x 5 pressed steel wheels. The front fenders were half-fenders, the rear section of which butted up against a metal step for entrance to the cab. The main fuel tank was located beside

The same column travelling under the Ghibli towards the Marmarica region in spring 1942. (ACS)

A vehicle equipped with a Schwarzlose M. 07/12 machine gun employed by the *4ª Divisione Camicie Nere* of the MVSN, in North Africa in September 1940. (ACS)

The Stazione A 310 R.E. radio van for the *Regio Esercito* assembled on the Dovunque. (Viberti)

Dovunques used as personnel carriers in Libya in the winter of 1940. Each truck could carry 25 men including the driver. (ACS)

Column of Dovunque 35s equipped with 20mm Breda 35 cannons. (ACS)

The Dovunque 35 seen from below.

Two spare wheels, mounted one on each side just behind the cab and free to rotate, assisted in bellying.

Italian and native soldiers of the *Regio Corpo Truppe Libiche* in Libya, September 1940. The number plate of the Dovunque in the foreground is 'RCTL 620' with red letters and black digits. (ACS)

novel idea but which never went past the experimentation phase. There were two spare wheels, one on each side, mounted just behind the cab and free to rotate, which assisted in bellying. Special tracks could be placed on the rear wheels. They consisted of 20 jointed steel shoes; a box located under the cargo bed held them when not in use. Cord Artiglio 32 x 6 tyres were mounted on 20 x 5 pressed steel wheels with four lightening holes; in Africa, where possible, Superflex Sigillo Verde tyres were preferred.

The cab itself was a cab-over-engine type, partially enclosed, with half-doors and a canvas top and side curtains covering the area behind the door opening; *Regia Aeronautica* required Dovunques with a closed cab. The front portion of the cab was

The Dovunque 35 shows few external differences compared to the Dovunque 33. This is a Coloniale example with Superflex Sigillo Verde tyres. (Fiat)

The Dovunque 35 with and without coachwork.

a smoke-laying vehicle as well as being equipped with 20mm Breda 35 cannon on the bed for anti-aircraft duties. An unknown number of Dovunque trucks also served in the *Regia Aeronautica* and in the *Regio Corpo Truppe Libiche*.

According to some sources, 701 examples were exported in 1938 to Hungary and, maybe, to Poland. The Dovunque 35 continued to be produced for the Germans following the September 1943 Armistice. It was used until the mid–1950s by the post-war Italian Army.

Technical Description
The Fiat Dovunque 33 and its sister truck, the SPA Dovunque 35, was a three-axle 6x4 all-terrain truck; both rear axles were powered. The rear wheels were dual sets, and there was also some experimentation with mounting dual tyres on the front axle, a

The series model of the Autocarro 612, aka Dovunque 33. It bears the circular SPA mark on the radiator. Note the Cord 32 x 6 tyres with early pattern Artiglio tread. (Fiat)

The Rear view of the Dovunque 33 without canvas top highlights the folding rear. (Fiat)

A Dovunque 33 in Ethiopia in 1936.

without unloading it). It should be noted that the term '*dovunque*' used to identify 6x4 cross-country trucks only appeared for the first time in official documents in January 1932.

Beginning in 1931, Fiat began developing a 6x4 artillery tractor, resulting in the 611 model and then the 611 C (*coloniale*), the forerunner of the Fiat 612. The 611 C was assigned to the *Regio Corpo Truppe Coloniali* which operated it in Tripolitania and Cyrenaica (two Italian possessions in the Libyan region) and served as the basis for the production of 10 Fiat 611 armoured cars.

In July 1931, Fiat presented a prototype of the 612 truck; testing and modifications followed. In January 1933 the Fiat 612 was redesignated as the Autocarro Dovunque 33, and a first batch was turned over to selected artillery regiments for initial testing.

Between January and July 1934, testing had revealed a number of shortcomings of the Dovunque 33; Fiat continued to make modifications and refine the design of this off-road truck in order to produce an improved model. In 1935–1936, 82 examples of the vehicle took part in the campaign in Italian East Africa, but performance was in some aspects disappointing, mainly due to the engine being underpowered. Accordingly, production of the improved series with a more powerful engine was sped up. The Dovunque 35 was the name of the new model, but Fiat handed over production responsibility to its subsidiary company, Società Piemontese Automobili (SPA), also located in Turin.

Although expensive and not easy to drive, the Dovunque 35 remained in production from 1936 to 1948, but the number of vehicles made was limited compared to expectations. On the eve of the war, a total of 557 Dovunque trucks (both 33 and 35) were in service, issued to chemical companies as well as to field artillery units as ammunition carriers. By the end of 1940 the total had risen to 971 units.

The Dovunque saw fairly extensive service in North Africa in 1940–41, first with the Libyan divisions and later with Bersaglieri units. It was subsequently issued to tank units because of its cross-country capabilities. In North Africa, it was used as

Another Ursus in the mud. Olgopol-Balta road, Ukraine, summer 1941.

An OM Titano 137, recognisable by its elongated cabin with two windows on each side.

- Minimum turning radius: 7,000mm (22ft 11in), estimated
- Tyres: 10.50 x 20
- Engine: OM six-cylinder water-cooled, 7,980cc, 100 HP @2,100 rpm
- Fuel: Diesel
- Transmission: four speeds forward, one reverse
- Fuel capacity: 160 litres (42.3 US gallons, 35.2 Imperial gallons)
- Drive layout: 4x2
- Speed: 52km/h (32mph)
- Range (on road): 480km (298 miles)

Autocarro Fiat Dovunque 33 and SPA Dovunque 35

Note
The concept of the Dovunque (in Italian, *dovunque* means anywhere or everywhere) truck was born in the late 1920s with the aim of making available, for military as well as civilian needs, a vehicle that was capable of performing both on roads and cross-country, to be used mainly in Italy's African colonies. To that end, the *Regio Esercito* acquired and tested a British 6x4 vehicle, a Morris Type D registered in 1929 with number plate RE10041 Subsequently, similar 6x4 trucks were tested, among them a truck produced by Garner and a Czech Tatra 72.

Developmental and Service History
In accordance with specifications issued by Italian military authorities, the new truck was to serve to transport men and materiel, but also as an artillery tractor as well as an artillery portee (the gun carried in the bed of the truck, at times capable of being fired

An Ursus with a cab with full doors and glass windows. There are also emergency lights on the sides of the windshield.

Trying to put back on the roadway, an OM Ursus bogged down in the mud in Italy, in September 1943. To make the operation easier its trailer has been removed. (Bundesarchiv: Bild 101I-305-0654-32)

Variants

Although it is not a variant, in 1937 OM also designed a more powerful truck than the Ursus, the Titano 137 (not to be confused with the post-war model of the same name). Compared to the Ursus, it had a powerful engine (6 cylinders, 11,540 cc, 137 HP @ 1,600 rpm), a payload of 7,500kg and a towable weight of 18,000kg. It was produced for two years in limited quantities and little used in the Italian armed forces.

Specifications

- Designation: Autocarro Militare Pesante Unificato OM Ursus
- Producer: Officine Meccaniche (OM), Milan
- Years produced: 1940–1942
- Number produced: Not known
- Length: 7,832mm (25ft 8in)
- Width: 2,330mm (7ft 7in)
- Height to cab roof: 2,880mm (9ft 5in)
- Unladen weight: 5,600kg (12,346lbs)
- Carrying capacity: 6,700kg (14,771lbs)
- Wheelbase: 4,500mm (14ft 9in)
- Front track: 1,910mm (6ft 3in)
- Rear track: 1,690mm (5ft 6in)

- Producer: Officine Meccaniche (OM), Milan
- Years produced: 1938–1945
- Number produced: Not known
- Length: 6,230mm (20ft 5in)
- Width: 2,210mm (7ft 3in)
- Height to cab roof: 2,060mm (6ft 9in)
- Unladen weight: 3,500kg (8,730lbs)
- Carrying capacity: 3,000kg (6,614lbs)
- Towing capacity: 7,800kg (17,196lbs)
- Wheelbase: 3,800mm (12ft 6in)
- Front track: 1,600mm (5ft 3in)
- Rear track: 1,640mm (5ft 4in)
- Minimum turning radius: 7,000mm (22ft 11in)
- Minimum clearance: 270mm (10in)
- Bed, internal length: 4,000mm (13ft 2in)
- Bed, internal width: 2,000mm (6ft 7in)
- Bed, internal height: 650mm (2ft 2in)
- Tyres: Superflex 8.25 x 20
- Engine: OM CR 1D four-cylinder water-cooled, 5,320cc, 67 HP @1,800 rpm
- Fuel: Diesel
- Transmission: five speeds forward, one reverse
- Fuel capacity: 65 litres (17 US gallons, 14.3 Imperial gallons)
- Drive layout: 4x2
- Speed: 62km/h (38.5mph)
- Range (on road): 280km (174 miles)

Autocarro Militare Pesante Unificato OM Ursus

Developmental and Service History

In 1937 Officine Meccaniche, which already produced trucks under Saurer licence, started to design a medium class standard-type military truck designated the Taurus (see separate entry) and, at the same time, a heavy truck named the Ursus (Latin for bear) which was quite similar in external appearance, but which was significantly larger dimensionally, had a more powerful engine, so it could carry a much larger payload. The Ursus was produced until 1942 and saw extensive use on the Eastern Front with the Italian expeditionary corps and later the Italian Eighth Army.

Technical Description

The Ursus was configured with a conventional cab arrangement and was a 4x2 layout with rear-wheel drive with dual rear wheels. The all-metal cab had full doors with glass windows or half-doors with canvas and mica covering. The truck had right-hand drive. The truck bed, like that on the earlier Taurus, was made of wood. The spare tyre was mounted underneath the bed, behind the cab, and wooden stowage lockers were mounted beneath the bed as well. The engine was a six-cylinder licence-built Swiss Saurer Diesel which developed 100 HP; the transmission had four forward and one reverse gear.

The OM Ursus was a heavier version of the OM Taurus. This example has a cab with half-doors, and canvas windows with mica or celluloid insert.

British prisoners in North Africa being transported on a Taurus. The truck is painted kaki sahariano over the existing dark grey-green.

Another OM Taurus, here employed by German troops to tow a 2cm Flak 30 cannon. (T. Anderson)

The petrol engine version was not employed by the Italian Army. Like many other Italian medium and heavy trucks, the Taurus chassis was also used for the production of buses.

Although not a variant as such, OM built a heavy truck, the Ursus which was a significantly larger truck with a more powerful engine (100 HP) and much greater payload.

Specifications
- Designation: Autocarro Militare Medio Unificato OM Taurus

Ukraine, summer 1941. An OM C 30 near the camp of the *52ª Divisione Fanteria Motorizzata 'Torino'*. It is recognisable by its rounded cab top and two-piece windscreen. (ACS)

A civilian C 30 with different bodywork, perhaps Orlandi, in Libya. Compared to the Taurus, the C 30 had a longer wheelbase and the fuel tank was placed beside the right longeron

In the C 30, the engine was substantially the same as in the 1 CRD, but the gearbox had five speeds forward and one reverse. The tank fixed beside the right longeron held 65 litres of diesel and had a pump. The starting was electric. The chassis lacked the rearmost cross-member and, therefore, the tow hook. The wheelbase, 4,200mm, was greater than that of the 1 CRD; as a result, the length of the vehicle reached 6,520mm, while the width and height remained the same. The tyres were Superflex 7.50 x 20.

Variants
The bed of the Taurus could be removed and the bed area modified to tow a semi-trailer.

A Taurus of the *Regio Esercito* employed by the *Opera Nazionale del Dopolavoro* (the OND, National Institution of the Recreational Activities) for the Italian armed forces. Note the Sigillo Verde Impero tyres. Tobruk, Libya, September 1940. (ACS)

An OM Taurus on the move in the summer of 1941, probably in Libya. The truck carries the Italian national flag painted on the roof of the cab for air recognition. (ACS)

wheels; the handbrake was mechanical on the rear wheels. The engine was a 5,320 cc four-cylinder licence-built Swiss Saurer Diesel which developed 67 HP at 1,800 rpm; the transmission had five forward and one reverse gear.

Finally, the main differences between the Taurus and the two models that preceded it are given below.

The OM 1 CRD had a 4,500 cc engine which delivered 50 HP @ 1800 rpm. The transmission was four speeds forward and one reverse. The 95 litre tank was located under the driver's seat, flanked by a 17-litre reserve in the dashboard. The starting was by crank. A tow hitch was attached to the last cross-member of the frame. The wheelbase was 3,800mm. Other measures were: length 6,120mm, width 2,020mm and height 2,900mm.

The OM Taurus, front view with canvas cover. Unlike the two previous models, the windshield was in one piece. (Negri Foundation)

Left side view of the Taurus, with tarpaulin and fitted with canvas and mica covers on the doors. Note the fuel tank located on the longeron side. (Negri Foundation)

Right side view of the OM Taurus, without tarpaulin. (Negri Foundation)

Area of the Little Saint Bernard, immediately before the attack on France in June 1940. This OM Taurus has been decorated with bunches of flowers. Note the circular bronze badge and the unusual number plate. (ACS)

Autocarro Militare Medio Unificato OM Taurus

Developmental and Service History

Officine Meccaniche (OM) from 1933 was a wholly owned subsidiary of Fiat. In 1935 the company began to produce a new medium truck that was the successor of the OM 3 BOD; it was a vehicle for military use manufactured in Italy under licence, the Saurer 1 CRD model (the 'C' series was a follow on to the 'B' – see OM 3 BOD section).

In 1937, the military truck 1 CRD had a civilian-only version called the C 30. The two versions showed external differences in bodywork, chassis length, transmission and other minor details, however both shared the same maintenance manual.

A short time later the C 30 truck was modified in the bodywork, engine, chassis and other parts creating a new model, the Taurus (Latin for bull), which immediately met with success in both the civilian and military fields.

The Taurus had a production run of about ten years, serving with the Italian armed forces until well into the post-war period. The Taurus turned out to be one of the best of the so-called standardised medium trucks and performed especially well in North Africa. Between 1944 and January 1945, 2,305 Taurus trucks were built under German supervision and issued to German units.

Technical Description

The Taurus was configured with a conventional cab arrangement and was a 4x2 layout with rear-wheel drive with dual rear wheels. Period photographs show two versions of the cab: one version, inherited from the C 30, was an all-metal fully enclosed cab with full doors with windows and rounded cab roof; the other version for military purposes was a wooden and metal cab with plain roof and half-doors with a removable canvas covering, which had a rather small celluloid or mica window.

It should be emphasised that at the beginning the bodywork was made by third-party companies, which is why there were differences in the external appearance of the civilian examples. Later OM began to build it in-house to better adhere to the specifications of the Italian Army.

The truck had right-hand drive. The truck bed, like those on most Italian trucks was made of wood, although civilian examples could have it with metal sides. Starting was electric, and the truck had two Marelli 12 volt batteries. The electric headlights were mounted on stanchions on the front bumper as well as the emergency acetylene headlamps forward of the cab doors. The spare tyre was located underneath the bed, behind the cab, and wooden stowage lockers were mounted beneath the bed as well.

Suspension consisted of semi-elliptical leaf springs with hydraulic shock absorbers on the front wheels. The wheels were six-spoked Dayton-type with removable rims and pneumatic tyres. The brakes were hydropneumatic drum brakes acting on the four

The OM 1 CRD, a military truck built under an agreement with the Swiss company Saurer.

The OM C 30, designed for the civilian market, was the forerunner of the Taurus.

OM 3 BODs stuck in Ukrainian mud in 1941. The tractor is a Fiat OCI 40. (ACS)

- Carrying capacity: 5,000kg (11,023lbs)
- Towing capacity: 10,000kg (22,046lbs)
- Wheelbase: 4,025mm (13ft 2in)
- Front track: 1,735mm (5ft 8in)
- Rear track: 1,668mm (5ft 5in)
- Minimum turning radius: 6,450mm (21ft 2in)
- Bed, internal length: 4,250mm (13ft 11in)
- Bed, internal width: 2,000mm (6ft 7in)
- Bed, internal height: 630mm (2ft 1in)
- Tyres: semi-pneumatic 195 x 720.5 or 205 x 720.5, pneumatic 36 x 8 or 38 x 9
- Engine: Type BOD four-cylinder water-cooled, 5,700cc, 70 HP @1,800 rpm
- Fuel: diesel
- Transmission: four speeds forward, one reverse
- Fuel capacity: 100 + 20 litres (31.7 US gallons, 26.4 Imperial gallons)
- Drive layout: 4x2
- Speed: 44km/h (27mph)
- Range (on road): 300km (186 miles)

MEDIUM AND HEAVY TRUCKS 95

More views of the OM 3 BOD.

A column of OM 3 BOD in Zadar, Croatia. In the background, the Porta di Terraferma Gate.

- Number produced: Not known
- Length: 6,910mm (22ft 8in)
- Width: 2,215mm (7ft 3in)
- Height: 2,810mm (9ft 9in)
- Unladen weight: 4,980kg (10,979lbs); 5,275kg (11,629lbs) including liquids

- Minimum clearance: 223mm (9in)
- Fording depth: 500mm (1ft 8in)
- Tyres: pneumatic 210x20
- Engine: Tipo 102B five-cylinder, 6,875cc, 80 HP @1,860 rpm
- Fuel: Gasoline
- Transmission: Manual transmission with four speeds forward, one reverse with reduction gear
- Fuel capacity: 138 litres (36.5 US gallons, 30.4 Imperial gallons)
- Drive layout: 4x2
- Speed: 62km/h (38.5mph)
- Range (on road): 350km (217 miles)

Autocarro Pesante Militare OM 3 BOD

Developmental and Service History

Officine Meccaniche (OM) had, since the twenties, produced trucks under licence from the Swiss company Saurer. The latter had in its catalogue a series of trucks called B-type with different kinds of diesel engines, including a four-cylinder (BOD) and a six-cylinder (BLD).

The OM Tipo 5 BOD was offered to the Italian military in 1933. The truck was viewed favourably and an initial batch of 30 trucks was ordered, later followed by a larger order of unspecified size. In 1935, the Tipo 5 BOD was redesignated as the 3 BOD. Total production figures are unavailable.

It is not clear in precisely which theatres, or to what extent, the OM 3 BOD saw service; based on photographic documentation it is known to have been in service with the Italian armed forces in East Africa, the Balkans and the Eastern Front.

Technical Description

The OM 3 BOD was a conventionally configured 4x2 rear-wheel drive truck, with dual rear wheels; the tyres were semi-pneumatic or pneumatic mounted on six-spoke wheels. The cab had half-doors; drive was right-hand. The wood and sheet metal cab had half-doors with canvas and celluloid closures that could be rolled up at the top. The windshield was split and could be opened forward. The windshield wiper had to be operated by hand. The wooden cargo bed could have a canvas cover and be equipped with benches for troop transport. Storage boxes were located on both sides of the vehicle. The spare wheel was carried under the rear of the cargo bed.

Suspension consisted of semi-elliptical leaf springs. Brakes were hydraulic with an air compressor; the parking brake was a drum brake and acted on the driveshaft. The engine was a four-cylinder diesel licensed by Saurer. The clutch and gearbox, four-speed manual with reverse, formed a single body with the engine block. In addition to the 100 litre main fuel tank, located on the frame longerons near the front seats, there was an auxiliary tank near the dashboard with a capacity of 20 or 25 litres. The electrical system did not include a battery and starting was by a crank, with a mechanism based not on the common inertia starter but with a rather complex system which also involved the withdrawal of a small quantity of fuel from the auxiliary tank and its injection into the cylinders by means of a small pump; this method proved impractical in cold climates.

Specifications
- Designation: Autocarro Pesante Militare OM 3 BOD
- Producer: Officine Meccaniche (OM), Milan
- Years produced: 1933–1946

The OM 3 BOD, born from the collaboration between Officine Meccaniche and Saurer.

A German soldier posing in front of a Lancia Esaro.

Two examples of Esaro used by German troops.

The engine was the same five-cylinder gasoline engine used by the Esaro's larger brother, the 3Ro, but horsepower was reduced to 80 because of the lower weight. The transmission had four forward gears and one reverse; a reduction gear resulted in eight forward and two reverse speeds. The front brakes were hydraulic while those in the rear were mechanical.

Specifications
- Designation: Autocarro Militare Medio Unificato Lancia Esaro
- Producer: Lancia & C. Fabbrica Automobili, Turin
- Years produced: 1943–1945
- Number produced: about 400
- Length: 6,250mm (20ft 6in)
- Width: 2,200mm (7ft 3in)
- Height: 2,960mm (9ft 8in)
- Unladen weight: 3,714kg (8,188lbs)
- Carrying capacity: 2,926kg (6,451lbs)
- Wheelbase: 3,650mm (12ft)
- Front track: 1,702mm (5ft 7in)
- Rear track: 1,710mm (5ft 7in)
- Minimum turning radius: 6,000mm (19ft 8in)

The Lancia Esaro without and with canvas top.

The military version of the Lancia Esaro was characterised by an inertia starter placed horizontally.

Technical Description

The Lancia Esaro was a conventionally configured truck with an enclosed cab with full doors with glass windows that could be raised and lowered. The Esaro produced for the Germans had, instead, the German-style wooden *Einheits* cab. The Esaro had an inertia starter; like most Italian military trucks, it did not have a battery. Suspension consisted of leaf springs, with shock absorbers in front. The Esaro was fitted with pneumatic tyres; it had electric headlights but lacked the acetylene headlamps of earlier models of Italian military trucks. The bed, sides and tailgate were wood; the bed could be covered with a canvas cover stretched over five bows, which were stacked behind the cab when not in use.

MEDIUM AND HEAVY TRUCKS

Two Lancia 3Ro tank trucks in a port during the procedures for loading or unloading fuel or other liquids. (D. Zambon)

- Bed, internal length: 4,780mm (15ft 8in); 4,850mm (15ft 10in) external
- Bed, internal width: 2,200mm (7ft 3in); 2,240mm (7ft 4in) external
- Bed, internal height: 650mm (2ft 2in); 680mm (2ft 3in) external
- Tyres: pneumatic Pirelli Superflex 9 x 20 or Pirelli Ultraflex or Michelin Stop 270 x 20; semi-pneumatic Pirelli Celerflex 225 x 720.5
- Engine: Tipo 102 five-cylinder, two-stroke, 6,875cc, 93 HP @1,860 rpm 3Ro NM; Tipo 102B four-cylinder, 6,875cc, 91 HP @1860 rpm 3Ro MB
- Fuel: diesel 3Ro NM; gasoline 3Ro MB
- Transmission: Manual transmission with four speeds forward, one reverse with reduction gear
- Fuel capacity: 135 litres (35.7 US gallons, 29.7 Imperial gallons)
- Drive layout: 4x2
- Speed: 45km/h (28mph) 3Ro NMP; 42km/h (26 mph) 3Ro NMSP
- Range (on road): 450km (280 miles) 3Ro NM; 300km (186 miles) 3Ro MB

Autocarro Militare Medio Unificato Lancia Esaro

Developmental and Service History

The Lancia Esaro was identified as series 267 in the Lancia nomenclature; it was also known as the 6 Ro, but this model should not be confused with the 6 Ro built post-war (1948), a military version of the civilian Esatau.

Differing from most other Italian medium military trucks, the Esaro was mass produced with a gasoline engine. Although the Esaro was adopted for service in mid–1942, series production did not begin until mid–1943 and consequently relatively few were delivered before the September 1943 Armistice. However, production continued under German control and between 1943 and 1945, approximately 1,900 were built. In late 1943 Lancia undertook to develop a 4x4 version, but that vehicle never entered into production. A very small number (22) of the Esaro were produced with a diesel engine. Production of the Esaro continued for a brief period after the end of the war, ending in 1948.

Operational employment of the Esaro was likely limited to Italy itself; most were issued to German forces, although some were also used by Mussolini's *Esercito Nazionale Repubblicano*. Surviving Esaros were used by the Italian Army in the immediate post-war period until they became no longer serviceable.

Water transport bowser on Lancia 3Ro chassis and medium standardised trailer. (Viberti)

Water transport bowser on Lancia 3Ro chassis, 'Libyan type'. (Viberti)

- Years produced: 1938–1945
- Number produced: 9,365 (other sources mention 9,460)
- Length: 7,250mm (23ft 9in)
- Width: 2,350mm (7ft 9in)
- Height: 3,000mm (9ft 10in) 3Ro NMP (with pneumatic tyres); 2,970mm (9ft 9in) 3Ro MNSP (with semi-pneumatic tyres)
- Unladen weight: 5,610kg (12,368lbs) 3Ro NMP; 5,890kg (12,985lbs) 3Ro NMSP; 5,315 (11,717lbs) 3Ro MB
- Carrying capacity: 6,390kg (14,088lbs) 3Ro NMP; 6,110kg (13,470lbs) 3Ro NMSP; 6,545kg (14,429lbs) 3Ro MB
- Towing capacity: 4500kg (9,920lbs)
- Wheelbase: 4,300mm (14ft 1in)
- Front track: 1,850mm (6ft)
- Rear track: 1,774mm (5ft 10in)
- Minimum turning radius: 7,000mm (23ft)
- Minimum clearance: 280mm (11in) 3Ro NMP; 250mm (10in) 3Ro NMSP
- Fording depth: 700mm (2ft 3in)

Some batteries of these gun trucks were used as close fire support to the scouting units, continuing to fight as far as Tunisia. (AUSSME)

The Autofficina Mod. 38, already seen on the Ro NM, was also set up for the 3Ro NMSP.

The Lancia 3Ro was also produced in a version fuelled with wood gas. As done in other countries, from 1944 the Germans ordered the production of Einheitsfahrerhaus (standard driver's cab) and other simplified components, to reduce the use of raw materials and time of manufacturing.

An early production 90/53 Lancia 3Ro/gun combination on show at a barracks.

An example captured in North Africa.

A First World War booty 100/17 howitzer mounted on the bed of a Lancia 3Ro in North Africa. The truck's cab has been removed. (AUSSME)

MEDIUM AND HEAVY TRUCKS

A Lancia 3Ro used for the transport of horses near Olhopil, Ukraine, in the summer of 1941. Both truck and trailer are still equipped with semi-pneumatic tyres. (ACS)

Suspension consisted of leaf springs on solid axles. Although most 3Ro were fitted with pneumatic tyres, some were produced with semi-pneumatic tyres. The 3Ro had electric headlights and dispensed with the outdated acetylene headlamps of the Ro. The bed of the 3Ro could carry up to 32 fully equipped troops or a light tank in the bed; a medium tank could be towed. A spare tyre was mounted underneath the rear portion of the bed and there were small double storage lockers under the forward portion of the bed on both sides.

The diesel engine, of Lancia design, was a water-cooled five-cylinder; from it was later derived a gasoline engine. The transmission, built under German Maybach licence, had four forward gears and one reverse; a reduction gear resulted in eight forward and two reverse speeds (although the drivers were not used to engaging the reduction gear for fear of breaking the gearbox). Brakes were mechanical drums on all four wheels, with a compressed-air booster. There was also a hydraulic emergency hand brake on all four wheels. The wheels had steel spoke rims, removable, like other unified heavy trucks; they could receive 225 x 720.5 Celerflex semi-pneumatic tyres or 270 x 20 Ultraflex pneumatic tyres.

Variants

As previously mentioned, the NM version had a diesel engine, and the MB had a gasoline engine. As on previous Lancia trucks, the suffix SP indicated a variant with semi-pneumatic tyres and the suffix P indicated pneumatic tyres.

In addition to the basic cargo body version, the 3Ro was produced as an animal (horse) transport, mobile repair shop, tanker truck with trailer (two 5,000 litre tanks for water). Most notably, the 3Ro was used as a platform for the 90/53 anti-aircraft gun, issued to the Italian armoured divisions in North Africa and also used with devastating effect as an anti-tank weapon.

A conversion carried out on some examples in North Africa at the end of 1941 involved the assembly of a 100/17 howitzer on the truck bed.

Following the September 1943 Armistice, 100 3Ro trucks were produced under German supervision and had a completely redesigned, very square Einheits cab.

Specifications

(Unless specifically noted, all measures apply to both the 3Ro NM and 3Ro MB versions)
- Designation: Autocarro Militare Pesante Unificato Lancia 3Ro
- Producer: Lancia & C. Fabbrica Automobili, Turin

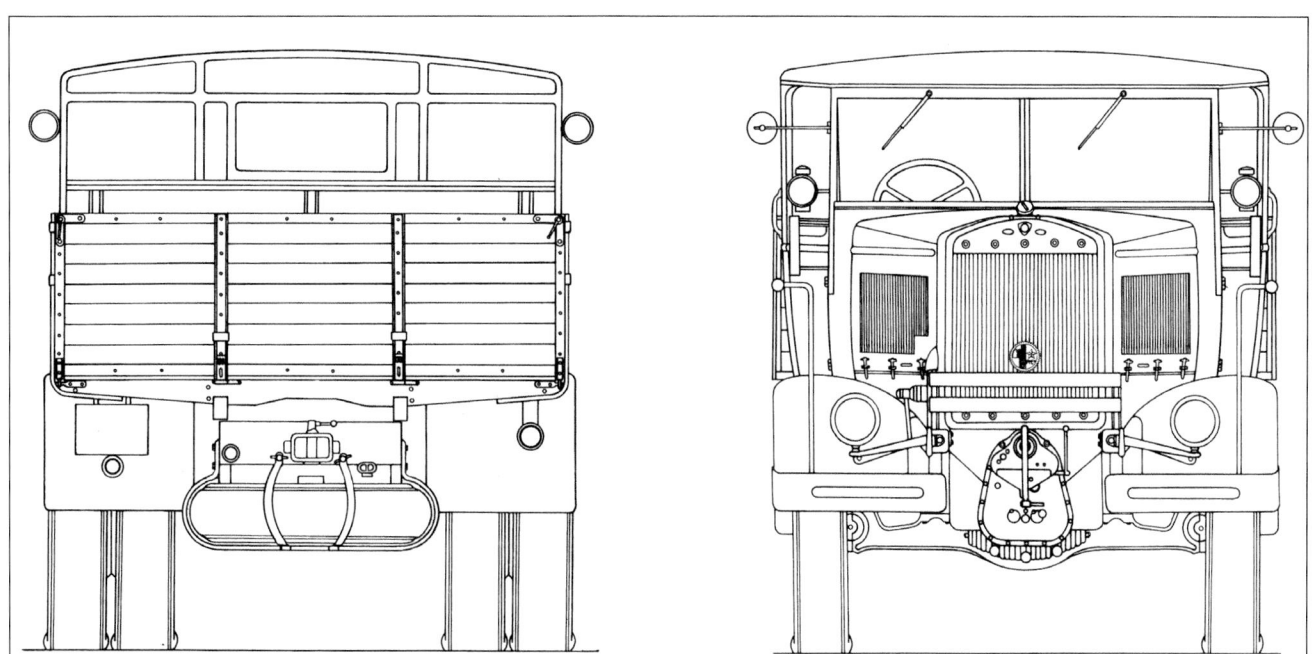

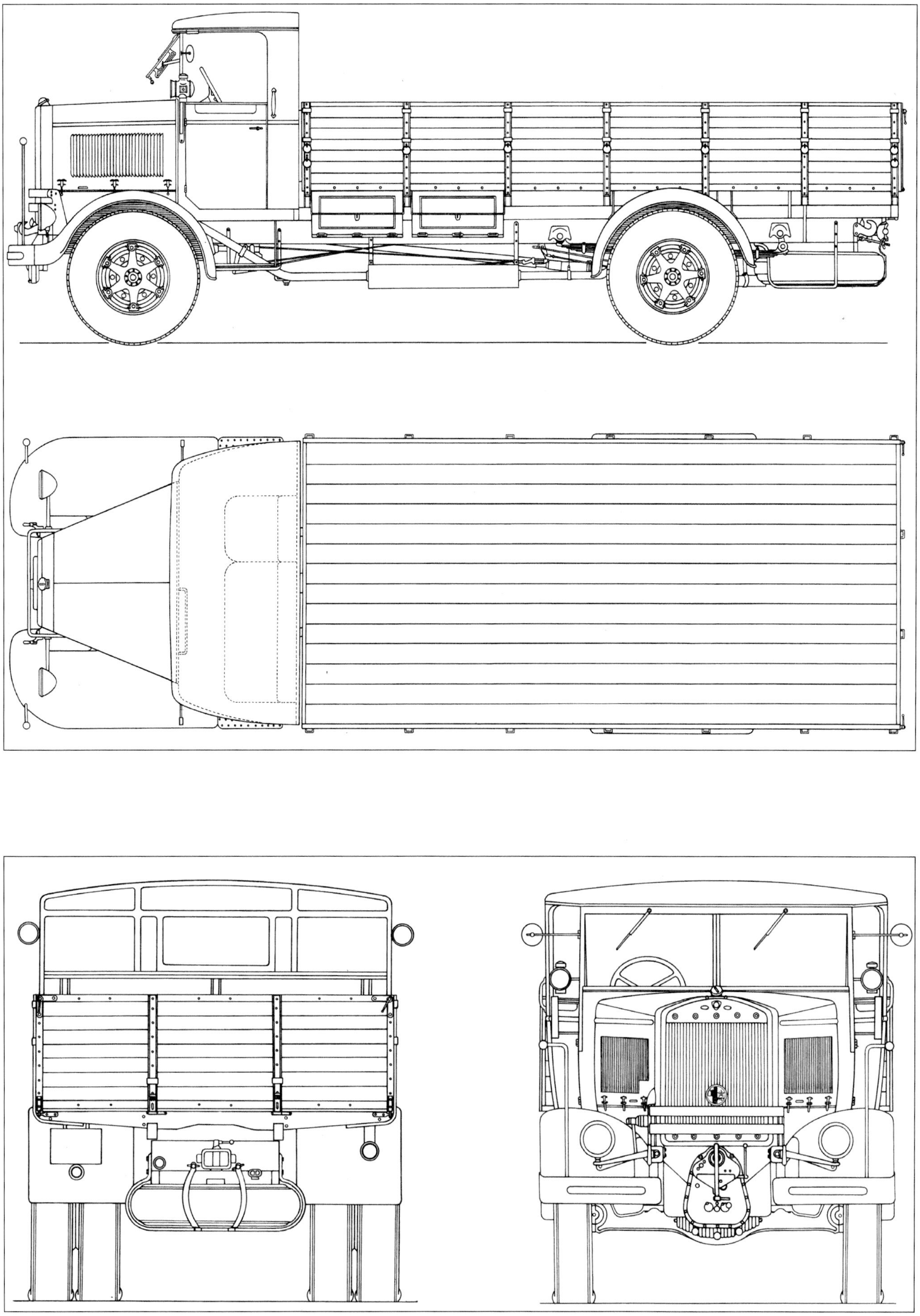

Lancia 3Ro. (Drawings by A. M. Feller – GMT)

Developmental and Service History

The Lancia 3Ro, originally designated as the Lancia 464 (civilian) and 564 (military), was an improved version of the earlier Lancia Ro series of heavy trucks (the model Ro of 1933 and Ro Ro of 1935) and is generally regarded amongst the best Italian heavy trucks of the war. Production of the 3Ro began in 1938; the major improvement over the Ro was an uncommon five-cylinder diesel engine, in place of the two-cylinder Junkers-made engine of the Ro and three-cylinder of the Ro Ro. Other changes included overall larger dimensions and increased carrying capacity and improved performance.

Between 1938 and 1943 a total of 9,365 3Ro were built (other sources mention 9,490). Another 772 examples were produced for the Germans between January 1944 and January 1945, 408 of which were of the gasoline-powered 564 MB version. In 1941 a small number of trucks powered by a gas generator was produced. The 3Ro continued to be produced for a brief period after the end of the war.

The Lancia 3Ro NM saw extensive use in North Africa, where it performed extremely well in the harsh desert conditions; an official report judged it to be the best Italian truck in the desert, performing better than any of the other heavy or medium trucks in that theatre. The truck was used to tow medium-calibre artillery pieces as well as towing two-axle trailers which served as tank transporters for medium tanks.

Technical Description

The Lancia 3Ro was a conventionally configured truck with an enclosed cab and half-doors; the two-piece front window could be opened forward for cab ventilation. The coachwork was built by Viberti. The ladder frame was, like that of the earlier Ro, very robust. Some 3Ro trucks were fitted with a winch; those so equipped were used to tow artillery pieces. The 3Ro had an inertia starter; early production models were fitted with a 6-volt battery, later upped to 12-volts. A limited number of the 3Ro were provided with an electrical starter. The truck was equipped with a backstop device. The differential could be locked to avoid slipping, for example, on muddy or snowy ground.

North Africa 1941 or 1942. A Lancia 3Ro towing a heavy Viberti trailer used for the transport of the M13 medium tank. (ACS)

Column of the *34° Raggruppamento Pesante* in Russia, spring 1942. (ACS)

Poor operating conditions for a 3Ro with canvas window. Russia, spring 1941. (ACS)

A heavy vehicle like the 3Ro often got bogged down in Soviet mud. The insignia of the *Corpo Automobilistico dell'Esercito* (Army Transportation Corps) is painted on the door of the trucks.(ACS)

- Carrying capacity: 5,000kg (11,023lbs)
- Wheelbase: 3,650mm (12ft)
- Front track: 1,810mm (5ft 11in) Ro MNSP; 1,850mm (6ft) Ro MNP and Ro MB
- Rear track: 1,700mm (5ft 7in) Ro MNSP; 2,300mm (5ft 9in) Ro MNP and Ro MB
- Minimum turning radius: 6,500mm (21ft 4in)
- Minimum clearance: 245 (10in) Ro MNSP; 295mm (11.5in) Ro MNP and Ro MB
- Bed, internal length: 4,210mm (14ft)
- Bed, internal width: 2,000mm (6ft 7in)
- Bed, internal height: 650mm (2ft 2in)
- Tyres: semi-pneumatic 195 x 720.5 Ro MN; pneumatic Superflex 9.75 x 20 Ro MNP and MB
- Engine: Tipo 89 two-cylinder in-line, 2-stroke, 3,180cc, 64 HP @1,500 rpm (Ro NM); Tipo 98 four-cylinder in-line side-valve, 5,120cc, 62 HP @1,700 rpm (Ro MM)
- Fuel: Diesel (Ro NM); gasoline (Ro BM)
- Transmission: Tipo 126 manual transmission with four speeds forward, one reverse with reduction gear
- Fuel capacity: 95 litres (25 US gallons, 20.8 Imperial gallons)
- Drive layout: 4x2
- Speed: 32km/h (20mph) Ro NMSP; 35,5km/h (22 mph) Ro NMP; 39km/h (24 mph) Ro BM
- Range (on road): 300km (186 miles) Ro NM; 235km (146 miles) Ro BM

Autocarro Militare Pesante Unificato Lancia 3Ro NM

A Lancia 3Ro heavy truck fresh from the production line.

Front view of an example with Superflex Sigillo Verde tyres. The inertia starter, the number plate painted on the bumper and the bronze circular badge are all clearly visible.

Rear view of a 3Ro NMP with Superflex S.V. Impero tyres.

Lancia 3Ro NMP of the second series with the compressed-air braking system (see the tank on the side) for the trailer. It lacks the headlights and was photographed in the Viberti workshops that manufactured the vehicle body.

The *Autoinnaffiatrice* (irrigator truck) based on a Ro chassis, built by Viberti.

Lancia Ro MB with field kitchen equipment.

Variants

In addition to the basic cargo body version, the Ro was produced as an animal (horse) transport, a mobile repair shop, a tanker truck and a heavy tow truck with a bed-mounted winch and boom.

The Lancia Ro Ro (or Ro-Ro), manufactured from 1935, was based on the same chassis as the Ro but powered by a Lancia Tipo 90 3-cylinder diesel engine, built under licence from Junkers. It was produced in approximately 300 units.

Specifications

(Unless specifically noted, all measurements apply to both the NM/MN and MB versions)
- Designation: Autocarro Pesante Lancia Ro
- Producer: Lancia & C. Fabbrica Automobili, Turin
- Years produced: 1933–1938
- Number produced: 5,186 (all versions)
- Length: 6,416mm (21ft) MN; 6,390 (20ft 11in) MB
- Width: 2,200mm (7ft 3in) Ro MNSP; 2,300mm (7ft 6in) Ro MNP and Ro MB
- Height: 2,900mm (9ft 6in)
- Unladen weight: 5,140kg (11,332lbs)

In the *Regio Esercito*, trucks were also used for the transport of horses and mules.

L'Autofficina Mod. 38 repair shop based on the Ro NM chassis.

A Ro NM tanker truck with trailer.

A Lancia Ro from the *1° Autogruppo Intendenza di Manovra* in Italian East Africa in the mid-thirties. Note the double row of cooling grids on the bonnet which differentiates it from the 3Ro that followed.

A Lancia Ro transporting British prisoners to Tripoli in autumn-winter 1941.

Towing 75/27 mod. 06 guns in North Africa. The trucks has Sigillo Verde low pressure tyres, while the gun carriages have stamped wheels and semi-pneumatic tyres.

A camouflaged Lancia Ro during the Spanish Civil War.

Technical Description

The Lancia Ro was a conventionally configured truck with a semi-enclosed cab; the half-doors were fitted with side curtains that had mica window inserts and the two-piece front window could be opened forward for cab ventilation. The frame was sturdy as would be expected for a heavy truck. Suspension consisted of leaf springs. In addition to electric headlights the Ro was fitted with supplementary – even though already out of date – acetylene headlamps. The cargo body had wooden sides and tailgate. The diesel engine was a two-cylinder Junkers type while the gasoline engine was a four-cylinder in-line. The transmission had four forward gears and one reverse; a reduction gear resulted in eight forward and two reverse speeds. The drum brakes operated with a mechanical air booster; the hydraulic handbrake acted on all four brakes. The electrical system was 6 V without battery; diesel versions had inertia starters, gasoline versions used a crank handle.

Two types of tyres were mounted on the Ro, semi-pneumatic (SP or S) and pneumatic (P); the two truck variants were identified by the designations Ro NMSP (or MNS) and Ro NMP (or MNP), respectively. In the first case the wheels were of disc type, in the second Dayton Gianetti with six spokes.

Autocarro Pesante Lancia Ro NM and Ro BM

The Lancia Ro NM was adopted by the *Regio Esercito* in 1934.

A Lancia Ro with semi-pneumatic tyres transporting a Pavesi P4 tractor.

Lancia Ro transporting a Pavesi P4 tractor. In this case the truck is equipped with pneumatic tyres.

Developmental and Service History

The Lancia Ro was the first of a series of heavy military trucks designed and produced by Lancia. Originally designated as the Lancia 264 in 1933, it was soon redesignated as the Ro. The company habitually baptised its trucks and heavy vehicles with Greek letters, such as Jota, Kappa, Omicron and – as here – Ro (or RO).

Two versions of the truck were produced, one with a licence-built German Junkers diesel engine and the other with a gasoline engine. Between 1934 and 1938 the Italian Army acquired 3,056 of the diesel version (Ro NM or Ro MN) and 1,701 of the gasoline engine version (Ro MB). A further 429 were built for the civilian market.

The Ro was initially issued to the Italian divisions stationed in Libya in the second half of the 1930s, to tank regiments and to transportation units. Among its uses were as a prime mover for divisional and corps artillery; it was also often used to tow tanks on a trailer. Later the Ro saw service in Italian East Africa, in Spain during the Civil War, as well as in North Africa. The truck performed very well in all theatres.

A civilian D65 after World War II.

Variants
The D65 was also built in a passenger bus version.

Specifications
- Designation: Autocarro Militare Unificato Medio Isotta Fraschini D65
- Producer: Isotta Fraschini, Milan
- Years produced: 1942–1955
- Number produced: Not known
- Length: 5,870mm (19ft 3in)
- Width: 2,160mm (7ft)
- Height: 2,320mm (7ft 7in)
- Unladen weight: 3,460kg (7,628lbs)
- Carrying capacity: 3,200kg (7,055lbs)
- Wheelbase: 3,300mm (10ft 10in)
- Front track: 1,642mm (5ft 4in)
- Rear track: 1,650mm (5ft 5in)
- Minimum turning radius: 6,500mm (21ft 4in)
- Minimum clearance: 225mm (9in)
- Bed, internal length: 4,000mm (13ft 2in)
- Bed, internal width: 2,000mm (6ft 7in)
- Bed, internal height: 650mm (2ft 2in)
- Tyres: Superflex 7.50x20 with different treads
- Engine: four-cylinder water-cooled MAN, 5,330cc, 75 HP @2,000 rpm
- Fuel: diesel
- Transmission: four speeds forward, one reverse
- Fuel capacity: 105 litres (27.7 US gallons, 23 Imperial gallons)
- Drive layout: 4x2
- Speed: 55km/h (34mph)
- Range (on road): 380km (236 miles)

The Isotta Fraschini D65 with its peculiar cab-over-engine configuration.

An English language advertisement from the immediate post-war period featuring the manufacturer's flagship products.

Technical Description

The D70 M was a 4x2 truck characterised by a conventional cab. It had a fully enclosed metal cab with half-doors and was a two-axle truck with rear-wheel drive and dual rear wheels. Drive was right-hand. The engine was a six-cylinder in-line diesel developing 64 HP. The manual transmission consisted of four forward speeds and one reverse. The truck bed was wood with fixed sides and had a hinged tailgate. A canvas top was provided for the bed. There were small storage lockers under the bed on both sides, and the spare tyre was mounted under the bed behind the cab.

Specifications

- Designation: Autocarro Militare Medio Isotta Fraschini D70 M
- Producer: Isotta Fraschini, Milan
- Years produced: 1936–1942
- Number produced: Not known
- Length: 6,950mm (22ft 10in)
- Width: 2,150mm (7ft)
- Height: 2,850mm (9ft 4in)
- Unladen weight: 3,950kg (8,708lbs)
- Carrying capacity: 3,000kg (6,614lbs)
- Wheelbase: 4,200mm (13ft 9in)
- Front track: 1,450mm (4ft 9in)
- Rear track: 1,570mm (5ft 2in)
- Minimum turning radius: 5,000mm (16ft 5in)
- Minimum clearance: 225mm (9in)
- Tyres: Cord 34 x 7 with different treads
- Engine: six-cylinder water-cooled MAN, 6,754cc, 64 HP @1,800 rpm
- Fuel: Diesel
- Transmission: four speeds forward, one reverse
- Fuel capacity: 90 litres (23.8 US gallons, 19.8 Imperial gallons)
- Drive layout: 4x2
- Speed: 53km/h (33mph)
- Range (on road): 360km (224 miles)

Autocarro Militare Unificato Medio Isotta Fraschini D65

Developmental and Service History

Following the 1937 decree that called for standardisation of as many truck components and dimensions as possible for various weight categories, in 1940 Isotta Fraschini began to develop a new truck to replace its D70 M medium military truck whose series production had begun in 1936. The D65 represented a significant departure from the earlier D70 M and conformed to the requirements set out in the standardisation guidelines. The D65 diesel engine entered service in 1942, in two almost identical versions, the civilian UCN (*Unificato Civile Nafta*) and the military UMN (*Unificato Militare Nafta*). A gasoline version named UMB (*Unificato Militare Benzina*), also designated the D65 2/4, appeared in September 1943 and, for this reason, was used only by the German armed forces in Italy. The D65 proved to be a successful truck; production of the D65 began in 1940 and continued well into the post-war years – until 1955; it served in the Italian Army until the 1950s.

Technical Description

The D65 bore a close superficial resemblance to the Fiat 626 truck. It was a 4x2 truck that had a cab-over-engine configuration. The cab was fully enclosed with full doors and full glass side windows. It was a two-axle truck with rear-wheel drive and dual rear wheels. Drive was right-hand. The engine was a four-cylinder diesel developing 75–78 HP with electric starter and 24V battery.

The manual transmission consisted of four forward speeds and one reverse. A reduction gear increased the speeds to eight forward and two reverse. The suspensions used leaf springs with bumpers; the front springs were supplemented by hydraulic shock absorbers. The expansion brakes were hydropneumatic on all four wheels. The safety handbrake acted on the transmission. In the military version, locking the differential was possible to limit slippage on muddy or snowy ground.

The truck bed was wooden with fixed sides and had a hinged tailgate. A canvas top was provided for the bed. There were small storage lockers under the bed on both sides, and the spare tyre was mounted under the rear portion of the bed. The wheels were six-spoked Dayton-type with removable rims.

Variants

Some D80 trucks were modified in the field during the Spanish Civil War as tow trucks. The existence of a bowser version is known, albeit rare and is perhaps a post-war vehicle.

Specifications

- Designation: Autocarro Militare Unificato Pesante Isotta Fraschini D80 NM
- Producer: Isotta Fraschini, Milan
- Years produced: 1934–1945
- Number produced: Not known
- Length: 7,240mm (23ft 9in)
- Width: 2,350mm (7ft 8in)
- Height: 3,000mm (9ft 10in)
- Unladen weight: 5,500kg (12,125lbs)
- Carrying capacity: 6,500kg (14,330lbs)
- Wheelbase: 4,100mm (13ft 5in)
- Front track: 1,784mm (5ft 10in)
- Rear track: 1,770mm (5ft 10in)
- Minimum turning radius: 7,000mm (23ft)
- Minimum clearance: 310mm (1ft)
- Bed, internal length: 4,420mm (14ft 6in)
- Bed, internal width: 2,000mm (6ft 7in)
- Bed, internal height: 640mm (2ft 1in)
- Tyres: Celerflex 205 x 720.5; later Cord Sigillo Verde 38 x 9
- Engine: D 80 four-stroke six-cylinder in-line water-cooled licence-built German MAN Diesel with Bosch injectors, 7,300cc, developing 95 HP @1,900 rpm
- Fuel: Diesel
- Transmission: five speeds forward, one reverse
- Fuel capacity: 125 litres (33 US gallons, 27.5 Imperial gallons)
- Drive layout: 4x2
- Speed: 45km/h (28mph)
- Range (on road): 370km (230 miles)

Autocarro Militare Medio Isotta Fraschini D70 M

Factory photos of the Isotta Fraschini D70 M.

Developmental and Service History

The Isotta Fraschini D70 M medium truck was produced from 1936 to 1942. It followed the Isotta Fraschini D80, which in 1934 was that company's initial entry into the truck market. The D70 M was issued to transportation units and saw relatively little service; the D70 M began to be replaced in 1940 by the standardised model Isotta Fraschini D65.

The second series Isotta Fraschini D80 COM Autocarro Unificato Militare (standardised military truck). Note the spoked wheels and the pneumatic tyres with Superflex Sigillo Verde tread.

had a more streamlined all-metal cab, a different bonnet and side engine covers and a more commercial-looking radiator grille, although squared and not oval shaped.

The earliest D80 trucks had pressed steel wheels with semi-pneumatic tyres; an interim version had semi-pneumatic tyres mounted on six-spoke wheels, while the final version had pneumatic tyres on six-spoke wheels. The D80 NM had the right-hand drive that was standard on Italian military trucks. Suspension consisted of semi-elliptical leaf springs. The brake system included a compressed-air booster.

The engine was a six-cylinder diesel developing 105 HP made on a German model of the MAN company. The manual transmission had five forward speeds and one reverse. Starting was by an inertia starter; the late series (of 1940) had a battery and an electric starter. The truck bed was wood with fixed sides and had a hinged tailgate. Some late series trucks had hinged side bed panels. A canvas top was provided for the bed. There were small storage lockers under the bed on both sides on all series, and the spare tyre was mounted under the rear portion of the bed.

A 1938 advertising poster relating to the civilian Isotta Fraschini D80 CO (second series with oval grille).

Some examples of the same series are seen during a parade in 1939.

A D80 M with semi-pneumatic tyres and without the grille showing the radiator made up of separable elements, one of the requirements of the standardised military trucks. (ACS)

Later the trucks were upgraded to be part of the *Autocarri Unificati* (standardised trucks) category. Therefore in 1939 a second series was presented, in two variants: the D80 CO (*Calandra Ovale*, oval grille) and the military D80 COM (which however did not have the oval grille, and in the armed forces kept the same code NM). Actually, this second series had a few differences from the first, such as the compressed-air brake booster and the engine optimised for improved fuel consumption; the most evident change was in the bodywork and especially in the nose, with the very peculiar oval radiator grille in the civilian version CO. The military variant retained the crank starter, later transformed into an electric starter with a battery.

Production of the D80 NM continued following the Italian Armistice of September 1943 under German supervision until early 1945. Specific production numbers are unknown, as is the scale of issue to units.

The D80 NM served in North Africa and had earlier been issued (the first series) to the Italian contingent sent to Spain during the Civil War.

Technical Description

The Isotta Fraschini D80 NM was a 4x2 truck with conventional cab layout with rear-wheel drive. Although the D80 prototype had a fully enclosed all-metal cab with full doors, early production D80 trucks had a semi-enclosed cab with half-doors with canvas side curtains. By 1939 an all-metal cab made its appearance, although it still retained the half-doors with canvas inserts with transparent window openings. The 1940 version of the military D80 NM – corresponding to the second series COM –

Autocarro Militare Unificato Pesante Isotta Fraschini D80 NM

The Isotta Fraschini D80 M (military) of the first series.

This first series D80 M was converted into a recovery truck during the Spanish Civil War.

A D80 M of the intermediate series with spoked wheels and semi-pneumatic tyres. The vehicle belonged to the *8° Reggimento Artiglieria Guardie di Frontiera* (8th Border Guards Artillery Regiment). The task of these units was to garrison and defend the land borders of Italy.

Developmental and Service History

Isotta Fraschini was well-known for its high-quality luxury cars; although it had manufactured cars since 1900, it was not until 1934 that it entered into the truck market with the heavy diesel-powered D80. The military version D80 M (NM according to the army's nomenclature), was launched the next year, and underwent a series of modifications throughout its production history, involving two kinds of wheel and tyre combinations, and different cab configurations.

The Fiat 665 Protetto or Scudato armoured personnel carrier.

Specifications
- Designation: Autocarro Militare Pesante Unificato Fiat 665 NM
- Producer: Fiat, Turin, together with the Arsenale del Regio Esercito, Turin
- Years produced: 1942–1943?
- Number produced: NA
- Length: 7,095mm (23ft 35in)
- Width: 2,670mm (8ft 9in)
- Height: 3,044mm (10ft)
- Unladen weight: 7,200kg (15,873lbs)
- Carrying capacity: 5,000kg (11,023lbs); 4000kg (8,818lbs) off-road
- Wheelbase: 3,760mm (12ft 4in)
- Front track: 1,855mm (6ft)
- Rear track: 1,910mm (6ft 3in)
- Minimum turning radius: 9,200mm (30ft 2in)
- Minimum clearance: 310mm (1ft)
- Fording depth: 650mm (2ft 2in)
- Bed, internal length: 4,700mm (15ft 5in)
- Bed, internal width: 2,100mm (6ft 10in), approximately
- Bed, internal height: 650mm (2ft 2in), approximately
- Tyres: Superflex Sigillo Verde or Superflex S.V. Libia 11.25 x 24
- Engine: Fiat model 365 six-cylinder in-line water-cooled direct injection, 9,365cc, 110 HP @2,000 rpm
- Fuel: Diesel
- Transmission: four speeds forward, one reverse
- Fuel capacity: 255 litres (67.4 US gallons, 56 Imperial gallons)
- Drive layout: 4x2
- Speed: 57km/h (35mph)
- Range (on road): 750km (466 miles)

The Fiat 665 was the first heavy four-wheel drive truck made by the Turin manufacturer.

Front and rear views of the Fiat 665.

Variants

A *Protetto* (Armoured) aka *Scudato* (Shielded) version of the 665 NM was conceived in 1942 as a personnel carrier. A total of 110 units, many of them operating in Yugoslavia, were in service before the Armistice of 8 September 1943. Most of these were captured and reused by the Germans and by Mussolini's *Repubblica Sociale Italiana* (RSI, Italian Social Republic) troops. The cab and body were protected by 7.5mm armour plate; each side of the body had eight firing slits and the body could hold 20 soldiers. The modification of the 665 standard version continued with examples with different armour plating and sometimes with upper cover, in some cases recycling the trench shields. One or more machine guns of various types and calibre (including war booty guns) were often installed in the upper portion.

The lack of all-wheel drive for movement over rough ground, such as that encountered in North Africa and Russia, was recognised as a serious shortcoming, a 4x4 version of the 666 designated the 665 NM was designed in March 1941 and adopted in November of the same year.

Production of a civilian version continued on into the post-war period.

Specifications

- Designation: Autocarro Militare Pesante Unificato Fiat 666
- Producer: Fabbrica Italiana Automobili Turin (Fiat), Turin
- Years produced: 1940–1948
- Number produced: Not known
- Length: 7,095mm (23'35")
- Width: 2,350mm (7ft 8in)
- Height with canvas bed cover: 2,850mm (9ft 4in)
- Unladen weight: 6,000kg (13,228lbs)
- Carrying capacity: 6,000kg (13,228lbs)
- Wheelbase: 3,850mm (12ft 7in)
- Front track: 1,840mm (6ft)
- Rear track: 1,750mm (5ft 8in)
- Minimum turning radius: 6,600mm (21ft 8in)
- Minimum clearance: 270mm (10in)
- Fording depth: 650mm (2ft 2in)
- Bed, internal length: 4,700mm (15ft 5in)
- Bed, internal width: 2,100mm (6ft 10in)
- Bed, internal height: 650mm (2ft 2in)
- Tyres: Superflex 10.50 x 20 or Ultraflex 270 x 20, with Sigillo Verde Impero, Sigillo Verde Raiflex or Artiglio tread, or Michelin Confort Stop 270 x 20
- Engine: Fiat model 366 six-cylinder in-line water-cooled, 9,365cc, 95 HP @2,000 rpm
- Fuel: Diesel
- Transmission: four speeds forward, one reverse
- Fuel capacity: 135 litres (35.7 US gallons, 29.7 Imperial gallons)
- Drive layout: 4x2
- Speed: 50km/h (31mph)
- Range (on road): 390km (242 miles)
- Range (cross-country): 350km (217 miles)

Autocarro Militare Pesante Unificato Fiat 665 NM

Developmental and Service History

The Fiat 665 all-wheel drive heavy truck was based on the 666 NM truck and closely resembled the 666 externally; the most readily distinguishable external characteristic between the two trucks was that the 665 NM front wheel hub was much larger than that of the 666. The 665 NM was developed in March 1941 and was ready for production in mid–1942. It was adopted in November 1942.

Technical Description

Like the Fiat 666 NM upon which it was based, the 665 NM was a cab forward (COE) vehicle; the cab was all metal and enclosed; the standard cab had full doors with windows. Drive layout was 4x4. The frame was a ladder frame; suspension consisted of leaf springs; the rear axle had dual wheels. The truck had the same right-hand drive arrangement as on its predecessor. The electrical system was fed by two Marelli 12 volt batteries. Brakes were hydraulic with a compressed-air booster. The truck bed was made of wooden planks; tools and a spare wheel were mounted under the bed.

The 665 NM was powered by a 110 HP Fiat a six-cylinder diesel; the transmission had four forward gears and one reverse gear; a reduction gear was present for cross-country driving. Guide rails in the engine compartment allowed the engine to be removed quickly and easily from the front for maintenance or replacement.

To make recognition easier, this 666 has the Italian flag painted on the cab roof and an identical one but made of fabric hanging from the rear-view mirror.

A trimotor S. 82 Marsupiale and a Fiat 666 NM of the *Regia Aeronautica* on the Tirana Airfield, December 1940. (ACS)

A Fiat 666 repair shop of the *Regia Aeronautica*.

Variants

In addition to the basic cargo body, variants included bus, fuel or water tank versions.

The 666 BM with petrol engine was designed for use in Russia, as it would have been easier to start in the cold weather but was never put into production.

The Fiat 666 NM is difficult to differentiate from the Fiat 626 NM, even though it was bigger; a distinctive element are the longer bed sides.

A Fiat 666 cargo truck leads an Italian column in North Africa.

a ladder frame; suspension consisted of leaf springs; the rear axle had dual wheels. The truck had the right-hand drive, normally associated with Italian military trucks. The electrical system was fed by two Marelli 12 volt batteries. Brakes were hydraulic with a compressed-air booster. The truck bed was made of wooden planks; tools and a spare wheel were mounted under the bed.

The 666 NM was powered by a 95 HP Fiat six-cylinder direct injection diesel; the transmission had four forward gears and one reverse gear; a reduction gear was present for cross-country driving. Guide rails in the engine compartment allowed the engine to be removed quickly and easily from the front for maintenance or replacement. The 666 NM trucks for the *Regio Esercito* and *Regia Aeronautica* mounted Trilex spoke wheels with three-section rim, or K-type spoke wheels with one-piece rim.

- Carrying capacity: 3,000kg (6,614lbs)
- Wheelbase: 3,000mm (9ft 10in) NM; 3,320mm (10ft 11in) NLM
- Front track: 1,712mm (5ft 7in)
- Rear track: 1,610mm (5ft 3in)
- Minimum turning radius: 5,800mm (19ft)
- Minimum clearance: 225mm (8in)
- Fording depth: 600mm (2ft)
- Bed, internal length: 3,650mm (11ft 12in) NM; 4,000mm (13ft 2in) NLM
- Bed, internal width: 2,000mm (6ft 7in) NM; 2,050mm (6ft 8in) NLM
- Bed, internal height: 500mm (1ft 8in) NM; 670mm (2ft 2in) NLM
- Tyres: Superflex 7.50 x 20 NM; Superflex 8.25 x 20 or Ultraflex 210 x 20 (with Sigillo Verde Impero, Sigillo Verde Raiflex or Artiglio tread) NLM
- Engine: Fiat model 326 six-cylinder in-line water-cooled, 5,750cc, 65 HP @2,200 rpm
- Fuel: Diesel
- Transmission: five speeds forward, one reverse
- Fuel capacity: 110 litres (29 US gallons, 24.2 Imperial gallons)
- Drive layout: 4x2
- Speed: 63km/h (40mph)
- Range (on road): 400km (249 miles)
- Range (cross-country): 340km (211 miles)

Autocarro Militare Pesante Unificato Fiat 666 NM

The civilian Fiat 666 N with Superflex Sigillo Verde Impero tyres.

Developmental and Service History

The Fiat 666 heavy truck was essentially a beefed-up version of the Fiat 626 NM medium truck and at first glance could be mistaken for the 626 NM. It too fell into the category of standardised military vehicles. The truck could carry 20 fully equipped soldiers on the bed, in addition to the driver and truck chief. Production began in 1940 and lasted until 1948. The 666 NM saw extensive service in Russia, North Africa and on the national territory and was issued to all three Italian military services.

Technical Description

The Fiat 666 was a cab forward (COE) vehicle; the cab was all metal and enclosed; the standard cab had full doors with windows, but some were made with window openings covered by canvas covers with small mica window inserts. The frame was

A camouflaged Fiat 626 of the *Wehrmacht* tows a Junkers Ju.87D Stuka bomber belonging to *Luftflotte 2* towards the airfield in central Italy in spring 1944.

Specifications
- Designation: Autocarro Militare Medio Unificato Fiat 626 NM / NLM
- Producer: Fiat, Turin
- Years produced: 1939–1945
- Number produced: 10,000+
- Length: 6,235mm (20ft 5in)
- Width: 2,133mm (6ft 11in)
- Height to cab roof: 2,500mm (8ft 3in)
- Unladen weight: 3,960kg (8,730lbs)

A short wheelbase Fiat 626 transformed into a military bus. This variant does not appear in the Fiat documentation.

Variants

The NC (*nafta, coloniale*) was a civilian version which was designed for overseas use, characterised by a higher capacity cooling system, an auxiliary 135 litre fuel tank in the rear portion of the frame, oil-bath filters, low pressure tyres and hydraulic shock absorbers on the rear axle as well.

In 1940 two more versions appeared, the NL (*nafta, lungo*, or diesel, long, a civilian model) and the NLM (*nafta, lungo, militare*, or diesel, long, military) which had extended frames and beds, oil-bath filter and 70 HP engine; other improvements were made to all models in production, such as larger tyres and the spare tyre moved to the rear of the frame. The RA version (*Regia Aeronautica*) was identical except for the presence of a second spare tyre and minor differences in the electrical system.

In 1941 the BM (*benzina, militare* or gasoline, military) and BLM (*benzina, lungo, militare*, or gasoline, long, military) versions made their appearance. In addition to a different engine, the gas tank had a larger capacity – 150 litres – because of the higher fuel consumption occasioned by the use of gasoline.

The RN (*ribassato, nafta*, or lowered, diesel), RNL (*ribassato, nafta, lungo*, or lowered, diesel, long) and RB (*ribassato, benzina*, or lowered, gasoline) were produced in limited quantities for use as special vehicles, for example fire engines, and a bus chassis, with seating for 27 passengers; the number of passengers could be increased thanks to a special trailer, however this was usable only on flat roads because of the lack of engine power.

In addition, the 626 chassis was used as a basis for communications vehicles, command vehicles, printing van, tanker trucks, mobile workshops, ambulances and fire trucks. The purpose-built bodies were made by specialised firms; some were delivered to the *Regia Aeronautica*. Originally intended for the civilian market but later adopted by the military was the Fiat 626 tanker truck which could carry around 3,000 litres of water or fuel, and the Fiat 626 wrecker. Some designs never led to series production, such as the 626 EL (*elettrico, lungo*, or electric, long) and the 626 Protetto (armoured), which was a true armoured transport vehicle. Some examples of the basic 626 NM were fitted with weapons, such as the 6.5mm Breda model 30 light machine gun, 8mm Fiat 35 and Breda 37 machine guns, and the 20mm Breda model 35 cannon.

As production continued, improvements were made to the 626 NM that were common on the civilian model, such as electric windshield wipers and turn signals, full side windows and the towing indicator on the cab roof. A G version (*gassogeno*, gas generator engine) was also made which was powered by a wood-burning gas producing device aimed at saving the increasingly scarce gasoline or diesel fuel, but with a significant decrease in performance. The shortage of tyres led to adoption of tyres of various sizes and sources, including foreign sources.

The lack of all-wheel drive was a serious shortcoming, at least over rough ground such as that in North Africa and Russia, and in late 1942 Fiat developed the Fiat 625 with two powered axles, but that truck was never produced in series.

Following the 8 September Armistice, production continued on behalf of the Germans, who introduced some limited modifications, particularly an all-wood cab. The Fiat 628 Einheits version, characterised by very economical building solutions such as a squared cab, metal parts reduced to a minimum, simplified wheels and truck bed and a simplified electrical system, never reached series production. In the post-war period, production of the civilian version of the 626 continued until newer trucks derived from the 626 entered service.

Two uncommon images of a Fiat 626 RB with bodywork by Viberti in the truck version. (Viberti)

The Fiat 626 RLN bus was manufactured from 1939 to 1947 and remained in civilian and military service for many years after the war. It could be equipped with a trailer for passengers.

tools and a spare wheel were mounted under the bed. The designed maximum 3,000kg cargo capacity was frequently exceeded with no significant problems.

The engine of the basic version was a six-cylinder in-line diesel which developed 65 HP at 2200 rpm; the transmission had a low first gear and four gears for normal driving, plus a rear gear; there was no reduction gear for cross-country driving. The drum brakes were hydraulic and acted on the four wheels, with a servo brake (the air compressor was driven by the engine). In addition, there was a mechanical hand parking brake on the transmission.

There were four tow shackles for lifting the truck and a hefty tow hook for towing heavy loads. Overall, maintenance of the mechanical components was simple and quick. As was the case for other Italian trucks, the almost artisanal construction based on many wooden parts resulted in minor dimensional and component differences among individual examples.

A Fiat 626 Autobotte (tanker truck).

Fiat 508 CM staff car and Fiat 626 truck from the *Regia Marina*.

Two uncommon images of a Fiat 626 RB with bodywork by Viberti in the truck version. (Viberti)

A Column of Fiat 626 Sanità ambulances.

A Fiat 626 Sanità van belonging to a column of the German Medical Corps in the Ravenna harbour in the autumn of 1944.

A Fiat 626 Autobotte (tanker truck).

A 626 NLM of the *Comando Superiore Forze Armate dell'Africa Settentrionale* (North African armed forces High Command) used for the transport of prisoners. Note the blackout headlights and the fuel tank located on the roof, possibly due to the failure of the standard fuel pump. (C. Pergher)

A Fiat 626 van with bodywork by Menarini employed as a mobile field printing press.

Technical Description

The Fiat 626 was a modern truck with a cab forward (COE) arrangement; the cab was all metal and enclosed. The frame was a ladder frame; suspension consisted of leaf springs and the front axle had hydraulic shock absorbers; the rear axle had dual wheels. The truck had right-hand drive, a feature common to all Italian military trucks. The split windshield could be opened forward to allow ventilation while the truck was moving. The truck bed was made of wooden planks and had two inspection hatches;

Column of vehicles in Ukraine in August 1941. The vehicles are in the regulation grey-green colour. (ACS)

A Fiat 626 NLM in Tobruk, Libya, autumn 1941. The example is painted in the kaki sahariano colour intended for the North African Front. (ACS)

In late 1939 France ordered 1,650 examples of the Fiat 626 in order to speed up motorisation of the army in anticipation of a military confrontation with Germany and also probably to gain favour with Italian industry and thus avoid the danger of a military attack by Italy. At the time of Italy's entry into the war in June 1940, about 700 Fiat 626 trucks had been delivered to the French, some of which equipped Italian and German units after the French surrender.

The 626 was used by the *Regio Esercito*, and to a lesser extent by the *Regia Aeronautica* on all fronts; delivery of many of the trucks to the Eastern Front further exacerbated the shortage of trucks in the North African theatre, leading to a supply crisis in Libya. Hundreds of trucks, many of which were fresh from the factory, were lost because of the terrible conditions of the Russian roads and the long distances that had to be covered, in addition to losses to enemy action.

Production of the Fiat 626 increased as the war dragged on, but even though more than 10,000 were made, it was never enough to satisfy all requirements for the army. Some captured 626 trucks were used by Allied troops, but the biggest non-Italian users were the Germans who took possession of many 626s after the September 1943 Armistice and who ordered production to be continued, with more than 3,500 delivered before the end of the war.

The Fiat 626 was generally very well-liked by drivers and mechanics, although it was not without its faults. In particular, the wheels slid easily on snow or mud because of the lack of all-wheel drive and the unfavourable distribution of weight. In North Africa, drivers reportedly reported that it was somewhat difficult to drive, especially on unmade up tracks. There were also problems with engine starting and fuel feed, and the cargo bed did not stand up well under hard use in military service. Other problems stemmed from the fragile nature of some mechanical and electrical components and the shortage of spare parts, which led to a low in-service rate at the front.

MEDIUM AND HEAVY TRUCKS 57

Fiat 626 NLM, still with Diesel engine but with a long wheelbase.

Fiat 626 BLM, similar to the previous one but equipped with gasoline engine; note the larger fuel tank.

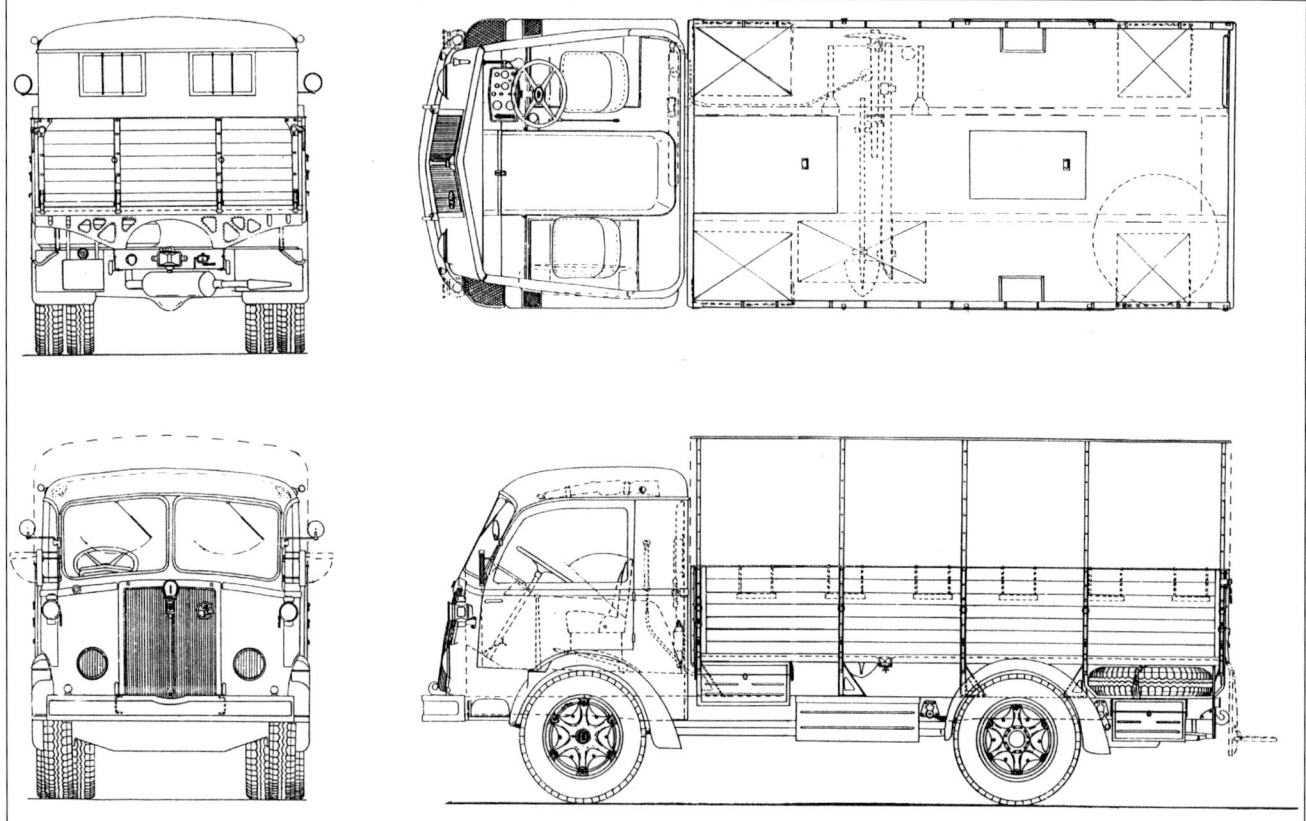

Fiat 626 NLM. (Drawings by M. Pieri)

That same year, the Fiat 626 entered production in two versions, the civilian N (diesel) version and the NM, military, version; the latter had fixed and higher body side panels, maintained the anachronistic acetylene headlamps in addition to the electric headlamps, directional signals and manual rather than electric windshield wipers. The 626 became the *Regio Esercito*'s standard medium truck; it could carry 18 men in the bed, in addition to the driver and truck chief.

- Rear track: 1,850mm (6ft 1in)
- Minimum turning radius: 7,750mm (25ft 5in)
- Minimum clearance: 320mm (1ft)
- Bed, internal length: 4,435mm (14ft 7in)
- Bed, internal width: 2,280mm (7ft 6in)
- Bed, internal height: 650mm (2ft 2in)
- Tyres: Pirelli Cord 42 x 9 or Superflex 9 x 24 with Sigillo Verde, Sigillo Verde Raiflex or other treads; also Michelin Stop were mounted
- Engine: Fiat 355C, six-cylinder in-line water-cooled, 8,355cc, 80 HP @2,100 rpm
- Fuel: Diesel
- Transmission: four speeds forward, one reverse
- Fuel capacity: 195 litres (51.5 US gallons, 42.9 Imperial gallons)
- Drive layout: 4x2
- Speed: 40km/h (25mph)
- Range (on road): Not Known

Autocarro Militare Medio Unificato Fiat 626 NM and NLM

The Fiat 626 N was the first civilian model of this truck. (Fiat)

Fiat 626 NM was built starting from the civilian 626 N. (AUSSME)

Developmental and Service History

In the late 1930s production of motor vehicles in Italy witnessed a significant increase for a number of reasons, including increased demand for civilian vehicles as well as new requirements for military vehicles to support ongoing operations in Italian East Africa, North Africa and later in Spain. In July 1937 a 'Standardisation' Royal Decree laid out the standards regarding the production of civilian trucks so that they might constitute a reserve for military use if needed (see the relative section for more details). The standard type of military trucks were preferably to use diesel engines, be no more than 235 centimetres wide and have at least 20 centimetres ground clearance. Fiat modified several designs that were being developed and in 1939 presented two new trucks, the medium 626 and the heavy 666, which were quite similar except for their dimensions; both were 4x2 trucks with rear-wheel drive.

Tanker variant of the 634 N2 employed by the *Regia Aeronautica* for water transport.

elliptical springs. Brakes were four-wheel drum brakes with a compressed-air booster. The 634 was the first Italian truck of its class to have a 24 volt electrical system. The bed had wooden sides and a hinged tailgate; there were two lockers under the bed between the cab and the rear wheel, and spare tyres were stowed under the rear portion of the bed. The fuel tank was on the driver's (right-hand) side. The engine of the 634 N1 was a Fiat diesel developing 80 HP (the early version 634 N had a 75 HP engine), and the manual transmission consisted of four forward and one reverse gear; there was no reduction gear. The engine was started by means of two electric starters.

Variants

Variants of the 634 NM included the 634 GM, which was powered by a gas generator mounted over the roof of the cab, and the 634 BM, which was powered by a Fiat 250M gasoline engine. There were also at least two tank truck versions of the 634 N1 and N2, mainly employed by the *Regia Aeronautica*.

A number of 634 NM trucks issued to the *Regia Marina* were modified in North Africa as platforms (*autocannoni*) for the 76/30 anti-aircraft gun or the 102/35 gun which was used in an anti-tank role.

Specifications

- Designation: Autocarro Militare Pesante Unificato Fiat 634 NM
- Producer: Fabbrica Italiana Automobili Turin (Fiat), Turin
- Years produced: 1931–1939
- Number produced: Not Known
- Length: 7,435mm (24ft 5in)
- Width: 2,400mm (7ft 10in)
- Height with canvas top: 3,245mm (10ft 8in)
- Unladen weight: 6,360kg (14,021lbs)
- Carrying capacity: 7,640kg (16,843lbs)
- Towing capacity: 9,000kg (19,842lbs)
- Wheelbase: 4,300mm (14ft 1in)
- Front track: 1,816mm (6ft)

Fiat 634 N2 ready for delivery in 1940. (LIFE)

A Fiat 634 N2 heavy truck from the *Regio Esercito* carrying a squad of soldiers in North Africa.

A 634 N2 in a North Africa port in summer of 1941. (ACS)

Well-known image of a Fiat 634 carrying two L3/35 light tanks, one on the cargo bed and the other on a special trailer.

The Fiat 634 N2 or second series. The triangle on the cab roof (the triangle sign on civilian trucks was also equipped with a light) had to be raised when a trailer was present. (Negri Foundation) A4 full width caption

Libyan Ascari ready for action aboard a Fiat 634.

Unloading procedures for Fiat 634 N trucks in the port of Durres, in September 1940. (ACS)

mounted headlights. It was a two-axle truck with rear wheel drive and dual rear wheels; unlike the early civilian versions, which were fitted with stamped rim wheels with semi-pneumatic tyres, the military 634 had advanced six-spoke wheels with pneumatic tyres. Drive was right-hand. The frame was made by steel longerons and the suspension consisted of four semi-

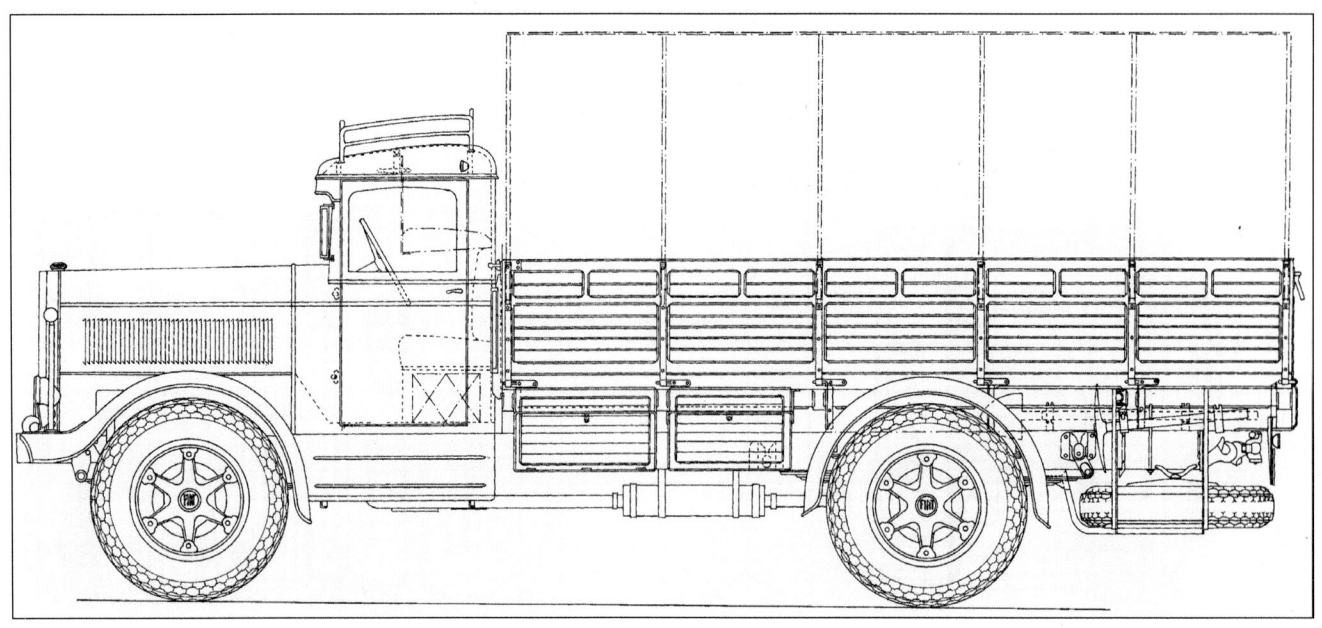
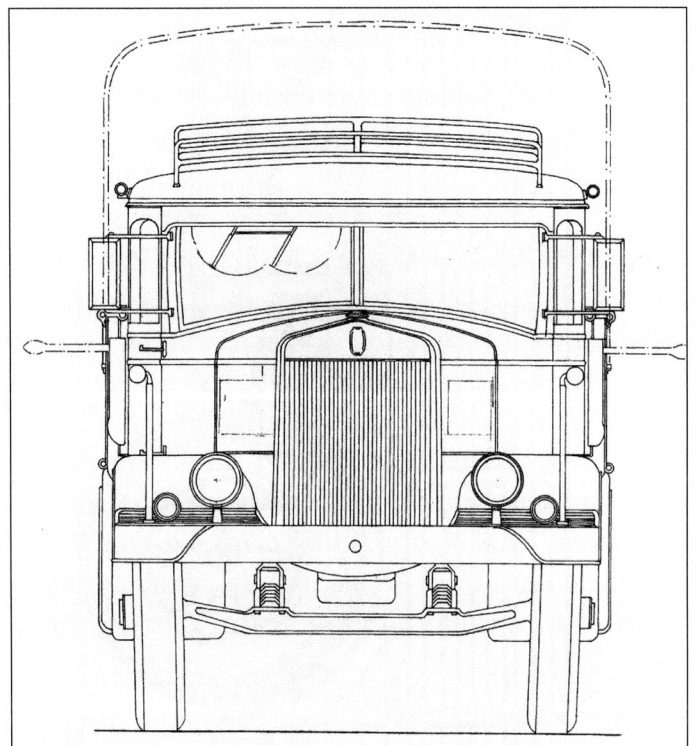
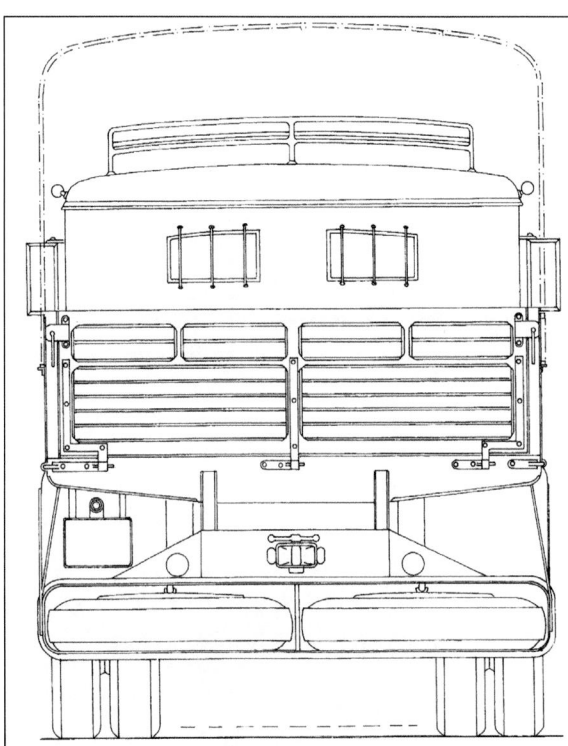
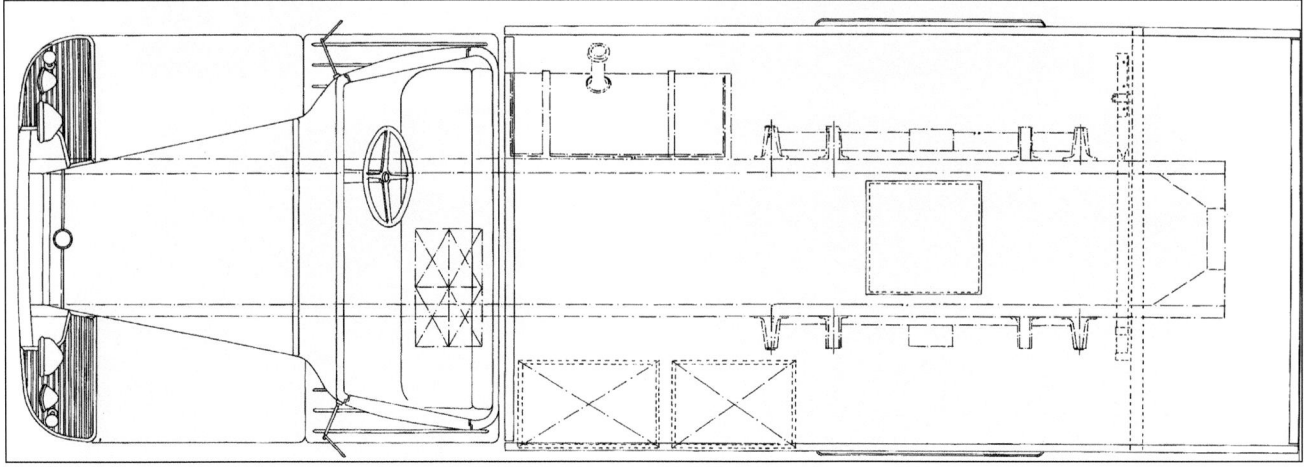

Original line drawings of the Fiat 634 NM. (Fiat)

Autocarro Militare Pesante Unificato Fiat 634 NM

Factory views of a Fiat 634 NM heavy truck. (Fiat)

A Fiat 634 N together with a Fiat Balilla Camioncino small truck; the massive size of the 634 earned it the nickname of the Gigante (giant). (Negri Foundation)

Developmental and Service History

The Fiat 634 N was a development of the earlier 632 N series of heavy trucks (see above) and differed in external appearance as well as in weight, payload and performance. Because of its size, being the heaviest Italian truck of that time (it was launched in 1931), it was referred to variously as the *Gigante* (giant) or *Elefante* (elephant). The 634 was designed to tow a 10-tonne payload, which was remarkable for the time. The military version, the 634 NM derived from the civilian improved version N1. The 634 N2 was a redesigned version of N1 and intended for the civilian market, but also used by the armed forces. It is easily recognised by the front and by the cab with more modern lines.

All these versions were acquired by the *Regio Esercito* and saw extensive service in Italian East Africa, Spain and in North Africa. Due to the total lack of specific vehicles for the transport of tanks, the 634 NM was one of the most used trucks in this role, being able to carry light tanks (L3 and L6 series) and their derivatives.

Technical Description

The Fiat 634 NM had a conventional layout with an all-metal cab with full doors. Compared to the Fiat 632 from which it was developed, the 634 had a greatly-redesigned cab and fenders, which were more aerodynamic. The 634 had four bumper-

Another Fiat 633 truck in Eritrea.

- Number produced: Not Known
- Length: 6,850mm (22ft 6in) NM; 6,820mm (22ft 4in) BM
- Width: 2,200mm (7ft 3in)
- Height 2,940mm (9ft 8in)
- Unladen weight: 5,250kg (11,574lbs)
- Carrying capacity: 5,000kg (11,023lbs)
- Wheelbase: 3,750mm (12ft 4in)
- Front track: 1,700mm (5ft 8in)
- Rear track: 1,700mm (5ft 8in)
- Minimum turning radius: 6,500mm (21ft 4in)
- Minimum clearance: 270mm (11in)
- Bed, internal length: 4,100mm (13ft 6in)
- Bed, internal width: 2,000mm (6ft 7in)
- Bed, internal height: 700mm (2ft 3in)
- Tyres: semi-pneumatic Celerflex 720.5 x 195
- Engine: Fiat 350C, four-cylinder in-line water-cooled, 5,570cc, 60 HP @1,800 rpm NM; Fiat 250M, four-cylinder in-line water-cooled, 6,647cc, 80 HP @1,800 rpm BM
- Fuel: Diesel NM; gasoline BM
- Transmission: four speeds forward, one reverse; no reduction gear
- Fuel capacity: 125 litres (33 US gallons, 27.5 Imperial gallons)
- Drive layout: 4x2
- Speed: 30km/h (19mph)
- Range (on road): 380km (236 miles)

Fiat 633 trucks in Eritrea, as shown by the civilian number plate. The vehicle on the right belongs to the *Società Nazionale Trasporti Gondrand* (Gondrand National Transport Company).

Developmental and Service History

In 1931, Fiat introduced its first diesel-powered heavy truck, the 632 N. The 632 N was produced in two series, the N and the N1, the first had a conventional cab layout and was powered by a 55 HP Fiat model 350 diesel engine. In 1933 the N1 series made its debut, characterised by a slightly redesigned cab and an improved engine, the 350C, with horsepower increased to 60 HP.

The follow-on series, introduced in 1934, was designated the 633 N (N stood for nafta, or diesel). The new vehicle incorporated significant changes, with redesigned cab, bonnet and grille. The 633 N served as the basis for a military version, designated the 633 NM (nafta militare, or diesel, military), introduced in 1935. The 633 remained in production until 1939 when it was replaced by the Fiat 666 heavy truck. The 633 NM was used in Spain during the Civil War and primarily in the occupied Balkan territories from 1941 to 1943.

Technical Description

The Fiat 633 NM was a conventional layout with an all-metal cab. It was a two-axle truck with rear wheel drive and dual rear wheels. Tyres were semi-pneumatic Celerflex or, more rarely, pneumatic. Drive was right-hand. The ladder frame had five cross-members and reinforcing gussets; the front cross-member also acted as the bumper, and the rear cross-member held the towing pintle. There were also four towing shackles on the frame. Suspension consisted of four semi-elliptical springs, and the brake system consisted of four drum brakes and a compressed-air booster. The truck had an inertia starter.

Variants

In 1935 a version powered by a gas generator mounted on the roof, designated the 633 GM, was introduced. In the same year, the gasoline version 633 BM, powered by a Fiat 250M engine, was also produced in limited numbers.

There was also a tanker body version of the 633 N. The ultimate iteration of the 633 developed into the Fiat 634 NM (see below).

Specifications

- (unless specifickally noted, all measures apply to 633 NM version)
- Designation: Autocarro Pesante Fiat 633 NM and BM
- Producer: Fabbrica Italiana Automobili Turin (Fiat), Turin
- Years produced: 1935–1939

The Fiat 633 N represented the evolution of the 632 N, the first Fiat diesel-powered heavy truck. Here is the military version 633 NM.

The gasoline-powered Fiat 633 BM with and without canvas cover.

An interesting civilian version of the Ceirano 47 that belonged to the Ferrari racing team between 1929 and 1937. Note the advertising of Pirelli Moto Cord tyres for motorcycles.

- Transmission: four speeds forward, one reverse
- Fuel capacity: 120 litres (31.7 US gallons, 26.4 Imperial gallons)
- Drive layout: 4x2
- Speed: 45km/h (28mph)
- Range (on road): 345km (214 miles)

Autocarro Pesante Fiat 633 NM

The Fiat 633 N represented the evolution of the 632 N, the first Fiat diesel-powered heavy truck. Here is the military version 633 NM.

The actual mobile bath truck contained a water boiler, a 2,000 litre tank and a pump for filling it in 15 minutes, plus pipes for the showers. A second vehicle carried two tents and a third carried clothes and equipment. It was used for the decontamination and disinfection of clothing, as well as for the personal hygiene of the troops.

A Ceirano 47 Autobagno mod. 1939 destroyed in Egypt in 1942. Its number plate was 'RE 29982'. (Museums of the City of Paris, www.parismusees.paris.fr/en)

- Rear track: 1,722mm (5ft 8in)
- Minimum turning radius: 7,000mm (23ft)
- Minimum clearance: 270mm (10in)
- Bed, internal length: 3,690mm (12ft 1in)
- Bed, internal width: 2,000mm (6ft 7in)
- Bed, internal height: 640mm (2ft)
- Tyres: Cord 34 x 7
- Engine: Ceirano 50 C four-cylinder water-cooled in-line, 4,720cc, 53 HP @1,750 rpm
- Fuel: Gasoline

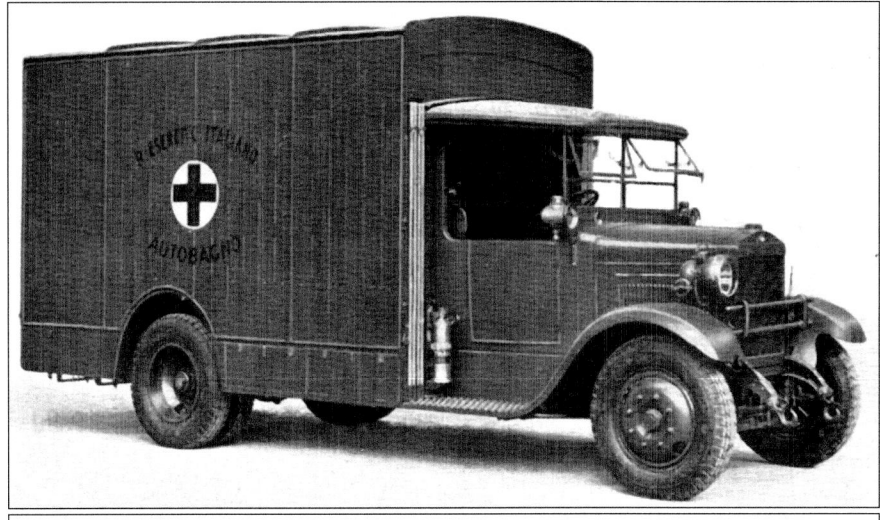

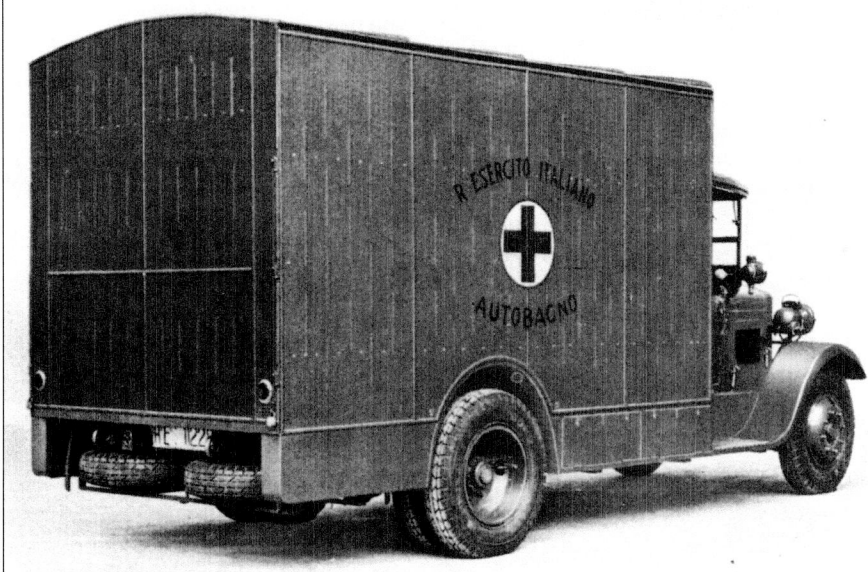

The Ceirano 47 Autobagno (mobile bath truck).

frame by shackles and bronze bushings. Brakes were mechanical. The engine was the same 53 HP four-cylinder Ceirano as on the larger 50 CM. The transmission was a four-speed manual with reverse and was fitted with a reduction gear; the clutch was a single dry disc.

Variants

There were several variants of the 47 CM. These included the 47 C (Coloniale) which was optimised for use in the African colonies and which, among other modifications, was fitted with improved air filters; a mobile bathing unit for the decontamination and the disinfection of clothing and personal hygiene of the troops; a mobile workshop; an aircraft recovery truck (for the *Regia Aeronautica*) and a tractor truck (also for the *Regia Aeronautica*).

Specifications

- Designation: Autocarro Militare Medio Ceirano 47 CM
- Producer: Giovannni Ceirano Fabbrica Automobili, Turin
- Years produced: 1935–1939
- Number produced: Not Known
- Length: 6,100mm (20ft)
- Width: 2,200mm (7ft 3in)
- Height 2,820mm (9ft 3in)
- Unladen weight: 3,875kg (8,543lbs)
- Carrying capacity: 3,000kg (6,614lbs)
- Wheelbase: 3,800mm (12ft 6in)
- Front track: 1,655mm (5ft 5in)

Personnel of a Ceirano 47 CM recovery truck observe a Messerschmitt Me 323 'Gigant'. The vehicle was equipped with an air compressor for starting the engines (up to three at the same time), which was also used for pneumatic tools and, if necessary, for the production of fire fighting foam. There were also portable fire extinguishers. The emergency landing gear was used to support the skid or the tail wheel of the aircraft. (Bundesarchiv: Bild 101I-303-0589-27A)

Ceirano 47 CM of the *Regia Aeronautica*.

Developmental and Service History

The Ceirano 47 CM was developed in 1927 as a lightened version of the Ceirano 50 CM and bore a very strong physical resemblance to it. In addition to being lighter, the 47 CM also allowed a higher road speed and was fitted with pneumatic rather than semi-pneumatic tyres. It did not have the locking differential of the 50 CM. Production ended in 1939.

The 47 CM was issued to the *Reggimenti di Artiglieria Contraerei* (anti-aircraft artillery regiments) and to the *autoreparti* (transport units). The 47 CM saw extensive service in Italian East Africa; a very small number served with the Italian contingent that was sent to Spain during the Civil War there. In addition to being issued to the *Regio Esercito*, the 47 CM was also adopted by the *Regia Aeronautica*.

Technical Description

Like the Ceirano 50 CM on whose design it was based, the Ceirano 47 CM was a conventionally configured 4x2 rear-wheel drive truck, with dual rear wheels; the tyres were pneumatic fitted on stamped disc wheels. The cab had half-doors which could be fitted with canvas side curtains. The frame was a lighter version of the riveted steel frame of the 50 CM; a towing pintle was affixed to the rear cross-member. The wooden body had a canvas cover. Storage lockers were located on both sides of the vehicle. The spare tyre was carried under the cargo bed, just behind the cab. Suspension consisted of leaf springs attached to the

Autocarro Medio Militare Ceirano 47 CM

The Ceirano 47 CM. (MSGR)

A Ceirano 47 CM aircraft recovery truck for the *Regia Aeronautica*.

canvas cover and could carry 18 men seated on five transversally mounted benches; the truck could also carry seven or eight horses or mules. Storage lockers were located on the running boards on both sides of the vehicle; the main fuel tank was under the driver's seat. The spare tyre was carried under the rear of the cargo bed. Suspension consisted of leaf springs attached to the frame by shackles and bronze bushings. Brakes were mechanical. Starting could be either by hand crank or (in later models) electrical. The engine was a petrol four-cylinder Ceirano that produced 53 HP. The transmission was a four-speed manual with reverse and was fitted with a reduction gear and a locking differential; the clutch was a single dry disc.

Variants

Variants of the 50 CM included a heavy mobile repair shop, a bowser, a recovery vehicle, a communications truck and a shower truck.

The 50 CMA (1931) had a strengthened frame and was modified to carry, on a platform equipped with a revolving mount, the 75/27 CK anti-aircraft gun, which, at the outset of the war, was the most numerous mobile anti-aircraft gun (166 examples) in the Italian inventory.

Specifications

- Designation: Autocarro Militare Pesante Ceirano 50 CM
- Producer: Giovannni Ceirano Fabbrica Automobili, Turin
- Years produced: 1926–?
- Number produced: NA
- Length: 6,420mm (21ft)
- Width: 2,100mm (6ft 10in)
- Height 2,910mm (9ft 6in)
- Unladen weight: 4,510kg (9,943lbs)
- Carrying capacity: 5,000kg (11,023lbs)
- Wheelbase: 3,600mm (11ft 10in)
- Front track: 1,630mm (5ft 4in)
- Rear track: 1,630mm (5ft 4in)
- Minimum turning radius: 6,300mm (20ft 8in)
- Minimum clearance: 320mm (1ft)
- Bed, internal length: 3,880mm (12ft 9in)
- Bed, internal width: 1,860mm (6ft 1in)
- Bed, internal height: 620mm (2½in)
- Tyres: Celerflex semi-pneumatic 175 x 720.5 or 195 x 720.5
- Engine: Ceirano 50 C four-cylinder water-cooled in-line, 4,720cc, 53 HP @1,900 rpm
- Fuel: Gasoline
- Transmission: four speeds forward, one reverse
- Fuel capacity: 125 litres (33 US gallons, 27.5 Imperial gallons)
- Drive layout: 4x2
- Speed: 24km/h (15mph)
- Range (on road): 235km (146 miles)

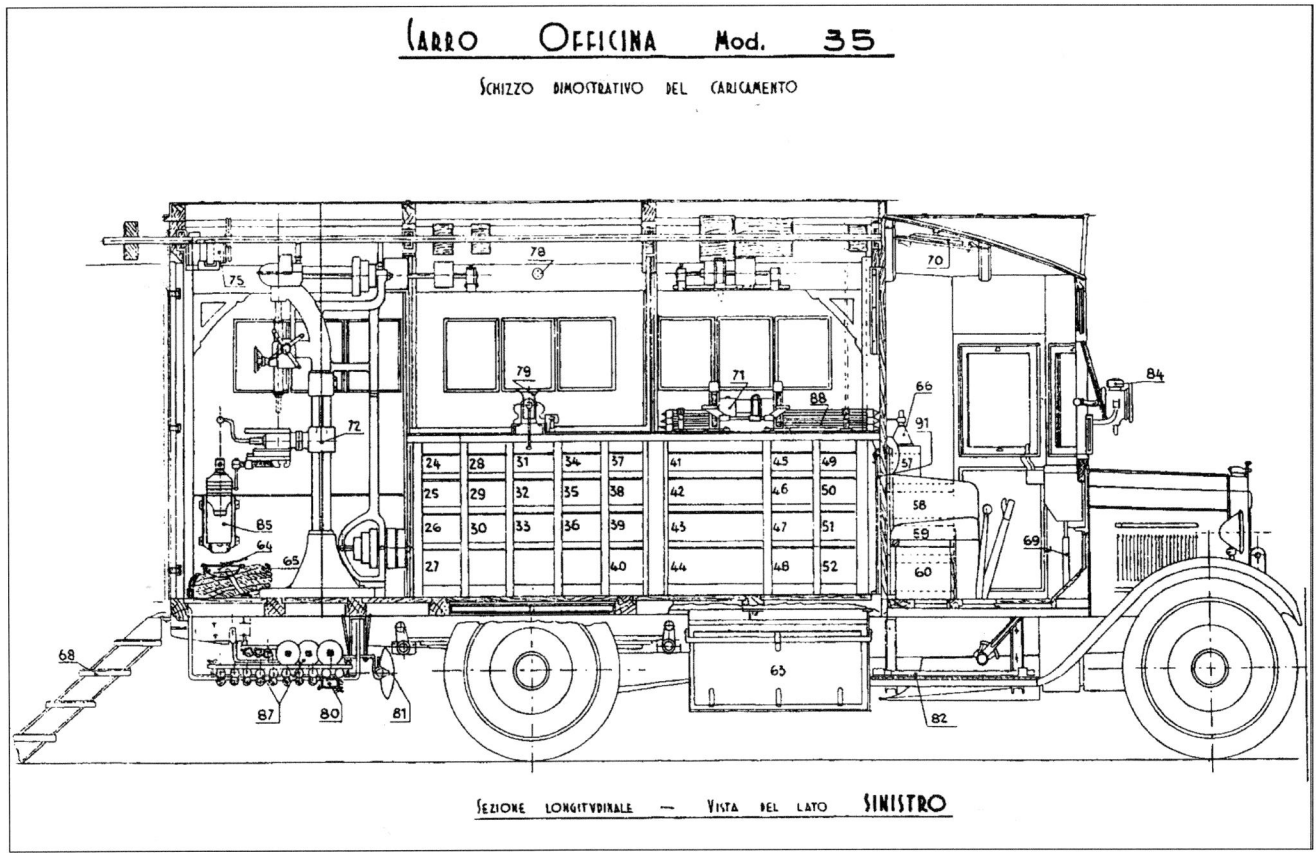
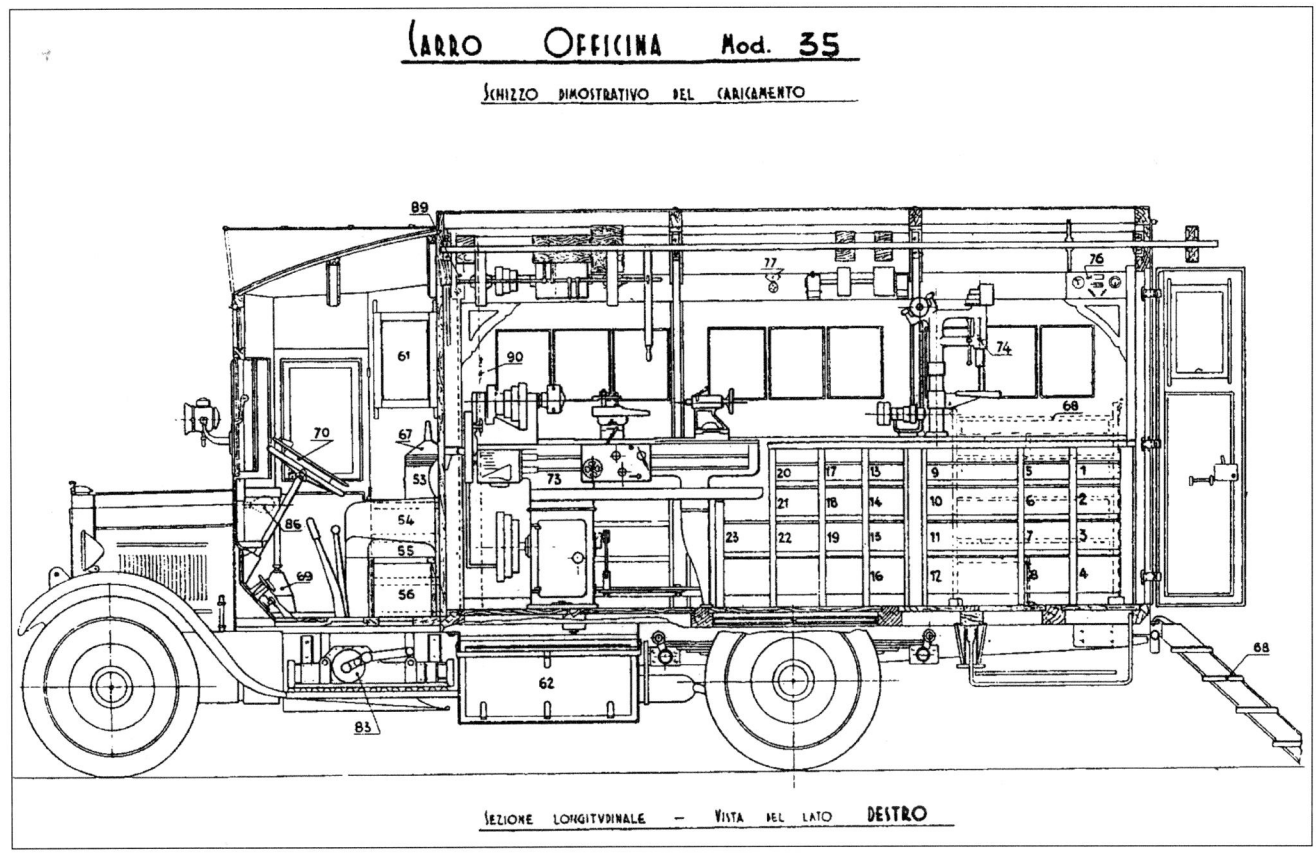

Sectional views of the Carro Officina Mod. 35.

Technical Description

The Ceirano 50 CM was a conventionally configured 4x2 rear-wheel drive truck, with dual rear wheels; the tyres were semi-pneumatic mounted on stamped disc wheels. The cab had half-doors which could be fitted with canvas side curtains. The frame was very robust with riveted cross-members; a towing pintle was affixed to the rear cross-member. The wooden body had a

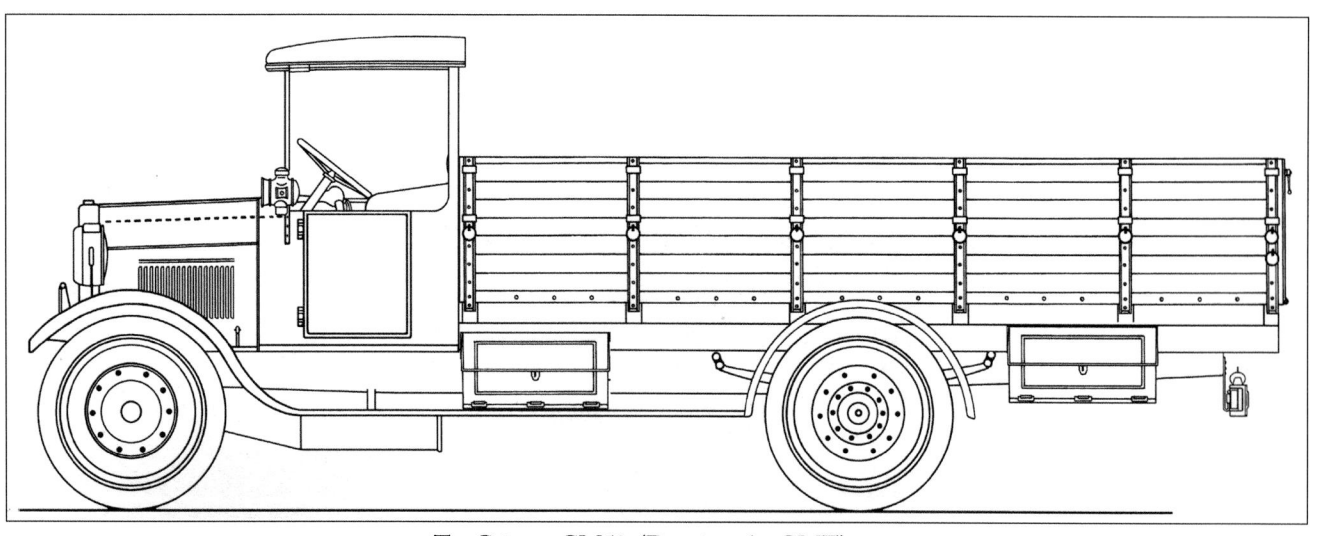

The Ceirano CM50. (Drawings by GMT)

The Carro Officina Mod. 35 mobile repair shop based on the Ceirano 50 chassis, ready for the use in Spain.

Inside view of a Carro Officina.

Rear view of the Ceirano 50 CM.

On the front of the truck, two cylindrical crossbars protected the radiator; the starter crank is connected to one of them. The example has only one acetylene headlight, on the right side, and one oil lamp, on the left. The wheels are fitted with Pirelli semi-pneumatic tyres. (Albertini via C. Pergher)

Developmental and Service History

The Ceirano 50 CM (*carro medio*, medium truck) was developed in 1926 to replace the First World War era Fiat 18 BL and BLR trucks. Following rigorous testing, the 50 CM was adopted by the *Regio Esercito* in 1927, as it fulfilled the requirements to be part of the medium truck category. In 1937 several modifications were made, the most visible of which was provision of a semi-enclosed cab; worthy of mention are the introduction of pneumatic (instead of semi-pneumatic) tyres, an electrical system and – in the version with electric starter – a battery pack.

Considerable numbers of the Ceirano 50 CM were produced until supplanted by diesel-powered heavy trucks. The 50 CM served in a civilian role as well as the military role; it performed well in both roles.

The 50 CM was issued to engineer units, to infantry division heavy transportation companies and to corps anti-aircraft artillery regiments. In 1934 they were issued to the Italian peacekeeping troops who had been sent to the Saar region, which had been contested by France and Germany. The 50 CM later served with the Italian 'volunteers' in the Civil War in Spain; it also served in Italian East Africa and in North Africa. The truck was also purchased by the *Regia Aeronautica*.

An inter-war photo of a line-up of 75/27 CK anti-aircraft systems mounted on the Ceirano 50 CM chassis and assigned to the 2° Reggimento Antiaereo. (Fiat)

- Width: 2,208mm (7ft 3in)
- Height: 2,810mm (9ft 2in)
- Unladen weight: 3,500kg (7,716lbs)
- Carrying capacity: 3,000kg (6,614lbs)
- Wheelbase: 3,350mm (11ft)
- Front track: 1,704mm (5ft 7in)
- Rear track: 1,642mm (5ft 5in)
- Minimum turning radius: 6,500mm (21ft 4in)
- Minimum clearance: 265mm (11in)
- Bed, internal length: 4,000mm (13ft 2in)
- Bed, internal width: 2,000mm (6ft 7in)
- Bed, internal height: 650mm (2ft 1in)
- Tyres: Ultraflex 210 x 20, with Sigillo Verde Impero or Sigillo Verde Raiflex tread
- Engine: MDU 35M four-cylinder, four-stoke water-cooled, 4,849cc, 65 HP @2,000 rpm
- Fuel: Diesel
- Transmission: four speeds forward, one reverse, with reduction gear
- Fuel capacity: 70 litres (18.5 US gallons, 15.4 Imperial gallons) plus 15 litres (4 US gallons, 3.3 Imperial gallons), or 83 litres (22 US gallons, 18.25 Imperial gallons)
- Drive layout: 4x2
- Speed: 64km/h (40mph) on level road
- Range (on road): 350km (217 miles) on level ground
- Range (cross-country): 300km (186 miles)

Autocarro Pesante Militare Ceirano 50 CM

Ceirano 50 CM truck second series. Note the canvas and celluloid panel instead of the glass window, the acetylene headlights and the oil lamp.

The definitive version of the Ceirano 50 CM with electric headlights and stamped disc wheels with eight holes, although still equipped with semi-pneumatic tyres.

The close-up images allow us to observe the engine, the inside of one of the storage boxes, the fastening cable of the tarpaulin, the headlights, the windshield and the canvas and mica or celluloid covers for the half-doors. (L. Valente)

cab. Lubrication was by a geared pump in the oil sump; the engine was liquid-cooled and consisted of a military-type radiator divided in several elements, each of which could be closed off in case of damage.

The clutch was a twin, dry disc type that could be dismantled and replaced relatively easily. The manual transmission had four forward and one rear gears, which could be doubled by means of a reduction gear. The transmission was not synchronised and required some care by the driver to avoid grinding gears. It was fitted with a self-locking differential. *Regio Esercito* requirements called for a backstop feature for starting while on hills; this feature was activated by a lever on the dashboard. Brakes were hydraulic with a compressed-air booster, while the manual handbrake acted on the rear brakes.

Limited modifications were introduced during the production run. The early simple electrical system was gradually replaced by a battery with starting motor, retaining the hand-cranked starter for emergencies, such as under very cold weather conditions. The electrical system was 12 volts, except for the starter which was 24 volts. External lights consisted of two electric headlights on the fenders plus a military taillight on the rear number plate. There were also two emergency acetylene lights on the cab sides (later removed). Directional signals were mechanical, although there were also provisions for electrical signals. There were provisions for an electrical connection to a trailer.

The truck bed was wood with fixed sides and had a hinged tailgate with mounting steps. A canvas top was provided; when not in use, the bows were stacked and stored behind the cab, while the longitudinal stringers were stored on the outside of the bed in various positions, depending on the truck variant.

Variants

The Miles was a robust vehicle, and several variants of the Miles were produced in addition to the standard cargo body: refrigerator van; shower truck (for decontaminating soldiers exposed to chemicals or gas, but also used for personal hygiene); stretcher truck for wounded soldiers; passenger bus and ambulance. In Russia the Miles was used as a tractor for 75/46 anti-aircraft guns.

Specifications

- Designation: Autocarro Unificato Medio Bianchi Miles
- Producer: Edoardo Bianchi, Milan
- Years produced: 1938–1944
- Number produced: Approximately 10,000
- Length: 6,052mm (19ft 10in)

An example belonging to an Autoraggruppamento in action on the Eastern Front is overtaken by a German Sd.Kfz. 221 armoured car.

The close-up images allow us to observe the engine, the inside of one of the storage boxes, the fastening cable of the tarpaulin, the headlights, the windshield and the canvas and mica or celluloid covers for the half-doors. (L. Valente)

panels to the engine compartment. The side panels could be completely removed to allow greater cooling for the engine in hot climates. The cab had half-doors without windows but could be fitted with a canvas cover with celluloid or mica windows. The Miles was a right-hand drive vehicle, typical for Italian trucks of that era. The two-piece windshield had an electric windshield wiper on the driver's side and a manual wiper on the passenger side. Suspension consisted of semi-elliptical springs, doubled at the rear.

Two types of engine were available, both direct injection diesel engines based on a Daimler Benz type built under licence. The first was an MDU 35 with two 12 V batteries, starting motor, glow plug and pressurised fuel feed. The second was the MDU 35M (military) with a dynamo, pressure and gravity feed (the gravity feed could take the place of the pressure feed if necessary), lacked a glow plug and had a hand-cranked Bosch external inertial starter. The MDU 35M was initially more widely issued, in two sub-versions, one on the Miles frame and the other on the Miles FG frame: the first type had a standard 70 litre fuel tank, of which 15 were a reserve located under the driver's seat, while the second type had an 83 litre tank located behind the

The Bianchi Miles. (Drawings by M. Pieri)

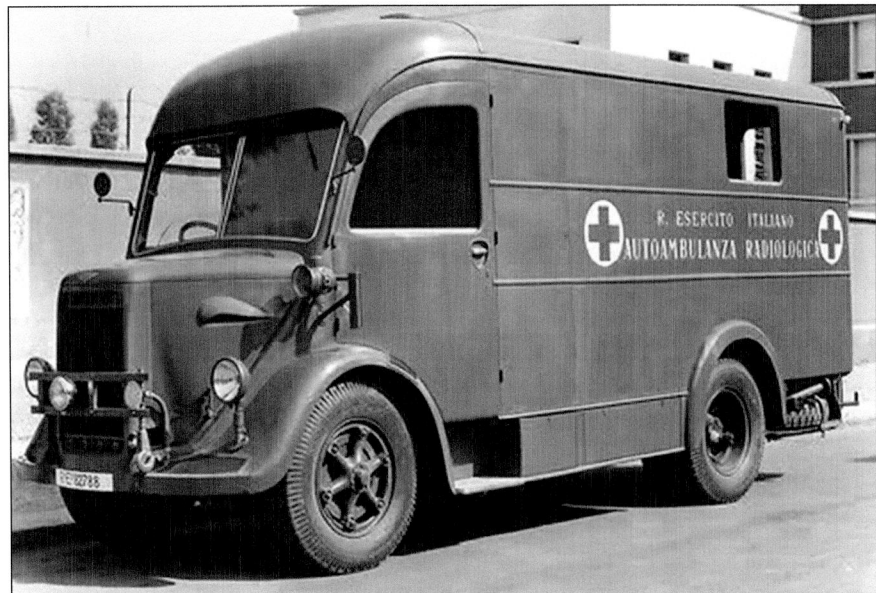

The radiological ambulances were already in use during the Great War. In the photograph is a version from the late thirties based on the Bianchi Miles. Among the specialised ambulance and van designers were Viberti, Fissore and Boneschi.

A Miles refrigerated truck, equipped with a trailer, waiting in a Ukrainian railway yard in the autumn of 1941.

cab characterised by a prominent 'snout', as on the Mediolanum. This arrangement allowed a tighter turning radius compared to similar vehicles, a decided advantage for a military truck.

The Bianchi Miles was employed in great numbers by the *Regio Esercito* (a total of about 10,000 were built), especially in North Africa and Russia. Smaller numbers were also used by the *Regia Marina* and the *Regia Aeronautica*. Following the 8 September 1943 Armistice between Italy and the Allies, the Germans captured many examples of the basic truck and its variants and continued production of the Miles, making some modifications to the body. It appears that about 90 examples were built between May and December 1944, but it is probable that quantities of new vehicles furnished to German units exceeded that number.

The truck was well-liked by the Italian drivers, both in Africa and on the Eastern Front. The various *Autoraggruppamenti* and *Autogruppi* of the *ArmIR* (the *Armata Italiana in Russia*, Italian Army in Russia, the successor of the *CSIR*) equipped with the Miles and other heavy trucks, were in charge of all logistical missions both during the advance and in the subsequent retreat. It was also appreciated by the Germans, who used it in theatres other than Italy.

During the post-war period, the surviving trucks were used by the *Regio Esercito* until they wore out and could no longer be supported. However, production of a civilianised model, designated the Civis (Latin for citizen) continued for some years after the war. Today, some museum examples of the Miles are in actuality the Civis that have been restored to resemble the Miles.

Technical Description

The Miles was a semi-forward cab truck; for its era, it was modern in concept, design and appearance. It had a conventional 4x2 layout with rear wheel drive, with dual rear wheels. The somewhat unique cabin arrangement made it easily identifiable, as did the side air intakes that resembled a horizontal comma or an eyebrow, which also served as handles for removing the side access

Autocarro Unificato Medio Bianchi Miles

Pre-war factory photos of a civilian Bianchi Miles, with and without tarpaulin, ready for delivery.

Driving on difficult terrain often led to the immobilisation of the truck, which was designed for driving on the road and equipped with only rear drive wheels. Here an example is being pulled by a German 8-ton half-track Sd.Kfz. 7.

A column of the *Regio Esercito* composed largely of Bianchi Miles on a track in North Africa, towards the end of 1941.

Crossing of the Donets, a river that traverses both Russia and the Ukraine, on a pontoon bridge built by Italian engineers, in the summer of 1942. (ACS)

Developmental and Service History

The Bianchi Miles (*miles* – phonetically pronounced mee-lez – is the Latin for soldier) medium truck entered production in 1938 as a purely standardised military truck, replacing the previous civilian model designated the Mediolanum (see above) which had been in production since 1935 and which was very similar both mechanically and in layout. An almost identical variant, except for some components, and aimed at the civilian market was called Mediolanum Miles.

The Bianchi company had been interested in a truck of limited dimensions and for that reason had opted to adopt a semi-forward cab type that included some of the mechanical components, rather than the more traditional standard rear-mounted

One of the derivatives of the truck was the Miles bus, which was fitted with bodies by various coachbuilders, such as Luigi Dalla Via and Menarini. The military version is shown here.

MEDIUM AND HEAVY TRUCKS 29

A column of Bianchi Mediolanum 68 together with Bersaglieri cyclists in preparation for the invasion of southern France, in June 1940.

Technical Description

The Mediolanum had a conventional cab layout; it was a 4x2 with rear wheel drive, with dual rear wheels. It was a right-hand drive vehicle. The wooden body could be covered by a canvas cover. There were two storage lockers on the left-hand side of the vehicle, while the exposed fuel tank was on the right side behind the cab.

The engine was a four-cylinder diesel that produced 57 HP; the engine of the 68 A increased the horsepower to 60. The transmission was a four-speed manual with reverse and was fitted with a reduction gear.

The Mediolanum mobile cinema in North Africa, 1942, followed by a SPA 38 R.

Variants
In addition to the cargo body, the Mediolanum was built as a refrigerated truck and was also fitted out as a mobile cinema for troops.

Specifications
- Designation: Autocarro medio Bianchi Tipo Mediolanum 1936 Militare
- Producer: Edoardo Bianchi, Milan
- Years produced: 1935–1938
- Number produced: NA
- Length: 6,305mm (20ft 8in)
- Width: 2,080mm (7ft)
- Height: without tarpaulin 2,600mm (8ft 6in); with tarpaulin 2780mm (9ft 1in)
- Unladen weight: 3,730kg (8,223lbs)
- Carrying capacity: 3,000kg (6,614lbs)
- Wheelbase: 3,800mm (12ft 6in)
- Front track: 1,704mm (5ft 7in)
- Rear track: 1,630mm (5ft 4in)
- Minimum turning radius: 6,500mm (21ft 4in)
- Minimum clearance: 235mm (9in)
- Bed length: 3,715mm (12ft 2in) internal; 3,800mm (12ft 6in) external
- Bed width: 1,915mm (6ft 3in) internal; 2,000mm (6ft 7in) external
- Bed height: 650mm (2ft 1in) internal; 700mm (2ft 4in) external
- Tyres: Cord 34 x 7 (930 x 198) or Superflex 7.50 x 20, both with Sigillo Verde tread or other tread
- Engine: MD35 four-cylinder, four-stoke water-cooled, 4,950cc, 58–60 HP @2,000 rpm
- Fuel: Diesel
- Transmission: four speeds forward, one reverse, with reduction gear
- Fuel capacity: 70 litres (18 US gallons, 15 Imperial gallons)
- Drive layout: 4x2
- Speed: 55km/h (34mph) on level road
- Range (on road): 280km (173 miles) on level ground

- Fuel capacity: 75 litres (19.8 US gallons, 16.5 Imperial gallons)
- Drive layout: 4x2
- Speed: 65km/h (40mph)
- Range (on road): 370km (230 miles)
- Range (cross-country): 330–350km (205–217 miles)

Autocarro Medio Bianchi Mediolanum

A civilian Mediolanum Tipo 35 (aka first series). Note the stamped disc wheels.

A civilian Mediolanum Tipo 36 or Mediolanum 68 (aka second series), with body made by Viberti and the definitive spoked wheels.

The militarised version of the Mediolanum 68.

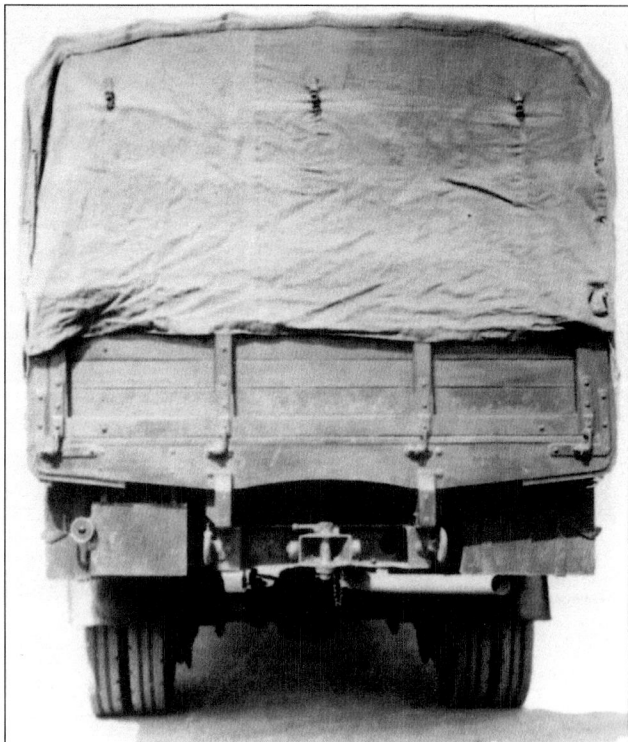

The Mediolanum 68A.

Developmental and Service History

The Bianchi Mediolanum (Mediolanum was the Roman name for Milan) was a civilian truck built by Bianchi from 1935 to 1938 under licence from Daimler Benz. It was the precursor to the Bianchi Miles military truck tractor (see separate entry), which shared many of the mechanical components of the Mediolanum. Two series were built, the Tipo 35 or 1935 (of which only a few were produced) and the Tipo 36 or 1936, which had an extended wheelbase, enlarged body, spoked wheels and slightly more powerful engine; this second version was later designated Mediolanum 68.

A militarised version was developed for the *Regio Esercito* and the *Regia Aeronautica*. An improved version of the Mediolanum, designated as the Bianchi 68 A, was produced in limited numbers prior to production of the Bianchi Miles.

The Mediolanum served in East and North Africa, where it was found to be quite satisfactory for military service, including in off-road journeys; it was found to be simple to maintain and easy to drive and had a low fuel consumption rate. Following the September 1943 Armistice, the Germans impressed a number of Mediolanums into their service.

The 430 RE without its body and Superflex Sigillo Verde Impero tyres.

Variants
Some Alfa Romeo 430 trucks were fitted out as anti-aircraft platforms with the 20mm Scotti/Isotta Fraschini cannon.

Specifications
- Designation: Autocarro Unificato Medio Alfa Romeo 430
- Producer: Alfa Romeo, Milan
- Years produced: 1942–1948
- Number produced: Not Known
- Length: 5,955mm (19ft 6in)
- Width: 2,130mm (7ft)
- Height: 2,580mm (8ft 6in)
- Unladen weight: 3,350kg (7,385lbs)
- Carrying capacity: 3,150kg (6,945lbs)
- Wheelbase: 3,300mm (10ft 7in)
- Front track: 1,797mm (5ft 10in)
- Rear track: 1,734mm (5ft 8in)
- Minimum turning radius: 5,800mm (19ft)
- Minimum clearance: 250mm (10in)
- Fording depth: 500mm (1ft 7in)
- Bed, internal length: 4,000mm (13ft 1in)
- Bed, internal width: 2,000mm (6ft 7in)
- Bed, internal height: 600mm (1ft 11in)
- Tyres: Superflex 7.50 x 20
- Engine: Four-cylinder water-cooled, 5,816cc, 80 HP @2,000 rpm
- Fuel: Diesel
- Transmission: four-speed forward, one reverse, with two-speed transfer gearbox

Rear views of the 430 RE.

The Alfa Romeo 430 RE was a *unificato* (standardised) military vehicle and was built from 1942 to 1948, with some modifications in the post-war period. Having arrived late, only a few examples were delivered to the Italian armed forces, while at least 186 were produced during the German occupation of northern Italy following the 8 September 1943 Armistice between Italy and the Allies.

Technical Description

The Alfa Romeo 430 was a 4x2 truck that was characterised by the same rounded cab-over-engine cab with a large two-piece windshield of the Alfa Romeo 800 RE heavy truck that inspired its design. It had a fully enclosed metal cab with half-doors and was a two-axle truck with rear-wheel drive and dual rear wheels. Drive was right-hand. The independent front suspension consisted of helical springs and shock absorbers, while the rear suspension had leaf springs. Brakes were hydraulic with a compressed-air booster.

The engine was a four-cylinder in-line diesel, developing 80 HP. The manual transmission consisted of four forward speeds and one reverse, with reduction gear.

The truck bed was wood with fixed sides and had a hinged tailgate. A canvas top was provided for the bed. There were small storage lockers under the bed on both sides, and the spare tyre was mounted under the left-hand side of the bed.

The prototype half-track version of the Alfa Romeo 800 RE. (CSM)

- Fording depth: 700mm (2ft 3in)
- Bed, internal length: 4,750mm (15ft 7in)
- Bed, internal width: 2,200mm (7ft 2in)
- Bed, internal height: 650mm (2ft 2in)
- Tyres: Ultraflex 270 x 20 or Superflex 10.50 x 20 with different treads
- Engine: Six-cylinder in-line water-cooled, 8,725cc, 108 HP @2,000 rpm
- Fuel: Diesel
- Transmission: Four-speed forward, one reverse, with reduction gear
- Fuel capacity: 142 litres (37.5 US gallons, 31.2 Imperial gallons)
- Drive layout: 4x2
- Speed: 50km/h (31mph)
- Range (on road): 500km (310 miles)

Autocarro Unificato Medio Alfa Romeo Tipo 430 RE

The civilian Alfa Romeo Tipo 430.v.

Developmental and Service History

The Alfa Romeo 430 RE was a scaled-down version of the Alfa Romeo 800 RE heavy truck, and copied the heavy truck's external appearance as well as many of its mechanical features. It was characterised at first glance by a two-part front bumper. The civilian version was identical, apart from some external details such as the absence of mechanical turn signals and acetylene emergency lights.

The first example of the Alfa Romeo 430 RE shown at the factory. It is recognisable by the emergency lights and the regulation mechanical turn signal. Note the 'prova' (test) front number plate. (AUSSME)

An 800 RE similar to the previous image stopped near Olgopol (today Olhopil) in Ukraine in August 1941; it is being overtaken by a platoon of L3/35 light tanks, while a column of Fiat 626 trucks passes in the opposite direction. (ACS)

An example of 800 RE in North Africa.

- Number produced: Approximately 1,400
- Length: 6,840mm (22ft 5in)
- Width: 2,350mm (7ft 8in)
- Height with tarpaulin: 2,850mm (9ft 4in)
- Unladen weight: 5,500kg (12,125lbs)
- Carrying capacity: 6,500kg (14,330lbs)
- Towing capacity: 12.000kg (26,455lbs)
- Wheelbase: 3,800mm (12ft 6in)
- Front track: 1,940mm (6ft 4in)
- Rear track: 1,940mm (6ft 4in)
- Rear track (on the centre line of the tyres): 1,734mm (5ft 8in)
- Minimum turning radius: 6,780mm (22ft 3in)
- Minimum clearance: 260mm (10in)

The Tipo 800 powered by a gas generator.

The Attrezzatura Trasporto Infiammabile Tipo A.S. su Alfa 800 RE. (Viberti)

Two Tipo 800 RE trucks with the Alfa Romeo logo painted on the front. (ACS)

The truck bed was wood with fixed sides, and had a hinged tailgate. A canvas top was provided for the bed. There were small storage lockers under the bed on both sides, and the spare tyre was mounted under the left-hand side of the bed. The military model RE featured protection bars in front of the radiator.

Variants

A version with a gasoline engine was conceived, as well as a version powered by a gas generator, but neither type went into production. A bus version, bodied by Viberti and other coachbuilders, was manufactured in small numbers.

Viberti proposed a tanker truck set-up for fuels, called Attrezzatura Trasporto Infiammabile Tipo A.S. su Alfa 800 RE, but there is no certain information on its actual production.

A half-track version of the Alfa Romeo 800 RE six-ton cargo truck was developed, although it is likely that only the prototype shown in CSM photographs was actually completed. The rear tracked unit vaguely resembled the French Kegresse system but was conceived and developed in-house by engineer Vittorio Locera.

After the Armistice the 800 RE was incorporated by the German forces with the name Lastkraftwagen 6.5 t Alfa Romeo (i) Typ 800 R.E.

Specifications

- Designation: Autocarro Unificato Pesante Alfa Romeo 800 RE
- Producer: Alfa Romeo, Milan
- Years produced: 1940–1943

The Tipo 800 RE tested with Sigillo Verde Impero tyres.

A civilian Tipo 800 with a *Regio Esercito* licence plate in the Balkans in January 1941; note the handle on the door and the unprotected radiator. (ACS)

occupation of France. Being a direct derivative of a civilian model designed for movement on paved roads, it was not particularly well suited for cross-country movement.

Despite some positive features, such as the good payload-to-weight ratio, the truck was used by the army in rather small quantities, just under 1,400 examples, unlike vehicles of other manufacturers with better political connections.

Technical Description

The 800 RE was a 4x2 truck characterised by a somewhat rounded cab-over-engine cab with a rather large two-piece windshield, reflecting its origins as a commercial vehicle. Unlike the civil version which had full doors, the Tipo 800 RE was equipped with half-doors without handles. It was a two-axle truck with rear-wheel drive and dual rear wheels. Drive was right-hand, typical for Italian military trucks of the era. The frame was made of pressed steel consisting of two longitudinal longerons connected by four electrically welded cross-members; the lifting hooks were fixed to the ends of the longerons and there was the regulation tow hook fixed to the rear cross-member. Suspension consisted of semi-elliptical leaf springs. Brakes were hydraulic with a compressed-air booster.

The engine was a six-cylinder in-line Diesel with Bosch, CIRSA or Bosio injectors. Starting was either electrical or manual with an inertia starter. The manual transmission consisted of four forward speeds and one reverse, with reduction gear and self-locking differential; there was also a backstop feature. Starting was manual by means of a crank (the civilian version had electric starting and a 24 volt battery).

- Speed: 55km/h (34mph) Tipo 500; 45km/h (28mph) Tipo 500 RE
- Range (on road): 400km (249 miles)

Autocarro Unificato Pesante Alfa Romeo Tipo 800 RE

The Alfa Romeo Tipo 800 RE. (AUSSME)

The general appearance of the Alfa Romeo 800 RE was clearly inspired by a commercial vehicle. (AUSSME)

Developmental and Service History
The Alfa Romeo 800 was also known as Tipo 800 or T.800. The military version 800 RE (*Regio Esercito*) was almost identical to the civilian one. It was a standardised heavy truck which likely accounts for its flowing rather than angular cab style. The 800 RE was produced from 1940 to 1943 and was used primarily in North Africa and on the Eastern Front, but also during the

MEDIUM AND HEAVY TRUCKS

An Alfa Romeo 85, the predecessor of the 350, with bus bodywork from the *Regia Aeronautica* photographed in East Africa. The Viberti logo is present on the radiator grille.

An advertising poster for an Alfa Romeo truck.

vehicles for communication cables and accessories that were able to cover distances up to one kilometre between the individual units. This motor train was employed in France, the Balkans and the Eastern Front.

To meet contingent domestic needs, Alfa Romeo also developed two versions with wood gas generator (G) and methane (M) engines.

Specifications
- Designation: Autocarro Medio Alfa Romeo Tipo 500 and Tipo 500 RE
- Producer: Alfa Romeo, Milan
- Years produced: 1937–1945
- Number produced: Approximately 3,000
- Length: 7,205mm (23ft 8in) Tipo 500; 7,020mm (23ft) Tipo 500 RE
- Width: 2,400mm (7ft 10in) Tipo 500; 2,200mm (7ft 3in) Tipo 500 RE
- Height: 2,250mm (7ft 4in) Tipo 500; 2,640mm (8ft 8in) Tipo 500 RE
- Unladen weight: 3,750kg (8,267lbs) Tipo 500; 3,800kg (8,377lbs) Tipo 500 RE
- Carrying capacity: 4,250kg (9,370lbs) Tipo 500; 3,200kg (7,055lbs) Tipo 500 RE
- Wheelbase: 4,500mm (14ft 9in) Tipo 500; 4,200mm (13ft 9in) Tipo 500 RE
- Front track: 1,660mm (5ft 5in)
- Rear track: 1,680mm (5ft 6in)
- Minimum turning radius: 7,200mm (19ft)
- Fording depth: 700mm (1ft 7in)
- Tyres: Superflex 8.25 x 20 or Cord 34 x 7 Tipo 500; Ultraflex 210 x 20 Tipo 500 RE
- Engine: AR F6M 313 six-cylinder water-cooled, 6,126cc, 75 HP @2,000 rpm
- Fuel: Diesel
- Transmission: four-speed forward, one reverse
- Fuel capacity: 100 litres (26.4 US gallons, 22 Imperial gallons)
- Drive layout: 4x2

The model preceding the 500 was the Alfa Romeo 350, which was bigger and squarer. Here a civilian model without cargo bed in the first post-war period. The 350 is recognisable immediately by the openable air intakes on the sides of the bonnet, which have a different shape and are more numerous (four) than on the 500.

An Alfa Romeo 350 in service with the *Regio Esercito*.

The truck bed was wooden with fixed sides and had a hinged tailgate. A canvas top with five bows was provided for the bed. There were small storage lockers under the bed on both sides, and the spare tyre was mounted under the left-hand side of the bed. The engine was a six-cylinder Deutz diesel developing 85 HP. The manual transmission consisted of four forward speeds and one reverse. The suspension used semi-elliptical longitudinal leaf springs (shock absorbers were optional) and on the four-wheel acted drum brakes.

Variants

The 500 chassis was used as the basis for many models of passenger bus, with a two-axle or three-axle chassis and lengthened frame (respectively, the 500 A, AP and AL) and the 500 civilian version was also used as the basis for a fire truck. A three-axle version 500 P was fitted out as a mobile repair shop with a trailer, with a body by Viberti and intended for use by the *Regia Aeronautica*, but was probably never manufactured in series.

The 500 RE had a modest degree of success as an *Autotreno Comando* (Command Motor Train) created in 1939 by Viberti and consisting of 12 camouflaged bus-bodied vehicles on the Alfa Romeo 500 chassis, plus three trailers, fitted out as a sort of mobile headquarters for an army corps. The motor train components were made by Macchi and were painted in a multi-tone camouflage scheme. Specifically, the units consisted of a tactical headquarters vehicle, a kitchen vehicle, a mess vehicle for 15 officers, one vehicle with living and sleeping quarters for the commanding general, one vehicle for the chief of staff, two other vehicles with sleeping quarters for other officers, four vehicles for communications, two electric generator vehicles, and two

The Autotreno Comando on parade.

Column of vehicles of the 'Command motor train'.

one of the most notable differences being the shape and appearance of the radiator grille area. In addition to the fender-mounted headlights of the 500, the 500 RE also had the outdated oil lamps mounted on the sides of the firewall, and mechanical turn signals. There were three unusually configured horizontal vents on each of the engine compartment sides that could be fully closed or opened at an angle to increase engine cooling.

The mess vehicle and the kitchen vehicle were connected by means of a serving hatch when in service. (ACS)

Side views of the Tipo 500 RE. The presence of oil, emergency headlamps and mechanical turn signals is evident, as well as the lack of air intake on the doors.

collaboration with the German companies Büssing-NAG and Deutz. About 3,000 examples of all variants were manufactured from 1937. The truck was widely used in the Italian colonies in Africa.

Technical Description

The Alfa Romeo 500 was a conventional truck with a fully enclosed metal cab and was a two-axle truck with rear-wheel drive and dual rear wheels. Drive was right-hand. The military version was somewhat simplified and had a slightly shorter wheelbase,

An Alfa Romeo 500 bogged down in the mud in Ukraine. (ACS)

The mobile repair shop assembled on the three-axle chassis 500 P. (Viberti)

5

Medium and Heavy Trucks

Autocarro Medio Alfa Romeo Tipo 500 and 500 RE

The civilian Alfa Romeo Tipo 500. Note the oval grille and the air intake on the door.

The military Tipo 500 RE, recognisable by the different shape of the radiator grille.

Side views of the Tipo 500 RE. The presence of oil, emergency headlamps and mechanical turn signals is evident, as well as the lack of air intake on the doors.

Developmental and Service History

The Alfa Romeo 500 was a medium truck produced by the Milanese factory from 1937 to 1945. The basic Tipo 500 was a commercial vehicle, many examples of which were operated in their civilian configuration by the *Regio Esercito*, while the Tipo 500 Militare or 500 RE was a militarised version. The Tipo 500 was the last conventionally configured truck produced by Alfa Romeo before it switched to the COE configuration. It was developed, together with the previous model 350, from the

Prefixes and suffixes used in vehicle designations

AS	Autocarro sahariano (desert truck)
B	Benzina (petrol, gasoline)
BM	Benzina, Militare (military vehicle with petrol engine)
C	Coloniale (tropicalised vehicle or equipment)
C	Corto (short wheelbase)
CL	Carro leggero (light truck)
CM	Carro militare (military truck)
CV	Carro veloce (fast tank, actually a tankette)
G	Gassogeno (gas generator engine)
GM	Gassogeno, Militare (military vehicle with gas generator engine)
L	Lungo (long wheelbase)
M	Militare (military vehicle)
N	Nafta (diesel oil)
NM	Nafta, Militare (military vehicle with diesel engine)
P	Pneumatici (pneumatic tyres)
PC	Pesante Campale (heavy field)
R	Ribassato (lowered chassis for use for buses and other special vehicles)
S or SP	Semipneumatici (semi-pneumatic tyres)
TL	Trattore leggero (light tractor)
TM	Trattore medio (medium tractor)
TP	Trattore Pesante (heavy tractor)

Motocarrozzetta: motorcycle/sidecar combination
Motocicletta, motociclo: motorcycle
Mototriciclo: three-wheeled motorcycle
Pesante: heavy
Polizia Coloniale: original name of the *Polizia dell'Africa Italiana*
Polizia dell'Africa Italiana (PAI): Italian African Police, the police corps of Italian North Africa and Italian East Africa colonies from 1936 to 1945, reporting directly to the Ministry of the Colonies, later renamed the Ministry of Italian Africa. Until 1939 the corps was named *Polizia Coloniale*
Regia Aeronautica (RA): Italian Royal Air Force
Regio Corpo Truppe Coloniali (RCTC): Royal Corps of Colonial Troops, Italian military unit which included troops stationed in the African colonies of Eritrea, Somalia, Tripolitania and Cirenaica (Tripolitania and Cirenaica were later merged into Libya)
Regio Corpo Truppe Libiche (RCTL): Royal Corps of Libyan Troops (1938–1943); formerly Regio Corpo Truppe Coloniali della Libia (1935–1938)
Regio Esercito (RE): Italian Royal Army
Regia Marina (RM): Italian Royal Navy
Rimorchio: trailer
Semicingolato: half-track
*Superflex (*aka *Superflex Cord):* low pressure pneumatic tyre for light and heavy vehicles
Sigillo Verde: special tread for heavy vehicles tyres suitable for soft soils
Sigillo Verde Libia (aka *Tipo Libia*): special tread for tyres designed for sand
Stella Bianca: special tread for light vehicles, similar to the *sigillo verde*
Trattore: tractor
Trattrice: tractor (usually heavy)
Ultraflex: very low pressure 'balloon' pneumatic tyre for heavy vehicles

Glossary

Italian terms
Aerflex: very low pressure 'balloon' pneumatic tyre for cars and light vehicles
Artiglio: pneumatic tyre with large treads ('artiglio' literally means 'claw')
Autobus, autocorriera: bus
Autocarro: truck, lorry
Autocarro unificato medio: standardised medium truck
Autocarro unificato pesante: standardised heavy truck
Autogruppo: transportation battalion, consisting of several *autoreparti* (transportation companies)
Autoraggruppamento: echelon consisting of several *autogruppi* (transportation battalions); transportation brigade
Autoreparto: transportation company, consisting of several *autosezioni* (transport sections)
Autosezione: motor transport section
Autovettura: motor car
Autovetturetta: compact motor car
Biposto: two-seat motorcycle
Camion: truck, lorry
Camioncino: small truck
Camionetta: light truck
Carrello elastico: a single-axle two-wheel bogie trailer on which antiquated artillery pieces were placed in order to make them suitable for high-speed towing
Carro: initially the term indicated a truck or lorry; later it was used for the *carro armato* (tank) and therefore the truck became *autocarro* to avoid misunderstandings
Celerflex: a type of semi-pneumatic tyre
Cingolato: tracked
Cingoletta: light tracked vehicle
Coloniale, Col.: modified versions of a civilian or military vehicle in order to operate in desert and tropical environments, typical of Italian African colonies
Cord: standard pneumatic tyre for light and heavy vehicles
Furgoncino: small van
Furgone: van
Grigioverde: standard grey-green colour for Italian Army materials in the European theatre
Kaki sahariano (or *giallo sabbia*): standard sand-yellow colour for Italian Army equipment in the North African theatre from middle of 1941
Leggero: light
Medio: medium
Militare, Mil.: military
Milizia Marittima di Artiglieria (MILMART): naval artillery militia, normally coastal artillery, but also manned truck-mounted naval guns
Milizia Nazionale della Strada (MdS): branch of the *Milizia Volontaria per la Sicurezza Nazionale* with traffic police functions
Milizia Volontaria per la Sicurezza Nazionale (MVSN): Volunteer Militia for National Security, a Fascist militia organisation
Modello, Mod.: model
Monoposto: single-seat motorcycle

Abbreviations

AOI	Africa Orientale Italiana (Italian East Africa)
AS	Africa Settentrionale (North Africa)
MdS	Milizia della Strada, Milizia Nazionale della Strada (National Road Militia)
MVSN	Milizia Volontaria per la Sicurezza Nazionale (Volunteer Militia for National Security)
PAI	Polizia dell'Africa Italiana (Italian African Police)
RA	Regia Aeronautica (Royal Italian Air Force)
RCTC	Regio Corpo Truppe Coloniali (Royal Corps of Colonial Troops)
RCTL	Regio Corpo Truppe Libiche (Royal Corps of Libyan Troops)
RE	Regio Esercito (Royal Italian Army)
RM	Regia Marina (Royal Italian Navy)

Documentation sources

The documents that appear in this volume come from the repositories and archives cited in the text, or from the authors' private archives. The authors are willing to settle any form of copyright issues pertaining to images and documents, the original provenance of which it has been impossible to determine.

ACS   Archivo Centrale dello Stato, Italy
AUSSME   Archivio Ufficio Storico Stato Maggiore Esercito, Italy
BAMA   Bundesarchiv, Militärarchiv, Germany
CSM   Centro Studi della Motorizzazione, Italy
CTM   Centro Tecnico della Motorizzazione, Italy
ECPAD   Établissement de Communication et de la Production Audiovisuelle de la Défense, France
LIFE   *Life* magazine, USA
GMT   Gruppo Modellistico Trentino di Studio e Ricerca Storica, Italy
ISR   Istituti Storici della Resistenza, Italy
IWM   Imperial War Museum, UK
MMM   Museo della Motorizzazione Militare, Italy
MSGR   Museo Storico Italiano della Guerra di Rovereto, Italy
NARA   National Archives and Records Service, USA
USMM   Ufficio Storico della Marina Militare, Italy

Acknowledgements

The authors and the publisher would like to give thanks to the following individuals for the precious collaboration granted in the creation of this book: Thomas Anderson, Massimo Bartolini, Luigi Carretta, Flavio Chistè, Stefano Di Giusto, Enrico Finazzer, Andrea Olivero, Claudio Pergher, Alberto Pirella, David Zambon, Ennio Zanetti. In particular, we are grateful to the Gruppo Modellistico Trentino di Studio e Ricerca Storica (www.gmt.tn.it – info@gmt.tn.it) and Claudio Pergher again for providing photographs, drawings and other material from its publications and to Flavio Chistè for his constant assistance.